Cases in Reward Management

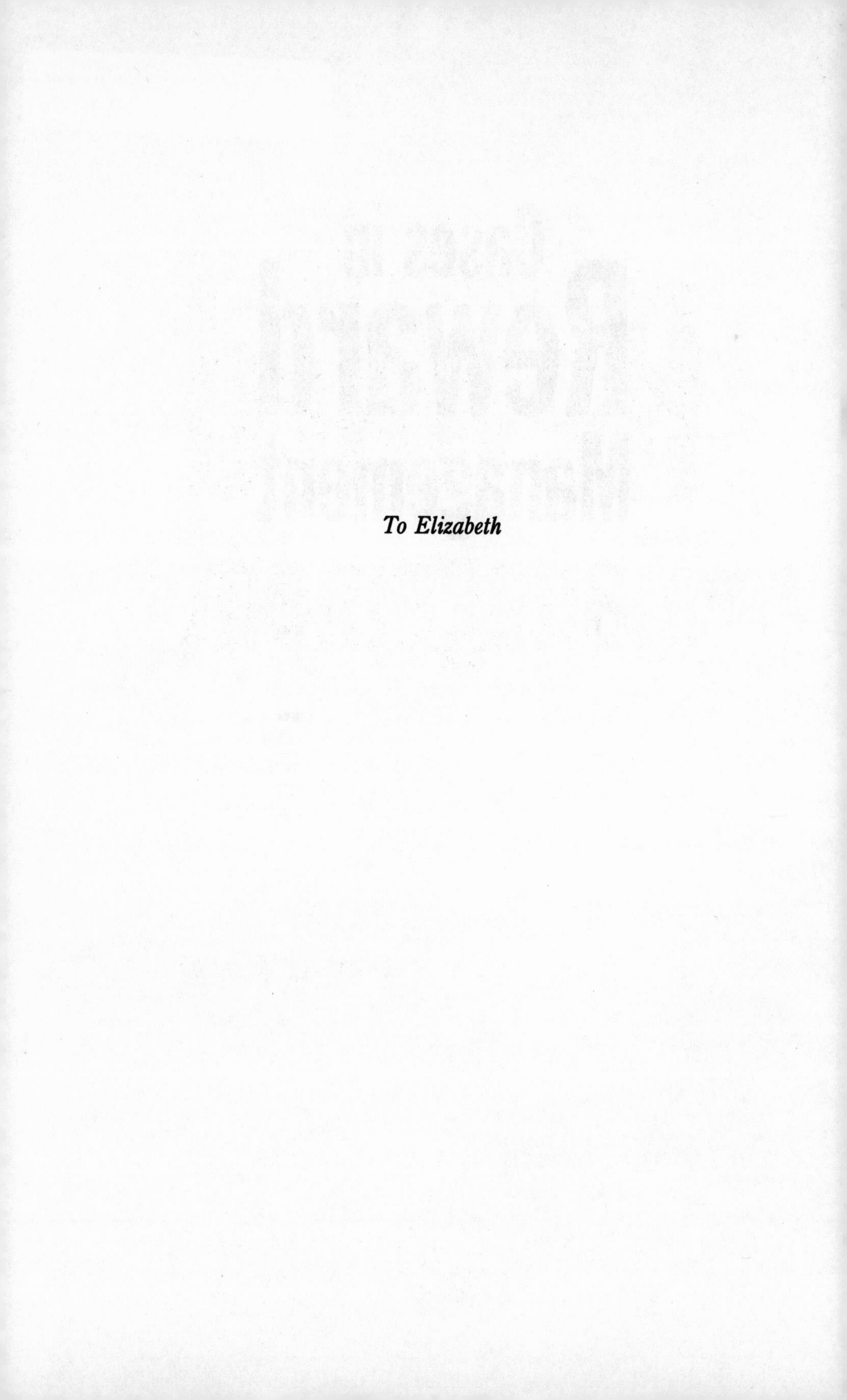

To Elizabeth

Cases in Reward Management

John Stredwick

First published in 1997

Kogan Page Limited
120 Pentonville Road
London N1 9JN

British Library Cataloguing in Publication Data

A CIP record for this book is available from the British Library.

ISBN 0 7494 2127 4

Typeset by BookEns Ltd, Royston, Herts.
Printed and bound in Great Britain by Biddles Ltd, Guildford and Kings Lynn

Contents

Foreword		9
Acknowledgements		11
The Contributors		13
Introduction		15

PART 1 REWARD STRATEGY

Introduction		23
Case Study 1	Strategic Reward Practice at Glaxo Wellcome	27
Case Study 2	Pay and Total Involvement at Everest Double Glazing	42
Case Study 3	The Importance of Pay in Compulsory Competitive Tendering: The David Webster Experience	51
Case Study 4	Leading Change with Compensation at Newsday Corporation	61
Case Study 5	Changing the Reward System at Blane and Rivershire Building Society	67
Case Study 6	With the Woolwich in a Take-over	76

PART 2 DEVELOPING PAY STRUCTURES

Introduction		84
Case Study 7	Movement to Broad Banding at MSD	88
Case Study 8	Devising a New Job Evaluation Scheme at Strand Housing Association	96
Case Study 9	From Job Evaluation to Salary Structure at Strand Housing Association	110

PART 3 PAYING FOR PERFORMANCE

Introduction		123
Case Study 10	Introducing Performance Pay at Associated Telecommunication Ltd	127
Case Study 11	No Panacea – a Failed PRP System at Midland Shire Council	145
Case Study 12	Piloting Appraisal-related Pay in the Police Service	152
Case Study 13	Performance-related Pay in Action at Barland Bank	163
Case Study 14	Incentives for Teleservicing Staff at Welton Insurance	171
Case Study 15	Restructuring and Rewarding the Sales Force	178
Case Study 16	A High Flying Sales Contest at Gate Products	189

PART 4 – PAYING TEAMS

Introduction		197
Case Study 17	Team Pay at Dartford Borough Council	201
Case Study 18	Gainsharing at BP and Ingersoll-Rand	210
Case Study 19	Profit-related Pay at the Burton Group	216
Case Study 20	Profit Sharing at the John Lewis Partnership	222

PART 5 – BENEFITS

Introduction		229
Case Study 21	Flexible Benefits at Mercury Communications	231
Case Study 22	Family-friendly Benefits at Hascot Western Langley	238
Case Study 23	The Pensions Paradox	245
Case Study 24	SAYE – A Tool for Employee Involvement?	251

PART 6 – MISCELLANEOUS CASES

Introduction		257
Case Study 25	Executive Pay at RTZ PLC	261
Case Study 26	Paying for Innovation – The Vauxhall Experience	266
Case Study 27	An Equal Pay Claim at LCS	277

Case Study 28 Too Far Too fast? – The Telecorp Dilemma 289

Case Study 29 Ambitious Rewards at an International Investment Bank 298

Subject Index 305

Author Index 311

Foreword

Pay should be the oil in the works of society, but sometimes, very publicly, it is grit instead. Many well-intentioned reward strategies fail to deliver or produce results which threaten the integrity of broader human resource management policy and values. Some approaches which technically ought not to work do so because everyone is committed to them, they are well communicated and they feel 'fit for purpose' at the time they are implemented.

Reward is an area where there are no magic solutions, no absolute answers and few golden rules. But there are important lessons to be learned from experience, and *Cases in Reward Management* is an important and valuable contribution to learning on pay issues. It fills the gap between the useful, practical 'up to the minute' coverage of current pay trends found, for example, in *People Management, Personnel Today,* and the publications of Incomes Data Services and Industrial Relations Services and the standard 'how to do it' texts on reward management and its various technical components. It leads students (and the many other readers who will use the book as a 'quarry') to explore what is likely to work in which circumstances and why, and signposts the key thinking and influences on this.

John Stredwick and his fellow contributors provide helpful pointers on the critical links between business strategy, the key levers of organisation success and the reward and recognition policies needed to deliver results, drawing valuable lessons from both public and private sectors. What you can get from this very wide collection of cases is how people in Glaxo Wellcome, John Lewis or Dartford Borough Council think about pay and why they reach the conclusions they do on policy development. Or you can learn what building societies, investment banks, petrochemical companies or housing associations actually do about the need for change and what happens on implementation.

Many readers will recognise the issues of responding to current pay 'fashions' such as team pay, flexible benefits, competency-related pay and broad banding and the internal power struggles over these between traditionalists and radicals. They will also identify with the need for contingent decisions, ie deciding what you can get done this year and what you have to 'park' and pick up later in a better climate.

This book is, I believe, a real contribution to the sharing of expertise on reward management. It exposes the kind of material that is all too often locked away in the confidential archives of companies and the consultancies they work with, or held by academics and students doing a single piece of detailed research.

Effective reward policy development is all about assessing 'business' benefits and shrewd pattern recognition. This collection of case studies exposes the current patterns of reward practice, their textures and the influences upon them. I hope that a very wide range of readers, far beyond the student audience it has been shaped for, will find it valuable in building their understanding of the art of the possible in reward management. It will achieve much if it enables constructive approaches to managing more effectively the balance between the economic transaction at the heart of pay and the psychological contract that defines the quality of the employment relationship. It would be good if this convinces a few more people that reward is a challenging and fascinating subject; for it lies at the heart of recognising human endeavour and creating an environment where success breeds success.

Helen Murlis
Head of Government and Agency Consulting
Hay Management Consultants

Acknowledgements

First ventures in any field can be one of life's rough rides and publishing is no exception. I am therefore most grateful to all those who helped to calm the nerves, prepare me for the crossing and to assure me that it was all worthwhile in the end.

My thanks must start with Helen Murlis, whose enthusiasm for the initial proposal and suggestions for the direction of the cases gave me the confidence in the framework which has lasted from those early days. Tony Mason, at Kogan Page, continued this support and I also received valuable advice from Michael Armstrong.

I did not travel alone and I am indebted to the contributors Sarah Kelly, Chris Mills, Pam Stevens and Sharon Mavin Taylor who respected deadlines and provided the rich variety which comes from years of practical experience as lecturers, practitioners and consultants.

Collaborators for the 'live' cases were very generous with their time and interest. They corrected my errors, clarified my explanations and lent their diagrams and charts. Their contributions were invaluable and I am much in their debt. They are:

- Kath Yates, Head of Compensation and Benefits at Glaxo Wellcome UK
- Bill Griffiths, Manager, Compensation and Benefits at Merck, Sharp and Dohme
- David Webster and Neil Cooper, Directors of the David Webster Group
- Bill Price, Managing Director of MCB
- Nic Garrett, Human Resources Manager of Woolwich Property Services
- Richard Dore, Head of Personnel and Administration, Dartford Borough Council
- Chris Pryke, Manager, Compensation and Benefits, The Burton Group
- Russ Watling, Employment Benefits Manager, Mercury Communications
- Adrian Garner, Head of Pensions and Remuneration, RTZ CRA
- Gordon McPhail, Human Resources Manager, Vauxhall Motors

There are a number of my colleagues at Putteridge Bury, the Management Faculty of the University of Luton, to whom I must extend my thanks. To Angela Thody, formerly Reader in Education at Putteridge Bury and now Professor of Education Policy at Lincoln University, who excited initial interest in research and publication and to Professor Colin Coulson Thomas, who gave valuable advice on the subtle aspects of getting published. To Mary

Scott, who assisted with the layout and tables, to Audrey Stuart and her librarian colleagues and to all my lecturing colleagues, support staff and students who showed interest and enthusiasm in the project.

Lastly, to my long-suffering wife Elizabeth, and my children for their support and understanding, particularly Howard, who patiently and repeatedly left his GSCE revision to show me how to get to grips with the intricacies of Microsoft Works and a rebellious printer.

The Contributors

I have been very fortunate to have contributions from a number of colleagues:

Sarah Kelly (Case Studies 5, 13 and 29) is Senior Lecturer at Bristol Business School. She is a graduate of Modern History from Oxford University, holds a Diploma in Personnel Management from the University of Westminster and a Post Graduate Certificate in Education from Leeds University. Her work experience includes six years in Merchant and Investment Banking in the City as both Personnel and Training Manager, followed by consulting experience at Andersen Consulting in the area of change management. This was followed by a move to Hay Consultants where she was active in the fields of competency identification and performance management.

Christopher Mills (Case Study 28) is Managing Consultant, South East Asia, for Development Dimensions International. DDI is a provider of human resource programmes and consulting services with its headquarters in Pittsburgh, Pennsylvania, USA with offices world wide. Chris lives in Singapore and is the author of two recent national studies on performance management (PM) in Singapore and Malaysia. He has designed and implemented numerous PM systems in different industries in the region and is currently engaged on a PhD, based on this subject area, supervised by Henley Business School.

Pam Stevens BA, MA, MIPD (Case Studies 23 and 24) is Lecturer at Dearne Valley Business School, near Doncaster. She gained her BA from McGill University, Montreal then left Canada to spend the next 25 years in Britain. She spent ten years as a Company Secretary of a PLC in the computer industry before completing her Masters degree in HRM at Hull University. She is course manager and lectures on a range of IPD and HRM courses. Her research interests are focused on reward issues.

Sharon Mavin Taylor BA, MA, Cert Ed, MIPM (Case Study 12) is Senior Lecturer at Newcastle Business School, University of Northumbria where she lectures in HRM. She gained her MA in HRM from Newcastle University following six years experience in retail management. Her research interests are centred around performance management systems, including 360 degree appraisal and race discrimination.

Introduction

Early cases

Gifts to the Greeks

Some years ago, we took a family holiday in Corfu for the first time. To our surprise, this was a complete contrast to the bare, arid Greek landscape we had previously encountered – we landed on a large, green island completely covered in trees. I found out later, while reading a book on Corfu's history, that the reason for its arboreal splendour was an instructive lesson on reward management.

In 1386, the Venetians captured the island from the Turks and set about a new strategy for their prize. As the Mediterranean's leading trader, they had discovered an insatiable demand for olive oil in both the domestic Italian market and elsewhere. Corfu, they decided, would be an ideal site for large-scale olive plantation.

The implementation of this grand design could be achieved by two methods. The hawks recommended the imposing of a martial regime, the clearance of the inhabitants and the importing of skilled Venetians and slaves to cultivate the plantation. The doves (who included a human resource (HR) specialist) pointed out the shortage of trained Venetians, the extortionate market rate for slaves and the difficulty of tying up a large troop garrison on the island. The human costs of down-sizing the island was also mentioned.

Their alternative approach was to offer a reward to the current inhabitants to plant and cultivate olive groves, with the help of a few experts. The cost was much lower and it left the military free for further conquests. These compelling arguments convinced the Doge and his Council and the details of Plan B were finalised. The precise reward per tree planted and tended was agreed, in line with Northern Italian practice and a slick communication exercise undertaken with the bemused inhabitants. They were much taken by the offer, accepted the money willingly and planted olive trees all over the island. The scheme appeared a great success.

As it happened, an unfortunate snag appeared. Due to the size of the sum offered, nearly all the subsistence farming on the island was abandoned, goats and young trees not co-existing well together. The inhabitants' tree-planting money was quickly dissipated on imported food at inflationary prices and soon they began to starve, long before the olive trees began bearing fruit. To protect their investment, the Venetians had to support the inhabitants for many years at huge cost.

This was one of the first, and certainly not the last, recorded examples of a reward strategy leading to dysfunctional behaviour. The HR expert, whose advice on labour pricing in comparative cultures was woefully adrift, was dispatched to the galleys or, some say, academia. Which one is not recorded.

When in Rome

Organisations have set out reward strategies for their employees for a long time. McLaughlin[1] recounts Caesar's decision to triple the pay of his Centurions to attract the top talent. Caesar also introduced terminal bonuses at the end of successful campaigns to replace the undisciplined hunt for booty – 50 dinari for a legionnaire, 500 for a centurion. This pay reform was clearly introduced to change behaviour which would lead to better client relations.

There are many stories of the competitive hunt for the skilled masons to build the gothic cathedrals in the middle ages, leading the masons to form a strong organisation so they could bargain on pay and working conditions across Medieval Europe.

Later developments

Closer to home, reward management was not acknowledged as a separate subject area to study and research until the mid 1980s. It was either considered as 'pay determination' and dealt with as a negotiating issue under industrial relations, or it was to be found at the back of a general personnel or accounting manual under salary administration. It was as though the question of initiatives in pay and rewards had never been considered outside of smoked-filled bargaining rooms or the cost accountant's office.

Even as late as the early 1990s, it was not impossible for a complete set of Institute of Personnel Management (now IPD) examinations to exclude pay questions altogether. In the years where they did appear, they were encompassed within the 'Employee Resourcing' orbit.

Reward management today

A number of changes have recently occurred which have sharply brought into focus the key importance of the subject in its own right:

- The decline of Union bargaining, arising from the Thatcherite legal reforms of the 1980s and the much reduced size of the manufacturing sector, together with the virtual disappearance of national pay agreements in the private sector, have given much more freedom to organisations to establish their own reward structures which can reflect their own particular culture and vision. This may put more emphasis on quality rather than quantity; on contribution rather than seniority; on customer orientation rather than empire building.
- Many organisations have adopted human resource management (HRM) strategies and concentrated their reward strategy on encouraging and rewarding individuals through a form of performance-related pay (PRP).

This has not occurred without controversy, from both an ethical and practical viewpoint, with much delight in the press when schemes come to an inglorious halt.

- The increased emphasis on entrepreneurship both within organisations and through Compulsory Competitive Tendering (CCT) legislation has led organisations to adjust pay systems to try to mirror the flexible approaches which exist in many small companies.
- Boardroom pay has become a national debating issue. So much so that not one, but two committees of notables, Cadbury and Greenbury, have reported on executive remuneration in the last four years and a third is planned. There has been much publicity of the remuneration of Cedric Brown of British Gas and other top executives of privatised industries. Large pay packets have been awarded to top executives for many years but the trend has intensified as these rewards have increasingly been set up to reflect the organisation's performance and have led to some annual remuneration packages exceeding one million pounds. Interest has also been heightened when a company's poor performance is ***not*** reflected in the awards to directors.
- The apparently unstoppable spread of the company car and the increased Inland Revenue presence in the area, has lead to a more detailed analysis of what benefits are actually meant to achieve in the work place and whether personal choice should play a larger part in their distribution.

These examples have led to reward management developing a much higher profile in the personnel profession. In 1994, the Personnel Standards Lead Body selected reward management as one of the four main generic areas to lead to the NVQ awards in personnel. In 1996, the IPD followed this path in their new professional qualification scheme with the promotion of reward management to sit alongside employee resourcing, development and relations as the four main components of their revised syllabus. Reward management has therefore been accepted as a subject area in its own right.

Case studies

There have been a number of case study books which have included examples of reward management, but the part played is a very small one. In the much used Winstanley and Woodall[2] book of HRM cases, just two of the 29 cases feature reward topics. There is only one reward case in a similar book by McGoldrick[3]. Another case study book, Adam-Smith and Peacock[4] feature organisational behaviour studies with neither pay nor reward being mentioned in the index. Finally, there are collections of cases on industrial relations which feature ***bargaining*** on pay and conditions but little about the reward strategy or the payment systems themselves.

This book is a response to a major gap in the market and is the first dedicated book on reward case studies.

The purpose of the book

Cases in Reward Management has a dual role. For the personnel/HRM practitioner, it can be used as a sourcebook for exploring best practice approaches to selected reward areas, particularly where the reader has little or no experience, or where that experience has proved disappointing. For the tutor and student, it provides material which can be used to explore the full range of reward issues through discussion and role play. The student activities can be part of that discussion or can be adapted easily as assignments.

Using case studies

Case studies are now such a well-known vehicle of learning (and latterly, of examining) that it is no longer necessary to give detailed explanations of how they should be used. Sufficient to quote Easton[5] who promoted a seven-step process looking from the student's perspective:

Understanding the situation – stressing the importance of finding out the key facts of the case, what information is missing, what can be confidently assumed and what are areas of uncertainty.

Diagnosing the problem areas – distinguishing between the problems which are immediately apparent and those more major underlying problems which may be associated with the culture of the organisation. There may be problems which need immediate action and others that await integrated action with other aspects of HRM strategy.

Generating alternative solutions – carefully and creatively working out all of the options available (including doing nothing) rather than jumping to an immediate solution.

Predicting the outcomes – taking each option in turn and working out what may happen in each case, attempting to evaluate the probability of those events.

Evaluating the options – working out the advantages and disadvantages of each option both in terms of benefits to the organisation and its employees and the costs involved, both financial and emotional.

Round out the analysis – having chosen the preferred course of action, ensure the proposal is complete in terms of its justification and in the chronological action plan required. Include a contingency plan where necessary.

Communicate the results – using the appropriate communication media, ensure that the preferred solution is explained coherently and expertly, including dealing with any outstanding questions and issues.

Choosing the case study

There are 29 cases in this collection and they are divided into six broad categories:

- Strategic studies
- Developing pay structures
- Paying for performance
- Team pay
- Benefits
- Special reward situations.

The cases do not all fit neatly into these watertight boxes. In fact, one of the major themes of this book (often repeated without apology) is the necessity to have an integrated and holistic approach to make reward systems work effectively. Although each case may have a major theme, there are often a number of variations to help put the case into context.

To help practitioners, tutors and students identify areas of interest and relevance, Table 1 sets out, in the form of a matrix, the subjects which are dealt with as a major part of the case. This Table also gives the following additional information.

Size of company

Taken as number of employees in the organisation as a whole or the business unit in question.

L	= Large	Over 5000 employees	13 cases
M	= Medium	Between 1000 and 5000 employees	7 cases
S	= Small	Under 1000 employees	9 cases

Sector of economy

A simplified identification has been adopted as follows:

CH	= Charity	2 cases
CO	= Communications/media	4 cases
FS	= Financial services	5 cases
M	= Manufacturing or mining	8 cases
OS	= Other services	5 cases
P	= Public sector	3 cases
R	= Retailing, distribution	2 cases

Employee groups

A division is made into four main groupings:

Production (which also includes manual servicing activities)	9 cases
Sales	16 cases
Administration and other servicing activities	16 cases
Management and executive	21 cases

Table 1 *Matrix for contents of case studies*

		Size	Sector	Employee Groups				Subject Area: Structure						Payment Methods						
				Production/Manual Service	Sales	Admin/Service	Management/Executives	Strategic Links	Job Evaluation	Performance Management	Equal Pay	Broad Banding	Skills/Competence Based	Paying Individuals	Paying Teams	Non-Cash Payments	Competitions	Profit-Sharing/Share Options	Benefits	Salary Surveys
1	Strategic Reward at Glaxo Wellcome	L	M		X	X	X	X					X							X
2	Total Involvement at Everest	M	M	X				X		X					X	X	X			
3	CCT – Pay Effects at David Webster	S	OS	X				X		X				X		X			X	
4	Leading Change at Newsday	M	CO		X			X		X				X	X					X
5	Changing Rewards at Blane	L	FS		X	X	X	X		X			X							X
6	Takeover with the Woolwich	M	OS		X	X	X	X		X				X	X		X	X	X	X
7	Reward Changes at MSD	L	M		X	X	X	X	X	X		X		X	X			X		X
8	Job Evaluation at Strand	S	CH			X	X	X	X	X	X	X	X							
9	Salary Structure at Strand	S	CH			X	X	X	X	X	X	X	X	X						
10	PRP at AT	M	CO	X	X	X	X	X	X	X		X		X	X					
11	PRP at Midshires	L	P			X	X	X		X					X					
12	Pilot Appraisal in Police	L	P			X	X	X		X				X	X					
13	Rewards at Barland Bank	L	FS			X	X	X		X			X	X						
14	Incentives at Welton	M	FS		X	X		X		X			X	X	X	X	X			
15	Motivating Sales at Money Bank	L	FS		X			X		X				X						
16	High Flying Sales at Gate	M	OS		X			X		X				X	X	X	X		X	
17	Team Based Pay at Dartford	S	P	X		X	X	X		X				X	X					
18	Gainsharing Cases	L	M	X			X	X		X				X	X					

				Employee Groups				Structure			Subject Area Payment Methods									
		Size	Sector	Production/Manual Service	Sales	Admin/Service	Management/Executives	Strategic Links	Job Evaluation	Performance Management	Equal Pay	Broad Banding	Skills/Competence Based	Paying Individuals	Paying Teams	Non-Cash Payments	Competitions	Profit-Sharing/Share Options	Benefits	Salary Surveys
19	Profit Related Pay at Burtons	L	R		X	X	X	X		X					X			X		
20	Profit Sharing at John Lewis	L	R		X	X	X	X		X					X			X		
21	Flexible Benefits at Mercury	L	CO		X	X	X	X						X		X			X	
22	Benefits at Ascot	S	M	X	X	X	X	X						X		X			X	
23	Pensions Case	S	OS	X	X	X	X	X						X					X	
24	SAYE at GSS	S	M	X	X	X	X	X						X	X	X			X	
25	Board Room Pay at RTZ	L	M				X	X		X					X			X		
26	Innovation at Vauxhalls	L	M	X				X		X				X	X	X	X		X	
27	Equal Pay Case	S	OS			X		X	X	X	X			X						
28	PM in Malaysian Telecorp	M	CO		X	X	X	X		X			X							
29	Pay in the City	S	FS			X	X	X		X				X					X	X

A number of the cases deal with a selection of different groups of employees, and sometimes the whole workforce, so there are overlaps here.

Real or constructed?

The majority of the content of case study publications are anonymous but this book is an exception. It is equally divided between detailed studies of actual company cases and those which have been written specially, based closely on the writer's experience, but where there is a need for anonymity due to the company's reluctance to expose material to the public domain.

'Named' cases:	1, 2, 3, 4, 6, 7, 12, 17, 18, 19, 20, 21, 25, 26
'Constructed' cases:	5, 8, 9, 10, 11, 13, 14, 15, 16, 22, 23, 24, 27, 28, 29

Reading – compulsory and recommended

With a few notable exceptions, there is a dearth of literature on reward management which has presented problems when recommending further reading for the topic areas contained in the cases. There are three key texts, however, two British and one American, which stand out and should be consulted alongside each case. These are:

- Armstrong, M and Murlis, H (1994) *Reward Management*, 3rd edition, Kogan Page/IPM, London
- Armstrong, M (1996) *Employee Reward*, IPD, London
- Milkovich, G and Newman, J (1996) *Compensation*, 5th edition, Irwin, Chicago

Rather than listing these books with others at the end of cases, I have inserted them as essential reading at the end of each case detailing the appropriate sections to read.

References

1 McLaughlin, D (1991) 'The Rise of a Strategic Approach to Executive Compensation' in F Foulkes, *Executive Compensation – A Strategic Guide for the 1990s*, Harvard Business School Press, Boston
2 Winstanley, D and Woodall, J (1992) *Case Studies in Personnel*, IPM, London
3 McGoldrick, A (1996) *Cases in Human Resource Management*, Pitman Publishing, London
4 Adam-Smith, D and Peacock, A (1994) *Cases in Organisational Behaviour*, Pitman Publishing, London
5 Easton, G (1992) *Learning from Case Studies*, 2nd edition, Prentice Hall, London

PART 1
REWARD STRATEGY

Introduction

It could be argued that all of the case studies in this book should be in this section. They are all about attempting to influence employees' behaviour by using reward devices and methods so that the employee makes a better contribution to the goals of the organisation. At its simplest level, it is to pay employees enough to keep them from leaving. At its most complex level, it is to motivate employees to 'work beyond contract', to inspire their own teams of employees to higher performance and to permanently reinforce the organisation's mission.

Constituents of reward strategy

Milkovich and Newman[1] define four key reward policies which, when combined in one form or another become the organisation's reward strategy. These are:

1. *Internal consistency* – comparing jobs and skill levels within the organisation and producing a system which reflects the organisation's concept of equity. This can range from a consultant's complex and sophisticated job evaluated system for a multi-national organisation to the simple spot rates existing in a small company.
2. *External competitiveness* – how an employer positions its pay relative to the competition. Organisations mostly try to balance the need to recruit and retain the best employees against the need to watch costs in a competitive environment.
3. *Employee contributions* – whether and how employees' performance and contribution should be rewarded. Who should be included in bonus entitlements? Should annual pay increases be contingent on performance? What should be the balance between cash and non-cash rewards? These, and a dozen other questions combine to give a wide range of options in this area.

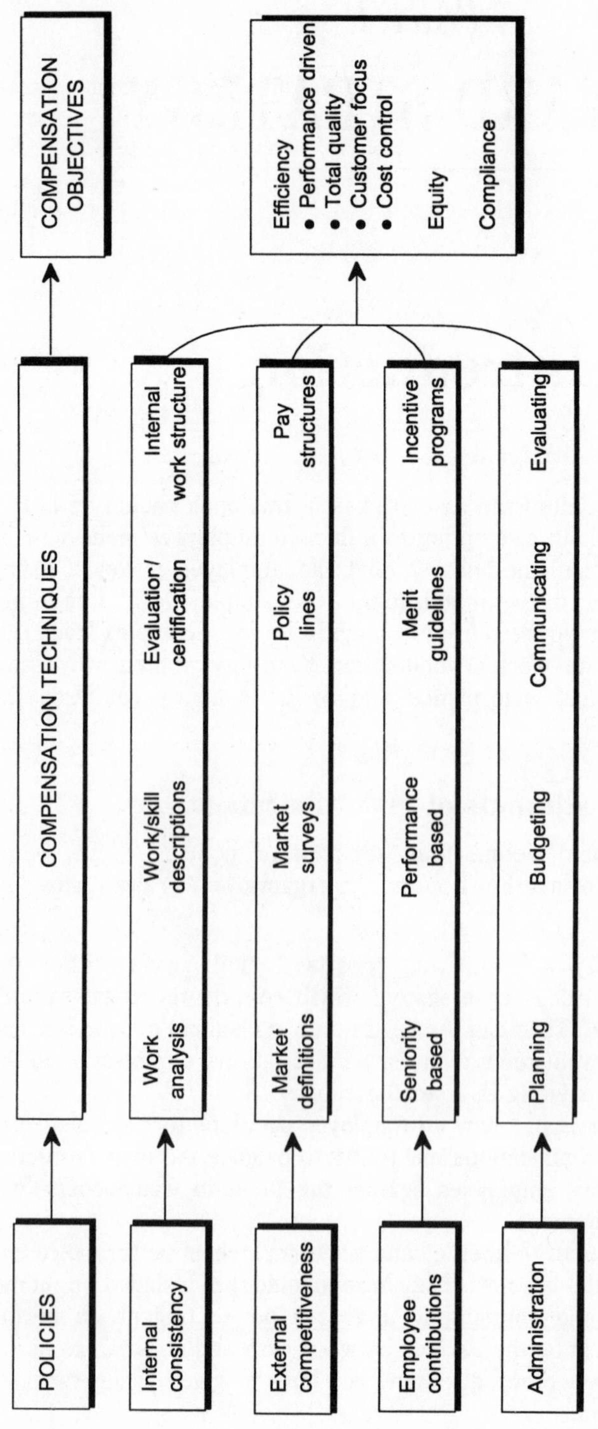

Figure 1.1 *The pay model*

Source: Milkovich, G and Newman, J (1996) *Compensation*, Irwin, Chicago.

4. *Administration* – how to manage and control the systems, including benefits.

These are shown in the pay model (Figure 1.1).

In some organisations, you have to hunt down an elusive reward strategy but it is still there somewhere. Until recently, organisations behaved reactively on rewards, only changing in response to union pressure or rapid market and employee movements. The combination of the decline in union power and the need to meet changing world economic realities has meant that a far more proactive stance has been adopted.

Reward is a phrase, not a whole sentence

This stance has been to tie reward strategies in with other business objectives: flexible benefits tie in with the need for employees to work flexibly; skills-based and competence based pay tie in with the increasing need for employees to learn skills and competences and learn them fast; pay for performance ties in with the need to produce 'just-in-time' and to customer requirements and team bonuses tie in with the need for teams to take their empowerment seriously and responsibly (Cannell and Wood[2]).

On their own, then, reward strategies have little value and a low success rate. Each of the cases in Part 1 show the part that reward systems play in change management: how they strengthen and reinforce the changes required in employees' behaviour.

In Case Study 1, Glaxo's evolutionary approach to reward management arose from a business process engineering exercise which, amongst other imperatives, put the emphasis on a quicker employee response.

Case Study 2 examines the experience of Everest Double Glazing in the 1980s where the complexity of its made-to-measure products and a more competitive market made it essential that employees competed to win business through a commitment to high productivity, top quality and goods delivered on time. The solution was a unique competition with some unusual prizes.

For the David Webster Group, in Case Study 3, the challenge was how to move away from traditional local authority methods of working while still delivering a high level of public service and making a profit. Sharing part of the risks with employees by increasing the variable pay element and reducing the standard benefits while increasing responsibility and the opportunity for high earnings was the preferred solution which produced the required results.

There is an American example of fundamental changes in the working relationship in a New York State newspaper group in Case Study 4 and the input of a renovated pay system, while Case Study 5 deals with the reward strategy in the substantial working changes in a building society's operations.

A different situation arises for a building society in Case Study 6 where the purchase and re-organisation of an estate agency group produces the need for some hard decisions on pay policies.

References

1 Milkovich, G and Newman, J (1996) *Compensation*, 6th edition, Irwin, Chicago
2 Cannell, M and Wood, S (1992) *Incentive Pay*, IPM, London

Further reading

Ashton, C (1995) *Pay, Performance and Career Development*, Business Intelligence, London
Schuster, J and Zingheim, P (1992) *The New Pay*, Lexington Books, New York

Case Study 1

Strategic Reward Practice at Glaxo Wellcome

Introduction

If one had to pick a single UK company that could be truly called 'world class' it would have to be Glaxo Wellcome UK. Currently valued at over £30 billion, its exports exceeding £1.4 billion in 1995, it is the leading world pharmaceutical company. Although its phenomenal growth since the 1950s has been due, in major part, to the success of its anti-ulcer treatment, it has successfully invested in a new generation of medicines which will guarantee its position in the premier league for at least the next 20 years.

No company can rest on its laurels, however, and GWUK has entered into a number of change processes in the last seven years to support its investment, manufacturing and marketing programme and to meet the needs of the market place in the 21st century.

This case study gives an overview of the part played by reward strategy in the change programme for GWUK and then deals in detail with three aspects of the change: the first two are linked with the performance management system and cover the movement towards a competency framework and the peer group appraisal method; the third looks at the gradual approach to paying for performance.

Background

GWUK is the commercial operating company, employing around 1500 staff. GWUK sits alongside other Glaxo Wellcome companies in the UK who employ a further 12,500 staff in research and development, manufacturing and at headquarters.

In 1989, GWUK first entered into a culture-changing process with a movement to considerably improve the communications throughout the organisation. A more substantial series of changes arose from the Business Process Re-engineering Programme that took place during 1994-5 which led to the re-alignment of a number of the HR strategies. The business imperative for change arose chiefly from the need for employees at all levels to respond much more flexibly to the changing business realities. This applied to all aspects of the business, including bringing new projects to completion, meeting the needs of a changing market place and establishing different long-term relationships with customers. The company had to move away from a traditional, functional, internally-driven approach and replace it with a way of working which puts the customer first.

New HR policies

The strategic HR approach was to design complementary approaches to reward and development to drive change in the level of organisational capability and deliver the highest level of competence.

Arising out of Business Process Re-engineering, structures had become much flatter and managers now had an average of more than 20 under their span of control. This, and the requirement for much greater flexibility, led to the following HR initiatives, which all had an ultimate effect upon the new reward system:

- Empowerment of work teams, driving through the concept that employees at all levels should be encouraged to reflect on their jobs, come up with ideas of doing them better and be able to implement them themselves within a broad remit. In reward terms, this meant that line managers would have much greater freedom to determine pay.
- Reinforcement of the future competencies required in the organisation, bringing in a competency framework to define the skills and behaviour required of all employees. This would be at the heart of the performance management scheme.
- Movement of employees across functional boundaries, doing away with the traditional job families (there were 25 of them at one stage!) and encouraging employees to take responsibility for their own learning and development. It was considered that there was too much reliance in total upon market-driven rates which had the effect of undermining internal balance and value. This led to a redefinition of the grading system and the introduction of six broad, overlapping salary grades. Each grade included roles of similar size from all areas of the company, linked to the competency framework, allowing the emphasis to be shifted from the narrow differentiation of roles and salaries in a traditional grading structure, to the emphasis on similarities which exist in the competencies required to do many jobs. New pay scales were attached to these grades. Figure 1.2 below, gives examples of some of these grades. The responsibility for the movement of salaries inside the bands has been shifted to the line manager who operates within budgets and the advice on market rates provided by the HR department. The pay information gathering still continues and managers are provided with a range of accurate comparative figures from a number of sources. The ultimate decisions on pay, however, now rest with the line managers who must balance the internal pressures against those from outside.

Grade	Starting Point	Maximum
	£	£
3	54,690	103,450
4	35,410	72,380
5	27,230	52,350
6	20,190	39,570
7	16,880	32,050

Figure 1.2 *Pay scales attached to grades*

The competency framework

Competency was defined as:

> What you know, what you do and how you do it which, when applied by an individual or a team, leads to positive outcomes for GWUK.

The framework was divided into core competencies, which were required by everyone across the business regardless of their individual roles and functions, and specialist competencies, which individuals and teams within a certain group of roles or functions had to demonstrate in order to be effective. Each of these groups of competencies had a **dimension** which was the level at which a competency needed to be performed with regard to the demands and requirements of the role rather than the individual's effectiveness in that role.

Core competencies

There were 20 core competencies, divided into five sub-groups. This is shown in Figure 1.3. These 20 core competencies are divided into two groups:

- those which are ***unidimensional*** and apply throughout their description to all positions (see Table 1.1); and
- those which are ***multi-dimensional*** where certain dimensions apply to some jobs and not to others (see Table 1.2).

The following is an example of each.

Example of unidimensional competency
Sub-group – personal qualities
Competency – personal accountability

(Figure 1.4 shows an extract from this competency.)

The first column (–) shows a negative response to each of the competencies, eg missing deadlines, using delaying tactics, etc.
The second column (+) shows a positive response to the competencies, eg sees things through to the end, takes responsibility for outcomes, etc.

1. PERSONAL QUALITIES	1.1 Personal accountability 1.2 Personal organisation 1.3 Self-development 1.4 Creativity and Innovation 1.5 Flexibility 1.6 Continuous Improvement
2. PLANNING TO ACHIEVE	2.1 Gathering, analysing and interpreting data to produce information 2.2 Problem solving and decision making 2.3 Establishing a Plan 2.4 Implementing and monitoring achievement
3. BUSINESS AND CUSTOMER FOCUS	3.1 Company environment 3.2 Business environment 3.3 Customer focus
4. SUPPORTIVE LEADERSHIP	4.1 Effective leadership 4.2 Empowering
5. WORKING WITH OTHERS	5.1 Team-working, managing conflict and being supportive 5.2 Developing colleagues 5.3 Giving and receiving feedback 5.4 Networking and building relationships 5.5 Communication

Figure 1.3 *GWUK core competency framework*

The third column (++) shows an extended positive response, eg has contingency plans, has a follow-up course of action, etc.

Whatever the job, this competency applies and the three responses detailed in the Table below communicate to job holders the required behaviour for all employees and particular behaviour that is to be rejected.

The following competencies are unidimensional:

Table 1.1 *Unidimensional competencies*

Personal qualities	Personal accountability Personal organisation Self-development Creativity and innovation Flexibility Continuous improvement
Supportive leadership	Teamworking, managing conflict and being supportive
Working with others	Giving and receiving feedback

Taking responsibility for your own actions, being pro-active and committed

–	+	++
• Does not commit to action or commits verbally when pushed, but still doesn't do it. • Blames others for personal failure – passes the buck. • Agrees unrealistic deadlines for themselves. • Misses deadlines or has to be chased to meet deadlines. • Doesn't respond to messages/mails. • Employs delaying tactics, making excuses or trying to conceal the situation when things go wrong. • Lets relatively unimportant tasks get in the way – what they like to do takes precedent. • Relies on others to complete action/task. • Builds their achievements up to be greater than they actually are. • Lets meetings drift on, with people revisiting points covered earlier.	• Takes responsibility for own actions and those of their team, eg – shows commitment to make it happen – does what says will do, ie actions match words – points out consequences of not getting the job done – keeps discussion on track in meetings • Does not 'blame' others. • Takes responsibility for outcomes, mistakes and triumphs. • Does not ask 'permission' before making decisions. • Asks for 'ground rules'. • Puts measures in place – sets guidelines for achievement with appropriate standards. • Sees things through to an end point; faces up to realities and accepts when things go wrong.	• Creates a high degree of personal accountability in others, eg encouraging others to take responsibility for their own actions. • Does everything within their means to ensure things are done to the best of their ability. • Always has a follow-up course of action. • Demonstrates the ability to make contingency plans, explaining why action is necessary.

Taking responsibility for your own actions, being pro-active and committed

–	+	++
• Complacent, slow to react or indifferent. • May not participate or contribute to discussion. • Responds aggressively to mistakes being pointed out. • Does minimum they can get away with. • Not concerned with – quality. No pride in 'the job'. • Gets on with their 'own job' keeping their 'heads down'.	• Doesn't make excuses when things fail – admits what have not achieved and explains why. • Meets deadlines or evaluates and revises deadlines where appropriate. • Committed/dedicated/enthusiastic to complete the task and communicates progress or changes of direction to others. • Is open and honest – no hidden agendas. • Is willing to trust others. • Challenges ideas and decisions in a constructive way. • Not afraid to say what they believe. • Able to confront difficult issues rather than skirt around them. • Prepared to seek help when 'out of depth'. • Acts to improve own behaviours/competence. • Actively seeks to improve things, eg 'how could this be done better'.	

Figure 1.4 *Personal qualities – personal accountability*

Example of Multi-dimensional competency
Sub-group – Planning to achieve
Competency – Problem solving and decision making

Figure 1.5 is an extract showing the three types of behavioural indicators similar to the unidimensional competencies. There are also four separate dimensions which can apply to some jobs but not others which are shown in Figure 1.6. For example, long-term focus will apply to more senior positions or project-type positions but not to more junior positions.

The following competencies are multi-dimensional:

Planning to achieve	Gathering, analysing and interpreting data Problem solving and decision making Establishing a plan Implementing and monitoring achievement
Business and customer focus	Company environment Business environment Customer focus
Supporting leadership	Effective leadership Empowering
Working with others	Developing colleagues Networking and building relationships Communication

Table 1.2 *Multi-dimensional competencies*

Matching competency to jobs

When the broad-banded grades were set up, a template was devised against each of the six grades which gave a definition of the typical job requirements in that grade. Figure 1.7 is the example of typical core competency profile for Grade 5 staff. Apart from all the unidimensional competencies which apply to all jobs, the dimensions vary for the other competencies. Taking again the competency 'Problem solving and decision making', Grade 5 staff would typically work in the weekly, short and medium-term areas (these are shaded) but do not always have the long-term focus.

Specialist competencies

There are a number of competencies which only apply to particular jobs. These are specifically related to, say, professional or technical areas and have been developed by the departments concerned.

Each manager works with staff members to identify the competencies required in the role they currently perform. This supports development and objective setting. The individual set is then compared to the typical core competency profile for each grade and the position would be placed in that grade which matched the best. Figure 1.7 also sets out some of the typical current role titles within Grade 5. Specialist competencies were then added, where appropriate.

Taking a broad approach to problem solving leading to practical decision making for the benefit of the organisation

–	+	++
• Sees symptoms but doesn't recognise problem. • Process of resolving problems is simplistic, eg – no alternative scenarios, no evidence of thinking problems through. • Does not clarify the issues so misunderstandings escalate. • Gets embroiled in detail and jumps in to solve the problem before doing the analysis. • Off loads decision on to someone else. • Does not consider the impact on others. • Is unable to back up decisions with reasons, data. • Decision making is limited to their 'comfort zone'. • Decisions made on short term basis only – no thought of long-term consequences. • Makes snap decisions with little foundation. • Finds solutions by themselves rather than getting others involved.	• Asks questions to gain a real understanding of the problem, clarifying understanding along the way. • States the problem clearly. • Looks at problems from different view points. • Uses experience of self, team and others to help solve problems. • Knows when to seek opinions/advice internally before making a decision. • Sorts out issues before getting into solutions. • Establishes boundaries for decision making. • Evaluates conflicting priorities to come up with a course of action. • Is able to make decisions rather than deliberations. • Does not waste time arriving at a decision/lets people know when decision will be made.	• Combines sound knowledge and intuition to make quality decisions. • If need be will make an immediate response to a crucial event, is aware of the implications.

Figure 1.5 *Behavioural indicators – problem solving and decision making*

Taking a broad approach to problem solving leading to practical decision making for the benefit of the organisation.

DIMENSION	DESCRIPTION
↑ Long-term focus	• Company wide, strategic level of problem solving and decision making • High risk issues, issues beyond organisation • Weighs up risk for all stakeholders • Long-term focus (likely to exceed 4 years)
Medium-term focus	• Problem solving/decision making for a department/function/defined area. • Issues may be high risk for dept/function. • Medium term focus (2/3 years) • Company focus
Short-term focus	• Team/group focus • Tactical problem solving/decision making based on own/shared experience and/or innovation.
Daily/weekly focus	• Solves problems and takes decisions on daily/weekly activities. • Little or no risk, refers on if higher risk.

Figure 1.6 *Dimensions – problem solving and decision making*

Staff within this band will have a broad understanding of what needs to be achieved, not only within their own role, but within the department or function. They will help develop objectives at departmental/function level taking into consideration the longer term aims of their role. They will require minimum direction and supervision and be starting to implement novel approaches to solving problems. They may well be leading cross-functional projects within a defined area. They may have responsibility for resources or be a technical expert in a field with little or no responsibility for resources. They will plan and control departmental/functional activities to ensure deadlines are met, delegating appropriately. May have budgetary responsibility. They will plan medium to long term, taking into consideration the potential impact on the rest of the organisation. They will have a strong awareness of the interfaces within the company and will be managing these relationships.

TYPICAL CORE COMPETENCY PROFILE

These competencies are unidimensional

DIMENSION

COMMON COMPETENCY AREA	COMPETENCY DESCRIPTOR
Personal Qualities	Personal Accountability
	Personal Organisation
	Self-Development
	Creativity & Innovation
	Flexibility
	Continuous Improvement
Planning to Achieve	Gathering, Analysing & Interpreting Data
	Problem Solving & Decision Making
	Establishing a Plan
	Implementing and Monitoring Achievement
Business & Customer Focus	Company Environment
	Business Environment
	Customer Focus
Supportive Leadership	Effective Leadership
	Empowering
	Teamworking, Managing Conflict and being Supportive
Working with Others	Developing Colleagues
	Giving & Receiving Feedback
	Networking & Building Relationships
	Communication

It is expected that roles within this grade will operate the majority of the time at the competency dimension shown above. There will be occasions when it may be necessary to operate at a higher or lower dimension, however these are the exception rather than the norm.

TYPICAL CURRENT ROLE TITLES	Project Leader, Financial Analyst, Development Accountant, Team Coach, Therapy Specialist, Account Manager, Senior Personnel Officer, Senior Market Research Executive, Principle Clinical Research Scientist, Brand Manager, Planning Manager, Senior Sales Executive, Senior Brand Manager, Technical Support Manager, Information Analysis Team Leader, Quality Control Manager, Media Manager, Chief Database Analyst, Manager Transitional Systems, Senior Communications Executive, Information Services Manager, IT Services Manager, Statistical Analyst, Senior Disease Management Advisor, Business Development Manager, Senior Customer Planning Manager, Marketing Services Manager, Technical Project Manager, Systems Support Manager.

Figure 1.7 *Grade 5 staff*

This method of evaluating jobs was considered to be far more flexible and user-friendly than the traditional rigid factor-points evaluation schemes. After thorough discussion with individual staff, it was agreed in an amiable and constructive fashion and although there was an appeals procedure, it was not used by any employee. If necessary, the company will use formal job evaluation techniques to help position borderline or disputed roles.

Performance management

Unlike most performance management (PM) systems, this new process starts from the employee's view. Each employee is issued with a complete set of the competencies which apply to their own position. This acts as a reference point, helping the employee to build up a picture of what they should be trying to achieve. It also acts as a development checklist, so employees and their manager can identify gaps or weaknesses which can be remedied through training or experiential learning.

The formal PM system has the following six stages.

Stage 1

At the start of the year, the manager sits down with their team to set out the team objectives for the next period, typically two years. In the pharmaceutical industry, the culture of long-term planning is highly developed, reflecting the long-term development of medicines and commercial relationships, so setting team objectives for just a year ahead is not acceptable or relevant. These are prioritised and put into a project planning format. The manager is expected to use their knowledge of the company business ambition and strategy to put their team contribution in context.

Stage 2

Once agreed, the manager works out with individuals their own contribution to achieving these objectives. Typically, individuals and teams will develop their ideas and plans for presentation to and review with their manager and other teams.

Stage 3

How the individual's contribution is to be measured is then worked out. This will be a combination of qualitative and quantitative measures. The sources of these measures are also agreed; they are often colleagues and internal customers.

Stage 4

During the course of the year, the employee will seek feedback from some of these sources as to how they are doing and they will keep records of the conversations and the outcomes either in their Personal Fact File issued to each employee or in a system they have devised themselves, perhaps using a Filofax. The employee will also be asked to provide feedback themselves to colleagues on a regular basis.

Stage 5

Meetings with their manager and team members take place on a regular basis, both formal and informal, not just once a year. Information arising from the feedback provided is discussed and any developmental needs decided then and there with no need to wait until the end of the year.

Stage 6

More formal reviews can take place to support career development and pay review processes. However, the emphasis is on ensuring that continuous review and assessment takes place. The HR function do not drive an appraisal process and do not require any standard forms to be completed unless there are performance problems where managers are required to follow best practice guidelines to monitor more formally.

Stage 7

Managers come together prior to pay reviews to discuss their assessments of staff to agree consistent approaches and to share information to support development moves.

Summary of PM system

The PM system is one that is 'feedback-rich' with the intention of this supporting the strong communication culture of the organisation. Due to the fact that the pay review is not directly connected to the developmental aspects of the PM system, then the process is not seen as one that is particularly threatening, but one which has become a very open, informal and two-way procedure. It is also seen by employees as one which is very supportive and encouraging. Assessments of performance and competence do contribute towards determining pay but the PM system has been successfully positioned as first and foremost an on-going development and monitoring tool.

Paying for performance

Senior managers

The final change dealt with in this case study is the move towards making pay more sensitive to the performance of the individual. Board members have worked under such an arrangement for some years and, in 1996, a system was introduced for a group of senior managers.

The essence of this payment is that a payment of up to ten per cent of their base pay can be made on the basis of target achievement as follows:

- a payment of between 0 per cent and 1.5 per cent related to company revenue;
- a payment of between 0 per cent and 1.5 per cent related to company profit; and
- a payment of between 0 per cent and 7 per cent related to individual performance.

It is not seen primarily as a motivator but one of reward for good performance. It is to reinforce the message that the impact of a senior manager has an ultimate impact on company performance. Neither is it seen as a particularly sophisticated scheme as the measures for individual performance are a mix of quantitative and qualitative factors.

Salesforce staff

There had been a variety of small scale non-cash benefits for the sales team for some years, including holidays, recognition dinners and certificates. By 1995, it was considered the time to extend these to include a pay element. The key element was considered the rewarding of the team, rather than the individual and to make these rewards reflect the performance of the company as a whole and the teams involved.

A bonus pool of 4.5 per cent of the sales force pay was created to be divided amongst the 30 business units making up the sales force. There was an average of 25 staff in each unit. Each unit was awarded a slice of the bonus pool depending on a number of performance measures including sales volume, market share and profitability. That sum of cash would be divided amongst the sales team at the discretion of the Business Manager reflecting the varied levels of contribution to the success of the teams.

Conclusion

As these changes are still bedding-in there has only been a limited amount of evaluation, but the overall employee feedback surveys indicate a ground swell of support for both the principles and the practice. There will be developments in the competency profiles, particularly in the specialist areas, as the organisation continues to learn about the differential competencies of the high performers. 360 degree appraisal will continue to develop, but complex paperwork and anonymity through third parties will be avoided as the organisation continues to press for the 'open and honest' approach. Bonus schemes will continue to be regarded with extreme caution and to be implemented only after very careful consideration and evaluation. There is nothing which fails quite as badly as a failed reward scheme and GWUK are extremely conscious of this.

Student activities

1. Identify ways that the GWUK performance management and reward

initiatives are aligned with the business imperatives. What other reward initiatives could be considered in this setting?

2. Write a short paper to your management team recommending 360 degree appraisal, making reference to the GWUK scheme and others.
3. How would you meet the criticisms of a line manager who argues that they are too busy to deal with the 'feedback-rich' scheme of performance management?
4. Construct a set of core competencies for a compensation and benefits manager and identify three areas of specialist competencies.

Standard reading

	Armstrong and Murlis	*Armstrong*	*Milkovich and Newman*
Pages	44–52 and 359–362	72–76 and 290–98	1–43 and 98–103

Further reading

Boam, R and Sparrow, P (1992) *Designing and Achieving Competency*, IPM, London
Connock, S (1992) *HR Vision – Managing a Quality Workforce*, IPD, London
Coulson-Thomas, C (1997) *Achieving Excellence through Business Transformation*, Kogan Page, London
Dugdill, G (1994) 'Wide Angle View', *Personnel Today*, September 27, pp 31–32
Haines, S and McCoy, K (1995) *Sustaining High Performance*, Kogan Page, London
Hay Group (1996) *People and Competences – The Route to Competitive Advantage*, Kogan Page, London
Fletcher, S (1992) *Competence-based Assessment Techniques*, IPM, London
Kossen, S (1994) *The Human Side of Organisations*, Harper Collins, London
Mitrani, A *et al* (1992) *Competency Based Human Resource Management*, Kogan Page, London
Prescott, B (1995) *Creating a World Class Quality Organisation*, Kogan Page, London
Summers, L *et al* (1991) 'Upside-Down Performance Appraisals', *Training and Development*, July, pp 15–20
Thatcher, M (1996) 'Allowing Everyone to Have Their Say', *People Management*, 21 March, pp 28–30

Case Study 2

Pay and Total Involvement at Everest Double Glazing

Introduction

Some of the best ideas in business come about from a carefully planned and well-executed initiative. Others occur by pure chance. A routine decision concerning a minor policy detail may suddenly turn into a major strategy with significant outcomes. This case study is one such example. It was not the main intention to totally align pay schemes with organisational objectives but that is how it eventually worked out. Moreover, the gains to the company and to the employees were substantial.

Background to the company

Everest Double Glazing began life in 1965 and immediately grew at a phenomenal pace so that turnover had reached £60 million by 1980. Originally set up by four entrepreneurs, the capital constantly needed to supply this high growth necessitated an outside investor and the company became a subsidiary of RTZ PLC in the early 1970s, although retaining the same highly successful management team.

The company had tapped the need of the rapidly growing property owning market to help protect inhabitants from the scourges of draughts, condensation and rotting timber windows. The original product had been a secondary single glazed window but this was followed by a range of double glazed entrance and patio doors and, by 1980, complete replacement double glazed windows. As competition grew in this expanding market, it was clear that the customer's needs had to be met with an even wider product range: the frames could be timber or aluminum; the aluminum could be grey or painted white; the glass could be toughened or incorporate any number of leaded or Georgian designs.

The most important feature of the entire market place was that each contract was unique. British construction methods had determined that there were no standard sizes for doors or windows except in new houses and these rarely incorporated double glazing. Every job, therefore, had to be made to measure and manufactured to order. Having signed up for the contract, the customer would be given an estimated delivery time which varied between five and 16 weeks depending on the product, the time of year and the current production backlog.

The key elements of the contract from the customer's viewpoint was that it was of high quality (no scratches, no condensation, operated smoothly), fit for the purpose (it was the right made-to-measure size) and delivered within a reasonable time, preferably that quoted at the time of sale.

These elements had always been part of the conscious production agenda but had not been reinforced until the early 1980s. A pause for breath from the apparently insatiable public in 1979-80 had thrown a number of companies in the industry into financial trouble and it was recognised that only those driven by quality as well as efficiency would survive and prosper.

Factory operations

By this time, Everest had expanded to ten factories in seven locations. Rather than expanding the factory at their base-site in Cheshunt, near Hertford, for reasons principally concerned with the heavy distribution costs and the generous start up incentives in development areas and in New Towns, new factories had been opened in Scotland, Wales (the Rhondda) the North-East, Yorkshire and Northampton as well as Sittingbourne in Kent. There was also the desire to replicate the original successful small factory team of about 100 employees. In all, there was a production labour force close to 1000 employees.

Throughout its short history, the board constantly looked at investing in more modern plants and equipment. When the demand for toughened glass increased sharply, through more stringent safety regulations on patio doors, the company was the first double glazing company to commission and operate a toughened glass plant. Each industry improvement in sealed unit manufacture and insulation was adopted as a matter of priority and shrink-wrapping finished products was adopted before the competition.

There was some limit to the degree of automation. The nature of the product, where every window and door has an almost infinite variety of style, shape, size and colour has meant that batch or continuous production was impossible. Much of the work remained in the hands of the individual operator to cut, collate, assemble, inspect and pack the product. Despite the individual nature of the product, and the importance of teamwork in the assembly process, much of the work remained repetitive. A few experienced glass-cutters were recruited but the bulk of the labour force were semi-skilled from a variety of backgrounds who had not worked in the industry before. The contract was one of flexibility where employees could be moved onto whichever job needed labour so training was a vital element. On a few occasions, this flexibility was tested by employees who wished to choose the jobs on which they worked but this was not acceptable and the clause needed enforcement as an essential part of their contract. Factory employees understood, accepted and supported this action as long as it was not enforced in an arbitrary or capricious manner.

Unions existed in the Welsh and Yorkshire factories but not elsewhere. Ballots took place occasionally but, in general, there was little enthusiasm to join. There were local informal arrangements for consultation purposes, particularly over questions of bonus.

Incentive arrangements

The experience of the entrepreneurial team had included 20 years in the furniture industry and they had a clear conviction that some incentive arrangement was necessary. Piece-work was discounted as being too divisive and complex to operate. From an early date, a factory-wide bonus scheme was operated, based on output. On balance the schemes appeared to be successful, resulting in a relatively low labour cost compared with the industry average. However, the schemes did not always operate smoothly.

Earnings plateau

A plateau seemed to be reached when employees appeared to agree collectively, but informally, that their earnings levels were sufficient and that they should not push any harder to increase productivity. This was despite small but continuous improvements in productivity aids. When this was discussed with the workforce, employees brushed it aside giving reasons of poor quality supplies, imbalance of workload, machine breakdown and other reasons. These excuses did all occur but in a very minor fashion and would not influence productivity improvement to any great extent.

Changeover of product mix

From time to time, factories had to be re-organized to meet the changing mix of product. This happened, for example, when the demand for the conventional secondary window dropped away and an increase for the replacement sealed unit window developed. As factories carried out this change, production targets for the new products were set up which the management considered quite easy to achieve. Surprisingly, they became difficult to meet even within the experienced workforce. Interim incentive arrangements, incorporating a sliding scale which took the changeover into account, hit trouble when the bonus level fell, causing systems of guaranteed bonus to operate far longer than was planned with the resulting increase in costs.

Quality

The bonus scheme was essentially one of output. Inspection at each stage of production controlled, to a large extent, the quality going out the door, but the inevitable pressures were placed on over-enthusiastic inspectors when production targets needed to be reached. As the market grew and the public became far more selective, the quality of the product became a much greater issue, particularly as Everest's prices were at the top of the range. Installers became progressively more unhappy at having to go back to a customer's house to replace a scratched glass or extrusion as it hit their own bonus. The company also lost sales through dissatisfied customers.

It was time, therefore, to reassess the bonus arrangement. It clearly no longer matched the business requirements of the organisation – it was too narrowly focused and its motivational impact was limited.

Incentives in other parts of the organisation

Everest had pioneered the direct selling approach employing salesmen on a commission-only basis. District and regional sales managers were also on a self-employed commission or over-ride basis. By itself, this was a substantial incentive to sell. On top of this, twice a year, there was an 12-week sales contest set out in a full colour brochure, supported by numerous prizes: holidays, hampers, luxury car loans and others of equal attraction. League tables of the top 100 district sales teams' performance were published each week stimulating competition. Nobody, after all, wanted to be seen in the lower grades.

Given the immense success of the sales incentives, a similar scheme was introduced in the 40 installation depots. At first a contest was set up which simply measured the productivity of the installers and the surveyors. Although this led immediately to higher installation levels, it did nothing for quality. On the second attempt, the scheme incorporated measurements of customer satisfaction, which included surveying within three weeks of sale and installation within three weeks of delivery to the depot. To deal with the quality issues, each replacement which needed to be ordered due to poor installation produced penalties. In the final version of the scheme, the issue of debtors was tackled. There had been a growing number of customers who had simply not paid their bills. In the vast majority of cases, this was due to dissatisfaction with some aspect of the work which had not been resolved. Into the scheme went penalties in proportion to the level of debt, to stimulate the depots to put these problems right.

League tables published throughout the year showed everybody the performance of each depot. The prize at the end of each year was a weekend abroad for all of the depot staff and their partners. In the first three years of the contest, the measured improvement in productivity and customer satisfaction was in the order of 30 per cent and this was maintained in subsequent years. What had worked for sales teams thriving on competition appeared to work for other teams of staff.

The new factory incentive scheme

The Personnel Manager was, therefore, given the task of planning and introducing a similar contest for the group of factories. Initially, there were a number of problems to overcome:

- some factories were more mechanised than others;

- distribution costs were different as some delivered to the whole country, others just to their region;
- some factories were multi-product, others single product;
- how was the issue of comparing quality to be assessed?
- could other issues of customer satisfaction be incorporated? and
- would factory employees respond to the challenge or regard it with cynicism?

The first scheme incorporated only productivity and quality elements. Productivity was measured by taking the factory output and dividing it by all the hours worked, not just those employees on the bonus scheme. Managers, cleaners and office staff were all included. This was to make sure every person working in the factory would become involved in the outcome. Taking evidence from the previous 12 months, simple factors were inserted for the products relating to their estimated comparative labour content. Ten per cent was deducted for entrance doors, 20 per cent for patio doors and ten per cent was added for replacement windows. A few extras were allowed, particularly for the detailed work involved in leaded and Georgian windows but extras were kept to an absolute minimum.

On the issue of quality, the measure chosen was the cost of replacements identified by the depots as factory faults. It was by no means realistic as depots would rarely blame themselves for such faults, but the effect was the same for each factory. Dependent on the value of replacements each week, points were added or deducted. These points came to be crucial in determining the winners.

Despite some uncertainty, no account was taken of the degree of mechanisation, area of distribution or any other factors unique to a particular factory as it was considered that none of them were so crucial to productivity to alter the result. This was confirmed after consultation with the factory managers who agreed, with some minor modifications, to enter into the spirit of the contest.

The first contest lasted for 24 weeks, divided into 6 × 4 weekly mini-competitions. Points for the main contest were won on the basis of ten points for the winner, six points for second place, down to one point for sixth place. It was called a 'Grand Prix' for obvious reasons! Employees in the winning factory for each mini-competition received £10 Marks and Spencers vouchers. (They could only win this prize twice out of the six mini-competitions.) A weekly league table of performance was published, arriving in the factories in the middle of the following week.

The results

As the first weeks passed, it began to catch everybody's interest and the results improved steadily. By the 12th week, there had been an overall ten per cent increase in productivity (20 per cent from the leading factory) and the quality measures had begun to improve. In the last four weeks of the contest, the leading four factories had increased their productivity by 30 per cent, producing output figures way ahead of expectations or the best predictions. These improvements generated additional profits estimated at around £500,000, quite sufficient to finance a weekend in Majorca enjoyed by all 100 employees and their partners from the winning factory.

The pattern continued in the following year. A 24-week contest in the first half of the year and a hamper contest in the second half, where targets were set for all the employees in a factory to win a variety of hampers, ranging from £20 to £50 in value. Every week's production therefore counted – there could be no slackness. The improvement in results continued, year after year. The overall performance in real terms increased from ten per cent in the first year to 20 per cent in the second and 25 per cent in the third. From there, it crept up to 35 per cent by the sixth year.

After the first year, the success of the scheme led to more company objectives being incorporated into the scheme. With the emphasis being on productivity and quality there was a temptation to concentrate production on those products which were more straightforward and leave the more complex items to build up. Customers waiting for these items became dissatisfied when they arrived for installation later and later. Producing on time became another target. Each week, a total summary of the products manufactured behind time was published, with penalties if those totals exceeded a target. Factories responded almost immediately, cutting their overdue backlogs by shifting labour to those areas of backlog and carrying out more training where it was required.

Other campaigns included factory cleanliness, with the unannounced director's visit and a materials cost saving scheme both of which gave the opportunity for more points and small prizes to be won.

Outcomes

Arising from the scheme a number of outcomes occurred, some predictable, some surprising.

1. Communication improved exponentially. By knowing their own performance, and knowing what the competition was doing, employees became much more focused on their output. Arising from the improved communication came a better understanding of corporate objectives. Employees understood when changes had to be made; they worked together much more closely as a team for the greater good and they did not need the management entreaties to work harder – more often than not, the greatest complaints of laziness were laid at the door of the fellow employees who were not captured by the competitive spirit. Moreover, having the medium of a weekly newsletter meant that up-to-date news on issues such as product development, holiday votes, quality improvements and a host of other features could be delivered each week.
2. Better communication led to a greater sense of trust and understanding. Letters from customers were published – some praised the excellent quality, a few were critical. A higher profile communication pattern was

established with more regular visits from directors and full meetings with all the factory employees for 15 minutes to inform them of longer-term developments, answer questions and congratulate success.

3. Problem solving. Having ten factories meant that few problems were unique. Having a constantly improved product meant that there continued to be a host of production problems to solve each year. Usually this was a 'management' problem but the contest started to change this. Anything that may work to help improve the position on the league table was a stimulant to employees, individually or in teams. The engineering team rarely had to spend time convincing employees of the necessity of change. If it meant the chance of higher production and better quality, they were in favour of it. There was a rich flow of successful suggestions which could be transferred across the factory spectrum. There was a clamour for investment and factories vied for the chance of implementing new equipment for automatic sealed unit making or glass cutting.
4. Competition also led to co-operation. The factory managers and depot managers met far more often to improve their service to each other. Quality problems were clearly explained and resolved and delivery arrangements were organised on the basis of need rather than the driver's convenience. Replacements were turned round much faster and depot complaints became far fewer. Sales personnel were invited to the factories to see the steps taken to improve the quality and to educate the salesforce on technical aspects. The 'blame' culture started to dissolve.

Conclusions

There is an inherent artificiality about such schemes. To award small prizes, to constantly monitor performance, to continually exhort employees to do better, can grate. If employees do not choose to take part, the scheme can fall flat on its face. The reason this did not happen was partly because it was a young and successful company and employees were trusting enough to be willing to give it a try and partly because there was always a light-hearted approach, despite the essence of the scheme being deadly serious.

The scheme threw an interesting light on motivation. The increases in productivity arising from the introduction of the contest produced a consequential increase in the earnings from the bonus scheme. Bonus earnings went up in real terms, on average by around 50 per cent (total earnings by 15 per cent). This meant that by 1986, five years into the contest, employees were earning about £20 a week extra bonus (£1000 a year), far more than the total prizes they could win in the contest, even including the weekend abroad. Why did they respond to the contest and not previously to opportunities to increase their bonus earnings?

The explanation is a complex one. Firstly, there was the increased excitement and interest which the contest brought. The newsletters were devoured the moment they arrived in the factory. There was a considerable air of tension in the last week of the contest one year where three teams fought it out to the finish and special prizes had to be thought up to cover the disappointment of the other two teams. Kohn[1] might believe that prizes devalue the intrinsic benefits of a job, but all shop floor jobs (and many white collar jobs) could do with enlivening from time to time.

Secondly, the objectives of the scheme made sense. Many employees themselves bought double glazing so all the pleadings on behalf of customers sounded true. They knew the market was very competitive and understood the need to succeed in a situation where there were no long-term contracts.

Thirdly, support came from an unlikely source – the employees' families. The hampers were extremely popular and families were very proud of the person who had 'won' them. The partners who went on the weekend abroad were particularly grateful and often rather dazed by the attention they received. They had heard of nothing like this before!

Finally, the scheme appeared to be fair. Most factories won something during the scheme's operation. Through a combination of good planning, research and luck, no negative factors entered to throw the scheme into disarray. No factory felt particularly disadvantaged, nor was another's success envied. The facts published each week seemed irrefutable. Being at some distance away from each other generally helped in this circumstance.

In this contest, everybody was a winner. Customers had a better quality, received products on time at a period when the expression 'customer care' was only a gleam in British Airways Personnel Director's eye; employees earned more money and won prizes; jobs were more secure in a competitive market and the holding company had a higher dividend.

Postscript

There were a few losers. The factories who tended to prop-up the table suffered most when RTZ decided to shed its peripheral activities in the late 1980s. The new buyer decided to concentrate production in a few sites and so a number were closed down. Sales started to suffer at around the same time and it was decided with some reluctance that the luxury of the contest could no longer be afforded. The recession, which followed shortly after, hit the double glazing industry very hard and Everest took some time to recover to the level of sales of the 1980s.

It was eight or so exciting years of operation. It is argued that transferability to other organisations is difficult as there are few who have such a geographical configuration. However, the concept itself is especially transferable. It is a message of involvement, excitement, effective teamwork, challenging targets and an integrated system of special rewards that, added together, supported a very successful era.

Student activities

1. How closely do you think this particular reward strategy is aligned to the organisational objectives?

2. Could such a contest be transferred to a one or two-site setting? Set out the possibilities and difficulties if this were to happen.
3. Compare the extrinsic and intrinsic rewards attached to the competition. Evaluate both types from the viewpoint of a factory employee in this study.
4. The team at the bottom of the league table wants a meeting with you as Personnel Manager as they are no longer prepared to take part in the contest. Draw up an *aide-mémoire* for the meeting.
5. Define the dangers that may be associated with the 'hype' of such a contest.

Standard reading

	Armstrong and Murlis	*Armstrong*	*Milkovich and Newman*
Pages	279–362	271–282	328–334

References

1 Kohn, A (1993) *Punished By Rewards*, Houghton Mifflin Company, Boston

Further reading

McAdem, J (1995) 'Employee involvement and performance reward plans', *Compensation and Benefits Review*, March/April, pp 45–55

Seaman, R (1995) 'How self-directed work teams support strategic alignment', *Compensation and Benefits Review*, July/August, pp 23–32

Stewart, G *et al.* (1993) 'Re-thinking rewards – responses to A Kohn's reward theories', *Harvard Business Review*, Nov/Dec, pp 37–49. (Also contains a short reply by A Kohn to his critics.)

Wood, S (1995) 'Can we speak of a high commitment management on the shop floor?', *Journal of Management Studies*, Vol. 32, March, pp 215–247

Wood, S (1996) 'High commitment management and payment systems', *Journal of Management Studies*, Vol. 33, January, pp 53–57

Case Study 3

The Importance of Pay in Compulsory Competitive Tendering: The David Webster Experience

Introduction

In their studies of pay systems in small and medium size non-union firms, Beardwell and Storey[1] found little evidence that pay and reward systems had a strategic foundation or any innovatory zeal which non-union firms are supposedly expected to display. The majority tended to have a conservative, traditional or merely pragmatic approach, nor did they appear to be particularly adept at avoiding the normal pitfalls of labour market pressures, internal differentials and the need to arrive at explicable pay structures.

This case study is a clear exception to their overall findings. It describes a quickly growing, clearly focused organisation where pay and rewards play a crucial part in motivating employees to achieve company objectives.

Background

Compulsory Competitive Tendering (CCT) is one of the more durable reforms of the Thatcherite era and has been adopted by the Labour party who share the vision of a cost effective and quality service improvement in the public sector.

The concept originated in Tory-controlled Home County local authorities who experimented in the late 1970s in putting small parts of their public services out to tender. The authorities were able to achieve this process because the number of staff involved was small (sometimes in single figures) and often because a deal was reached with the in-coming contractor to take on all staff who wished to transfer. On a few occasions, the union was in too weak a position, even in the 1970s, to rouse itself to outright opposition. The consequent savings made (some authorities quote 20 per cent or more) led the in-coming Thatcher administration to convert this voluntary process into a compulsory one, by passing the Planning and Land Act 1980 which was strengthened by the Local Government Act 1988. A strong current of anticollectivisation ran through this legislation as the administration wanted to remove the union stranglehold on vital public services and knew well that the successful contractors were often small and non-union.

The company

David Webster Ltd was founded in the early 1960s as a street lighting contractor in a buy-out from a family connected building contracting business. Its early years were spent erecting new street lighting units for a number of councils in Southern England with a small labour force varying from nine to 20.

In 1966 the quality of service provided was a key factor in the awarding of the contract for maintaining all the street lighting for Hatfield District Council in Hertfordshire. Like many local authorities, the contract had been carried out over a number of years by the Electricity Board. This was the first example in the UK of a local authority awarding a contract for day-to-day lighting service activities to a private contractor. This contract was for an initial three-year period but has been renewed in various forms every since and now exceeds 30 years.

Building on that experience, the company gradually won a small selection of maintenance contracts, and began to spread its activities around the Home Counties, including Bromley and Richmond. During the 1980s another arm of the business developed as work on civil engineering lighting grew, culminating in substantial contracts on the M25, the M1 and other major road works.

By the time the CCT legislation was passed, the company had grown to 200 employees with a turnover in excess of £10 million. CCT provided the opportunity to tender for contracts on a nationwide basis and a number of substantial contracts were won. These contracts and two strategic acquisitions allowed the organisation to more than double in size by the early 1990s. It remains a private company wholly owned by the founder and his family.

Operating a contract

A typical local authority contract involved remedying defects in the 20,000 or so lighting points in the district, mostly streetlights but also bollards and lighted signs. Each fortnight, a 'scout' drove around a fixed route at night making a list of the defects. This list would be passed to the contractor to remedy within a fixed time, usually five days. If a member of the public complained separately about a particular defect, this would be added to the list. An inspector working for the authority would inspect a selection of these defects to ensure that they had been remedied properly and on time. Other work involved the cleaning, painting of columns and bulk lamp replacements, planned preventive maintenance work and the repair work following traffic accidents. All of these activities had a fixed payment and financial penalties were applied if the work was not completed on time to the specification.

Traditional payment systems

From very early days David Webster had realised that the local authority pay system was inappropriate for his method of operation. Terms and conditions were negotiated nationally by local authority unions to cover a wide range of employees in a variety of services with some small local variations relating to working practices. In the interests of equity, employees working in street cleaning, cemeteries, grounds landscaping, etc would be on the same conditions and their pay would be determined by the national grading system. Lighting operatives would have a 40-hour week with hours from 7.30 am to 4.30 pm, Monday to Friday with an hour's unpaid lunch break. They would start from the depot and be allowed 30 minutes to load up and a further 30 minutes to unload, plus a short paid mid-morning break. They would work in two-man teams because this had been conceded as a general safety issue. They would be allocated work for the day, but bad weather, shortage of material, problems with the vehicle or a difficult remedial job could all be reasons given why the work was not completed. That might mean that overtime was required, paid at time plus a half.

Supervising the work and verifying the reasons given for poor performance was not easy, as the operatives were spread over a wide area and often without communication to their base. Bonus schemes were occasionally tried but were generally unsuccessful, due to:

- The schemes needed to be negotiated with the unions who were generally suspicious and demanded earnings safeguards before agreeing to their introduction.
- A major cause of disputes related to the external factors which hindered output. Unions would insist that allowances were given for vehicle breakdowns, bad weather, etc and claims in these areas provided difficulties for the unit manager. If they agreed to the claims, then this would lead to further claims, often difficult to authenticate which, in turn, would lead to wage drift. If they acted tough and turned the claims down then unions would become hostile to the scheme and may decide to terminate it. Worse, the claim could be taken over the manager's head to a meeting with higher management. If agreed at that forum it would do much to undermine the authority of the manager.
- An additional problem related to the potential extra pay coming from the scheme. High performance could give an employee an extra ten per cent in earnings. However, working a Saturday five-hour overtime shift could give an employee almost 20 per cent earnings increase. It was far more profitable for the employee to extend the time taken to do the work, allow it to accumulate then work the overtime. This was particularly true when such Saturday shifts were often on a 'job and finish' basis and could be completed in four hours or less!
- Artificial cut-off points or ceilings for the bonus which allowed only a limited amount of improvements.

Schemes were therefore difficult to agree, difficult to operate fairly, open to manipulation and unlikely to motivate. It was clear to David Webster that a system where lighting operatives were working on fixed hours, to a flat wage, with a fall-back overtime system and a closely defined job met only the requirements of the routine, predictable operations of a closed community. It did not fit the requirements of the flexible, profit-seeking, competitive environment in which David Webster worked.

The new pay scheme

The essential features of the new pay scheme which was to be at the heart of the company's operations is set out in Table 1.3.

Firstly, employees did not work under any fixed hours. They had keys to the main gates of the depots and could start work and finish work at whatever time suited them. They were expected to work a 45-hour week but the hours were not counted. Only complete days of sickness were noted. There were no official breaks, paid or unpaid. Employees could take as many or as few breaks as they wished. If employees wished to start at 5.00 am in summer to avoid traffic and finish at 3.00 pm they were free to do so. There was no time given for loading or unloading – the quicker this was done, the more time employees spent on the work to be done.

Secondly, the basic hourly rate was quite low. It varied a certain amount by geographical location but was generally around £4.00 an hour, much lower than the basic rate paid by the local authorities.

Thirdly, there was a substantial bonus scheme. The employee received a bonus for each piece of work priced on the basis of the amount that the authority was invoiced under the terms of the contract; so much for a lantern repair, so much for a repair to the electrics at the base of the column, etc. Details of these prices covered two pages of A4 paper and it seemed, at first, to be a very complex scheme. However, employees learn each job under

Table 1.3 *Comparing traditional local authority terms and conditions with David Webster scheme*

TRADITIONAL WORKING PRACTICES	DAVID WEBSTER SCHEME
Fixed hours of work	No fixed hours
Fixed loading and unloading times	No loading or unloading times
Fixed breaks	No fixed breaks
Two men teams	Team size to fit job requirement
High basic wage	Low basic wage
No bonus scheme	Bonus scheme a key factor
Overtime endemic	No overtime
No vehicle responsibility	Vehicle responsibility
No movement between contracts	Movement between contracts as required
No penalties for poor quality	Penalties for quality
'Permanent' contracts	Contract for life of contract
Generous sick pay	Limited sick pay
Involvement limited	Involvement crucial
Just a job	More like a small business

training and the 80/20 rules apply: 80 per cent or more of their work comes under 20 per cent of the work categories and many of the listed prices are rarely used. The employee records each job done and this is used to pay bonus and to invoice the authority.

No allowances were given for any special circumstances relating to the work, such as bad weather, difficult work, etc. The justification for this was two-fold. Firstly, that the authority paid no allowances to the company. When the contract was tendered, the company was to build into the price a sum to cover such circumstances. Secondly, the swings and roundabouts argument applied where an employee hit by difficult circumstances one month, by the laws of chance, would have some easier circumstances the following month. The on target earnings under the scheme aimed to allow the average employee to more than double their earnings through the bonus scheme. The benefits and potential drawbacks of this scheme are explored later.

Fourthly, there was no overtime. Employees who wished to work more hours did so by being issued with other work, if available, or by helping on other routes which were shorthanded through illness, when they had finished their allocated work. They did not receive any extra basic hours in these circumstances. For this reason, there was no incentive to spin out the work.

Fifthly, the job was enlarged somewhat by including the care of the vehicle. It is in the employee's interest that the vehicle is in good condition and does not break down. It is kept clean inside and out by the employee and they carry out simple maintenance (water, tyres, etc). They need to carefully liaise on regular servicing. This area of operation is important from the viewpoint of the image of the company and its relation with the general public.

Sixthly, their contract is one of flexibility. They could be moved about within the contract onto whatever work is available. Furthermore, they could be moved onto a nearby contract if the necessity arises. For example, employees based on Hertfordshire contracts were moved onto the London Borough of Ilford contracts. Flexibility extended to working as a one-man or two-man operation which were carefully delineated in terms of health and safety issues and terms of the contract.

Seventhly, there were downsides for the employees. The sick pay was very poor and the company recognised this. It was only a small contributory scheme dealing with the very occasional week-long absence. Overall, this was not regarded as too big a problem as sickness is very low and absenteeism negligible. There was no pension scheme and there were none of the additional benefits that a large organisation may offer such as private health insurance.

There has been a recent development which has changed one of the disadvantages for the employee. Previously, their contracts of employment were only likely to last as long as the company held the contract, except in those areas where a number of interlocking contracts operated. In a sense, this was a renewable short-term contract of three to six years. However, the operation of the Transfer of Undertakings regulations has made this mainly irrelevant and this is discussed later.

Discussion of the bonus scheme

On first sight, the bonus scheme looks like the old, discredited piece-work system which was, by and large, eliminated by the end of the 1960s in British industry. These old schemes were defective in an industrial setting for a number of reasons:

- they were divisive, setting one employee against another and discouraging teamwork;
- they were a barrier to the introduction of new products and systems as new prices had to be negotiated each time;
- employees concentrated on the work that paid well and neglected the remainder;
- there would be constant arguments over allowances when external factors stopped an employee producing as much as they wanted (poor materials, machine breakdown, etc); and
- production was encouraged at the expense of quality, safety or delivery on time.

The scheme at David Webster Ltd is set in a different context. It is not a large number of employees working on a production line on one site, each individual or team being reliant upon the other, nor is it in a heavily unionised environment.

The issues which caused piece-work to fail have mainly been overcome. Employees work singly or in small teams and are largely independent with their own area. They are not in competition or conflict with each other. In a unit, they all work under the same price list. Employees have a list of work on a defined route and must carry out every item, they cannot pick and choose the work. New and more efficient working practices, such as better vehicles, are welcomed as they improve bonus opportunities. There are only very occasional discussions over allowances where very special circumstances apply: heavy falls of snow and very difficult access to install columns are isolated examples.

Finally, although output is encouraged, quality and timing are essential. Should the local authority inspector discover that work claimed had not been carried out properly or on time, it would result in heavy penalties to the contractor. Add onto this control the random checks by supervisors, then employees appreciate quickly that skimping on the work is very risky and can quickly lead to their dismissal for gross misconduct. Safe working is also vital as time lost through a minor accident can be very costly to an employee through lost bonus. An award is made each year to the unit with the best safety record.

The bonus scheme encourages the arrangement to be more like a set of mini-contractors, each with their individual contractual responsibilities to provide a cost effective and profitable service to the public with the prime responsibility to help win the contract at the next renewal date. It is feasible to see the bonus as their slice of the contract's profits. There are standard operating instructions (the company has been awarded ISO 1902) but the time management and personal efficiency functions belong to the employee. A well organised, efficient employee earns high bonuses. The scheme overcomes the significant difficulties which usually apply when trying to supervise at a distance through the operation of a self-regulating system.

The bonus scheme has a further advantage. By linking it so closely to the prices agreed with the local authorities, employees are involved in the heart of the whole business operation. They can appreciate which individual items have higher margins than others and where savings can be made to benefit the organisation. The units are small enough for regular meetings to take place between the manager and their teams to discuss how to improve operations for their mutual benefit. Tips on efficient working are shared around. The entrepreneurial spirit also spills over to the attitude of the employees towards unions. David Webster has not been overtly hostile to unions and ballots have been held on union membership at the largest unit with full management co-operation on three occasions. Each time, a substantial majority of the employees voted against joining a union.

Bonus for managers and other staff

A recent development has been the introduction of bonuses for unit managers. This is based on the return on capital employed at each unit. A general target percentage return is set and for each one per cent above target, a bonus is paid. The nature of the local authority main contract is taken into account as some contracts were won with lower margins than others. The feedback to managers through this reporting system and the accounts which underpin the scheme have given the managers a far greater understanding of finance and unit profitability and rewarded them for efficient working. Recent developments include the movement to decentralize purchasing to business units, which gives managers greater opportunity to control their operations and improve their bonus by better planning and organisation. Other staff at the units also receive part of the bonus and this has been modified to include an overall bonus for Head Office staff. This has become a similar arrangement to gainsharing (see Case Study 18).

Transfer of undertakings regulations

Recent decisions by the European Court of Justice which have attempted to interpret the labyrinthine Acquired Rights Directive have presented problems for David Webster Ltd and other private contractors attempting to win local authority contracts. During the 1980s, when a contractor won the contract, the existing local authority employees were made redundant by the authority if no alternative work could be found for them. (After much political debate, the authority was allowed to incorporate these costs into their own tender.) It was up to the contractor if they then wished to choose to employ them. There was no obligation to do so. The contractor could also employ them on whatever terms and conditions they wished.

A number of decisions changed this situation. It was originally considered that the EC's Acquired Rights Directive applied only to businesses in the nature of a commercial venture but the European Court of Justice confirmed in their 1992 decision in the case of *Dr. Sophie Redmond Stichting* v *Bartol* that this was not so and applied to non-commercial businesses as well.

A second and more crucial decision was in the case of *Watson Rask and Christiansen* v *ISS Kantineservice A/S* in 1993 where the contracting-out of a canteen operation was seen as a transfer of an undertaking, not just a transfer of an internal service to an external contractor. This was despite the arguments that no assets were involved, no customers were transferred and there was no 'profitable object'. In the case of the transfer of a contract, therefore, it became a requirement on the contractor to take all the employees and continue to employ them on their existing terms.

This presents three problems. Firstly, all employees who wish to be transferred, have to be accepted. As the contractor is more efficient and generally employs fewer staff, this immediately presents a requirement for downsizing with all the attendant costs as the redundancy terms are also carried over.

Secondly, the contractor needs to change the terms and conditions of the transferred employees, especially those relating to pay, to the systems described earlier. As these changes are substantial, including a reduction in basic pay, an employee who does not wish to accept those new terms can claim constructive dismissal if those new terms are enforced. Moreover, these changes cannot be attempted until three to six months after the transfer.

Thirdly, as most local authority employees were union members, they have tended to carry over their union membership. The contractor is then faced with a decision as to whether to recognise the union for negotiating purposes.

The larger the contract, the more problematical are these issues. They have caused the contracting-out process to slow down while contractors continue to examine the consequences. Tender prices have risen as contractors now have to incorporate the redundancy costs, which are difficult to estimate. The reality of the transfer process is that local authority employees are informed by the contractor of the new terms of working and a number will try their best to stay with the authority, particularly those who have reasonable service and a pension expectation. (It has recently been established that pensions are not part of the regulations, illogical as this appears.) This may reduce the contractor's transfer costs. There may also be an interim arrangement where the transferring employees agree to the changed terms under some guaranteed earnings arrangement for the first year.

Conclusion

CCT has a number of attributes which give it a superior position in the pantheon of human resource management theory. It promotes flexibility in working practices, it has a clear unitary approach in its employee relations, it is customer focused, it encourages innovation, it has a positive employee involvement programme and performance pay is central to its operations.

Local authorities have not stood still and let contractors walk all over them. They have taken defensive action by changing their own way of working. They have adopted most of the these paradigms operated by the contractor and persuaded their unions of the essential requirements to change. The success here has been demonstrated by the majority of all competitive tenders still being won in-house.

It would appear that all sides are winners. The public have a better service, monitored far more effectively. If the public make substantial criticisms of the work of the contractor, then the contractor may, at worst, be immediately removed or certainly have their name removed from the list of companies invited to tender. The authority have a cheaper and more efficient service. More money is thereby released to invest in the lighting infrastructure or even reduce the council tax. The contractor makes a good living. The employees earn higher wages and gain more satisfaction through the improved intrinsic benefits (organising their own time, having control over their activities, etc).

As a postscript, a further development occurred in a recent House of Lords decision on equal pay. Here, North Yorks Council had persuaded the low paid catering ladies to accept a further pay cut so they could win the catering contract. After the contract was won, their union took up an equal pay claim as the staff were now paid less than male employees in the council who were on the same job-evaluated pay scale. The Council claimed that the difference was due to the business requirements in order to win the contract and not associated with discrimination. However, when the case eventually arrived at the House of Lords, it was decided that the public acceptance that catering staff should be very lowly paid was, in itself, discriminatory and the Council lost the case. The catering staff had their original pay rate restored.

Student activities

1. Your organisation is considering tendering for a local authority contract which is currently being run by the Direct Labour force. As Personnel Manager, draw up a list of the questions relating to personnel issues which you will need to ask the manager of the Direct Labour force before the tender can be drawn up.
2. After six months running the contract, you wish to change from the 'traditional working practices' to a scheme such as David Webster's. Draw up a briefing document to the 20 employees from the authority which have transferred to your organisation.
3. Your briefing document and determined persuasion has not been successful in the case of ten of the employees concerned. What action do you take now? Set out the possible options with advantages and disadvantages and signify your preferred option.

4. How do the operations of a company like David Webster Ltd match against the paradigm of HRM set out by writers such as Storey?

Standard reading

	Armstrong and Murlis	*Armstrong*	*Milkovich and Newman*
Pages	67–76 and 279–293	271–282	328–334

References

1 Beardwell, I and Storey, J (1996) 'Paying the piper – pay determination in the non-union firm', *Conference Paper, HRM – The Inside Story*, Open University, Milton Keynes, April

Further reading

Aikin, O (1993) 'Transfers are getting stickier', *Personnel Management*, Vol. 25, No. 5, May, pp 56–57

Ridgeway, C and Wallace, B (1995) *Empowering Change, the Role of People Management*, IPD, London

Fowler, A (1988) *HRM in Local Government*, Longmans, London

Hale, R and Whitlam, P (1995) *Target Setting and Goal Achievement*, Kogan Page, London

Maitland, I (1994) 'Getting a result', No. 3 in series *Managing People in Small and Growing Businesses*, IPD, London

Stewart, J (1996) *Managing Change Through Training and Development*, Kogan Page, London

Spence, P (1990) 'The effects of performance management and performance-related pay in local government', *Local Government Studies*, July/August

Case Study 4

Leading Change with Compensation at Newsday Corporation

Introduction

There are many effective ways to manage change. Some ways focus on systems and others on behaviours. To be successful, the change process itself must be multi-disciplined and holistic in nature. It must begin with clearly defined goals, objectives and strategies which serve as unifying principles.

Leading organisational change with a compensation initiative changes the very process itself by focusing the attention of those who will be affected by the end result. It can create an environment of anticipation and expectation that can, if properly handled, facilitate change. Leading change with compensation, however, is a little like moving mountains with dynamite. It beats the pick-and-shovel approach, but watch out for the side effects!

Background

During the 1980s, Newsday, a Long Island based publisher of two daily newspapers, enjoyed great prosperity linked to a general prosperity in the local economy. Advertising revenue is the dominant income for all newspapers with the cover price being of far less importance. At that time, one of the crucial success factors in a competitive publishing environment was the ability to generate and maintain large volumes of advertising revenue through teams of motivated sales representatives. The traditional managing process was to focus sales reps on managing accounts in the paper's best interest. For example, every week on the most desirable advertising days, newspaper editions would reach their maximum page limit so sales reps would try to persuade advertisers to switch their adverts to alternative days, even if it did not suit them.

Profitability at Newsday had been very high as the newspapers had been able to raise their advertising rates aggressively and exceeded their revenue goals year after year. In 1989, however, the local economy began to slip. Many advertisers, large and small, began to fall by the wayside. Those that weathered the storm had less money to spend on advertising. As the local economy struggled with a recession, the market itself became more competitive with the arrival of cable TV and the expansion of a cheaper direct mail service. Profits fell and action was needed to stem the decline.

Early attempts at change

Throughout the 1980s, the compensation of sales representatives at Newsday, as at most newspapers, was characterised by a high base salary. There were incentive plans, but they were fairly complex and very product-focused. Sales reps, assigned to geographical territories or sales categories, earned their incentives by hitting predetermined monthly revenue goals in each of a variety of sales categories. If they fell short in reaching a revenue goal, they received no incentive payout. Furthermore, if they exceeded the sales revenue goal, they did not earn any additional incentive. Thus, the compensation plan limited incentive earnings and sent a mixed motivational message to the sales reps. Although the intended primary roles of the sales force was service oriented – to keep the advertiser informed, to represent the advertiser's needs – in practice the perception by advertisers of the newspaper was as an unresponsive and monopolistic organisation whose staff placed service as only one section of their work agenda.

In 1990, Newsday changed the sales incentives to focus more attention on the customer's business needs. Although they retained some individual product goals, the incentive plans now gave sales representatives credit for any product sold. They also made revenue goals cumulative on a monthly, quarterly and annual basis and uncapped incentive earnings. In addition to maintaining a constant motivational message for the sales personnel, the changes were intended to encourage them to sell products which worked best for the advertiser.

Although the newspaper changed the sales incentive plans, it did not change the sales management philosophy and the supporting sales processes, such as goal-setting. As advertising revenue continued to decline, the dominant theme became controlling costs. The sales staff faced increasingly difficult and often unattainable goals and incentive earnings declined. Despite considerable efforts made in training and developing the staff, their motivation and outputs remained depressed.

Fundamental change

Another attempt at change took place in 1992 when management were convinced that the best performers were not being rewarded adequately, the overall sales effort was not strong enough and the selling effort did not adequately support the emerging marketing orientation of the newspapers.

Management considered re-leveraging the existing incentive plans but this would not have addressed the real issues of non-alignment with business objectives. An answer to some very basic questions was needed before fundamental change could begin. A project team was set the task of answering:

- who were the advertisers and what value did the newspaper provide to them?
- where would more effort and attention make a difference?
- did the sales reps have the skills and time to be successful in the new marketplace? and
- were the sales support systems effective?

An outside consultant, working with the management team and sales reps over a three-day intensive course, helped the organisation come to three clear conclusions:

- the bargain with the advertiser was to provide good value for the dollar spent, which was not always perceived to happen by either side;
- there were clear opportunities in the marketplace for the newspapers to increase sales revenue; and
- sales reps spent too much time in non-selling activities which gave no value to the advertiser or the organisation.

A new strategy emerged in order to get the sales reps to work much closer to the customer. It was hoped to transform the sales rep into a business consultant.

While this effort helped the business to understand the market better and to begin to change the working practices of the sales force, the basic questions of how to align sales efforts with both the sales strategy and the new emerging sales role, how to encourage and obtain a greater sales effort and how to reward sales performance more effectively, all remained unanswered.

Designing the new sales incentive scheme

In January 1993, management retained a team of two consultants specialising in compensation plans to help realign and refocus the sales incentive plans.

Step 1: Setting objectives and strategies

There continued to be differences amongst the key decision makers as to the focus of the sales strategy. However, amongst the mass of information gathered during the fact-finding process, a crucial piece of accounting data came to light. Through a profitability analysis, it was found that the profit margins on all Newsday products were not significantly different. It was therefore possible to adopt a non-differentiated selling strategy without significantly affecting profits. With that knowledge, it was agreed that the strategy would be confirmed as one of increasing sales revenue by focusing on the customers' needs and on building long-term relationships. Other conventional sales strategies followed naturally from this fundamental precept.

Step 2: Engaging the stakeholders

The intention was to make the design process highly visible and participatory, both to increase the quality of the decisions, and to gain the sales representatives' acceptance of the changes. Two groups generated the recommendations on the actual design of the new compensation plan. One, the Executive Task Force, consisted of the 17 sales managers; the other, the Sales Compensation Task Force, consisted of a similar number who were mostly sales reps but with a small number of sales managers. Although the groups were large, leaders emerged within each to form a core group of highly active members. It was these 'champions' who withstood a fair amount of peer pressure, embraced the change process and ultimately directed the outcomes.

Both groups' roles were defined as clearly advisory. Members were to review and consider facts, and then make recommendations on plan design. While they were being invited into the decision-making process, it was recognised that the ultimate authority lay with the executive board.

The Executive Task Force (ETF) looked at:

- definition of sales job classifications;
- the target compensation levels for each classification;
- the relationship between base and incentive pay; and
- the funding of the whole plan.

Members of the ETF made trips to other newspapers to examine their compensation schemes, including ideas on team payments.

The Sales Compensation Task Force reviewed:

- the proposals of the ETF;
- defining and weighting performance criteria for each incentive plan proposed; and
- communication processes.

More detailed information gathering and consultation took place over the next four months as the plans started to emerge. One of the early criteria was that the cost was to be no higher for the same performance as the previous year. Difficult discussions took place over issues such as:

1. The possible reduction of the sales reps' high base salary. While this provoked a strong reaction, severely testing trust in the organisation, this highly emotional issue was the key that opened discussion and resolution of many operational issues.
2. The goal-setting process had been much criticised as it appeared to rely simply on the previous year's result plus some growth factor. A new process was proposed which was a collaborative enterprise between managers and reps to try to produce a more level playing field.
3. In the old scheme, a 'windfall' clause existed whereby if a sales rep brought in a great deal of revenue not traceable to their direct efforts, then management would call it a 'windfall' and refuse to pay bonus on this

sum. Under the new proposals, this would be abolished but goals would be updated each quarter.

4. A 'discretionary' fund existed previously which allowed managers to reward effort to sales reps who had worked hard but not met their goals. However, as fair as this seemed, there were no well-defined criteria for these awards and most sales reps viewed them as capricious and arbitrary. All bonus payments subsequently were made on clear and transparent objectives.
5. Previously, sales reps had their bonus reduced due to mistakes made by other departments. For example, when an advert appeared produced wrongly (ie a wrong telephone number or address) and the advertiser refused to pay. Under new proposals, only sales related adjustments were charged against the rep.
6. The scheme would have no maximum payment.

Gaining acceptance

The latter four changes opened the door to the fundamental acceptance of the first proposal, a reduction of basic pay. Although this provoked a great deal of fear and uncertainty among the reps, their participation in the decision-making process assisted in convincing the group that the scheme was a viable one. A series of meetings took place to ensure everybody had a thorough understanding of the entire scheme and that all objections and doubts were addressed. Details of all the tests and dummy runs were given and nothing was held back. All the information was confirmed in an individually prepared package.

The final version was that the incentive target was roughly doubled, making it 40 per cent of the total targeted compensation for the job. The base salaries were reduced by $4500 (about ten per cent) and base rate increases were frozen for two years. The incentive scheme was relatively simple containing only four elements, rather than the eight or more in previous schemes. There were also additional team-based rewards which were a mix of cash and payments in kind. A special group was set up to consider the development and relevance of these rewards and the balance between team and individual payments. The performance management system was re-designed to support the incentive plan and provide better focused training and development for the reps, both those who met their targets and those who did not.

Summing up

This case study is not about a traditional sales compensation plan development. The plan was not designed behind closed doors and then rolled out to the sales staff. This was a highly participative and highly charged process. In placing pay at risk, the plan brought deep-rooted concerns of sales representatives forcefully to the surface which ultimately forced improvements in the goal-setting process and performance management system.

Initially there were difficulties when the scheme began as sales remained weaker than expected but sales reps quickly got into their stride and, by the end of 1993, the revenue exceeded the target for the first time for four years. At a year end evaluation, they confirmed that they felt the scheme to be fairer than any they had previously experienced.

The newspaper industry will be facing exhilarating and extensive change over the next 20 years. Electronic technology will revolutionize the collection, processing and distribution of information and the daily printed newspaper will face considerable rivals. New markets and subscribers will be found all along the superhighways. So continuing change will be required. Leading change, with pay as a vital change agent, can facilitate changes in others – training, staffing, flexibility, etc. Properly handled, pay sends the most powerful messages of when and what change is required.

Student activities

1. Why is this case study more than just about introducing an incentive scheme for sales reps?
2. Read Michael Armstrong's article on 'Change management' in *Human Resources*, Autumn 1993, pp 10–14. Who are the enemies of change in this example and who are the allies?
3. Can you identify any differences between the American context for change and the UK context?
4. What would you identify as the key criteria with which to measure a successful change process?

Standard reading

	Armstrong and Murlis	*Armstrong*	*Milkovich and Newman*
Pages	33–52	78–96	43–67

Further reading

Chaudhry-Lawton *et al*, (1992) *Quality: Change through teamwork*, Century Business, London

Dawson, P (1994) *Organisational Change: A Processional Approach*, Paul Chapman, London

Howarth, C (1984) *The Way People Work – Job Satisfaction and the Challenge of Work*, Oxford University Press

Nortier, F (1995) 'A new angle on coping with change: managing transition', *Journal of Management Development*, Vol. 14, No. 4, pp 32–46

Plant, R (1987) *Managing Change and Making it Stick*, Fontana, London

Case Study 5

Changing the Reward System at Blane and Riversshire Building Society

By Sarah Kelly, Senior Lecturer
Bristol Business School

Background

The Blane and Rivershire Building Society (BRBS) currently ranks in the top 20 building societies in the UK. However, in terms of the size and strength of its asset-base and its financial performance, it operates somewhere near the top of the 'second division' of the top 20 societies, employing about 2500 staff. Competition in this market is fierce. Organisations in the sector are subject to significant external pressures for change – many societies are considering mergers whilst some of the smaller societies are at risk of being swallowed up by larger societies or banks. Ten years ago there were 167 societies, now there are 83 and the trend looks set to continue.

A number of societies have already decided to convert their mutual society status to become quoted on the stock exchange as banks. The BRBS is a well-established organisation operating from headquarters in the Midlands and has branches across the Midlands and the South of England.

Strategic intentions

In the recent past, the Society attempted to expand its product and service range by acquiring an estate agency business. This was not a successful venture for the organisation as the estate agency business earned little in terms of extra revenue for the Society and was also considered 'difficult to manage'. The estate agency's values and norms did not fit well with the long established, paternalistic nature of the Society's culture.

Consequently, the organisation decided to concentrate on the two main areas of its business, savings and loans. The strategic plan is to focus on what the Society now views as its 'core business' and improve the quality of service delivery to its customers in these two areas. One of the key issues for the organisation is to improve its level of customer service both in the savings (deposit-taking business) and loans (mortgage lending business) operations. The executive team feel that it is vital for the Society to pursue a strategy of simplicity and focus. They feel that, in order to differentiate themselves in the market place, the Society must provide good products, delivered and processed at a low cost, and outstanding customer service. This will mean that traditional values will need to be revisited and a new focus on efficiency and customer friendly service will need to be introduced.

Strategy formation

Although the top team have held numerous off-site meetings in recent months to attempt to clarify their plans they have not, as yet, begun to think through the implementation of their ideas and they have not yet consulted the Personnel department about the implications of their plans. However, they have retained the services of a consultant, Harry Hargreaves, who is acting as a facilitator to the top team in their strategy formation process.

Harry's specialism is coaching executives and facilitating executive team decision making processes. He is concerned at the moment on a number of counts. Firstly, he sees that the changes that the Society plans to make will affect the way that the majority of employees operate. Harry feels that some more detailed consideration of the implementation issues will be vital to the success of any change. He also feels that very few employees have been consulted or involved in the change process. In particular, Harry is concerned about the role and involvement of the Personnel department.

Strategy implementation – the Board's proposals

Supported by Harry, the Board has been assessing the Society's competitive market place as well as what they believe to be the organisation's internal capabilities. They have come up with two key areas for improvement which will affect product processing and service delivery. They have spent a considerable amount of time discussing these ideas and have drawn together the following outline plans.

Customer service centre for loans business

Firstly the Board has decided to set up a central unit at headquarters to process mortgage applications. The intention is to create a dedicated group of 'case workers' organised into 'customer service' teams in the loans business. This means that one person (or 'case worker') will deal with the processing of a mortgage application from start to finish. Applications for mortgages will be referred from the branches to this area which will be dedicated to loans' customer service. The aim is to speed up the processing of mortgage applications and give the customer a single point of contact for this product. The intention is that this operation will be a flat, streamlined structure, dedicated to processing mortgage applications with maximum efficiency and effectiveness.

Branch restructuring and job re-design

The second major change will affect the branch structure. It has been decided that the servicing of savings accounts will continue to be done in the branch. However, customer service will be improved by the installation of a new customer information system into the branch network. The new computer system will mean that branch staff can process customer account enquiries easily and effectively using the system, but that the Society can maintain a 'high street' presence and provide a point of human contact for its customers and potential customers. This change will have a significant impact on the jobs and structure of the typical branch office.

Until now the branches have typically been staffed by a branch manager, a personal financial advisor (PFA), a customer service supervisor and three customer service representatives (see Figure 1.8). As a result of the changes in mortgage processing and in the branch, the role of the customer service supervisor in the branch will be redundant. The branch manager and the customer service representatives jobs will be 're-designed'.

In the future, the branch manager will have an extremely important co-ordinating role, making sure that customer service representatives provide the PFA with enough leads to generate significant income for the society. The branch manager will also have to take on a 'team manager' role and manage the customer service representatives on a day to day basis. In addition, branch managers will be responsible for bringing in new business through the use of campaigns and marketing events organised and carried out on a local basis. The customer service representative role will be enhanced, given that they should have all the information they need to deal with customers available through a new information system which will be developed and installed to support this change. However, the role of supervisor will be removed and it is anticipated that approximately 150 staff in the same number of branches will be affected.

Human resources strategy

From Harry Hargreaves' perspective the personnel function's activities could be described as reactive rather than proactive. The top priority appears to be to maintain the *status quo*, although there has been some recent progress in the area of training and development as the Society has recently received an Investors in People award. From what Harry knows about human resource management, he has a strong suspicion that the Personnel department, especially the Personnel Director, do not realise the nature and scope of the changes that are about to happen. In Harry's opinion, it would be difficult to accuse the Personnel department of thinking strategically!

The Personnel Director, George Evans, has been with the Society for a long time. He started his career as a management accountant and moved

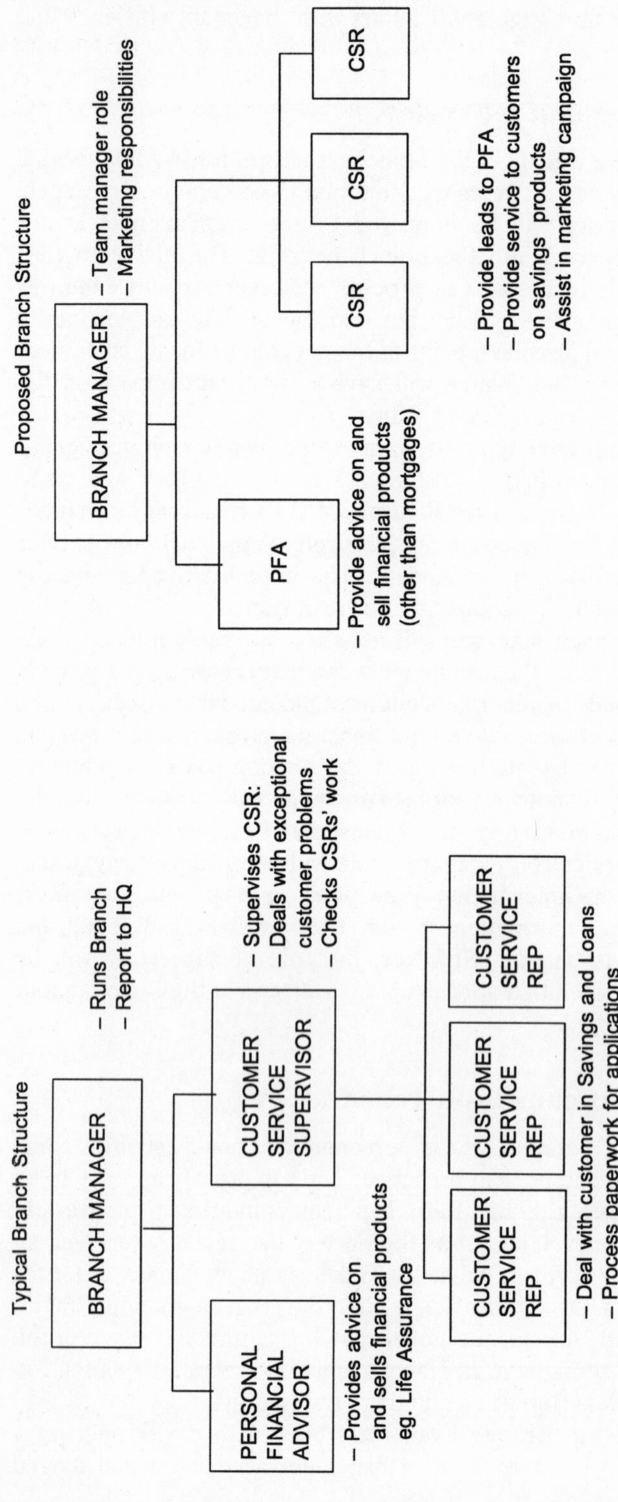

Figure 1.8 *Royal Midshires Building Society*

across to the personnel function about 15 years ago. Harry's assessment of George's position is that he is reasonably competent at maintaining existing personnel policies, but has a number of difficulties in trying to persuade the Board to re-think and adopt more radical and up to date approaches. George also suffers because the members of the Board do not tend to consult him with regard to people issues before they make decisions about the way forward for the Society. George has been present at some of the meetings where strategy has been discussed, but finds increasingly that decisions seem to be made without any real consideration of personnel issues.

New personnel staff

George Evans is well aware, therefore, that the Board is planning some significant changes which his department will have to support. He finds it difficult to make long-term plans or develop a strategy for the personnel function. He has, however, attempted to hire some new blood into his team, and one of these, Karen Ford, has recently joined the department. Karen has been appointed as the Personnel Manager for the branch network. She is based in the Society's headquarters in the Midlands, but has overall responsibility for all personnel matters in the branches.

Karen joined the Society from the retail sector and, at the time of her selection interview, took the opportunity to quiz George Evans about the organisation's human resource strategy. The Personnel Director's response indicated that the Society could expect significant changes in the competitive market place and in the way it would need to do business. Unused to high levels of turnover in the past, he intimated that the organisation would be likely to be recruiting more actively in the future.

He also intimated, however, that fundamental changes could be expected to occur in the financial services sector and that the Society should expect to be releasing staff in the near future. In fact, George's view was that the organisation should expect to have to carry out redundancy programmes, which would come as a significant cultural shock to the Society and its employees as no large-scale redundancy programme had ever been implemented by the Society.

On a more positive note, George anticipated that the Society would need to concentrate on making the most out of the existing resources. As a consequence of some of these factors, he had became convinced that training and developing the staff would be of paramount importance. George had heard a lot about competencies at conferences and workshops. He recognised their potential use in training and developing people, and was pleased that the organisation had already achieved a nationally recognised award for its training and development plans and activities.

Asked directly by Karen at her interview to assess the culture of the organisation, George had been forced to admit that, although there were significant changes afoot in the way the organisation approached its business, it was far from clear what or how these changes would be implemented.

George described the culture of the organisation to Karen as somewhat 'old fashioned' with a 'paternalistic' Board who tended to have a number of good forward thinking ideas. However, he was forced to admit that the organisation was not very adept at putting these ideas into practice. His feeling was that the Society's employees were quite unused to large scale, radical change and that communicating with employees was generally deemed to be quite difficult as the majority of staff were located at a distance from headquarters in the branches across the Midlands and South East.

The Personnel Director's assessment of the branch network was that each branch tended to operate with a good deal of local knowledge, but had only the vaguest notion of what happened at headquarters. Having said this, most employees were well aware of competitors' activities in the local market place and were becoming increasingly concerned about some of the rapid changes and somewhat worrying developments in the financial services labour market in general.

The new HR structure

The model adopted by George Evans for the Personnel department which Karen had just joined means that there are no specialist posts for training or reward management in the department. George's plan is for each of the Personnel Managers based at headquarters to develop a specialism and take particular responsibility for one of these areas. One of the other Personnel Managers has taken the responsibility for leading the IIP team and Karen has been hired because she has held this kind of dual role in her previous job. Although she does not class herself as a compensation and benefits expert, she has sufficient experience in this area to be able to analyse the existing situation and decide what would be needed to develop the appropriate reward strategies and plans.

George hopes that given Karen's experience elsewhere, the personnel team may be able to pull together a more proactive approach to human resource and reward management. He has already assigned a couple of projects to Karen in these areas and is hopeful that her expertise will help him to present well researched and persuasive arguments to the Board. His hope is that Karen's experience of up to date reward management practices will help influence the Board to take a more radical approach to the subject. So far they have been disinclined to review remuneration policies, as they do not believe that any problems exist in this area.

Reward management at BRBS

After only a short time in the job, several branch managers have already contacted Karen claiming that their staff are not paid enough and that many are leaving, particularly in the bigger towns and cities. This, they say, is causing retention problems – they feel they are losing their best staff members to other financial institutions and even into other sectors. Karen recognised this as a problem, but is unsure as to the root causes of the issue.

She has some personal views as to some of the possible causes. As a recent newcomer to the Society, she noted that salary levels across the branch network seemed somewhat inconsistent. Some time ago the Society introduced a job evaluation scheme but it was a very simple and informal one and was now looking long in the tooth. As new jobs were introduced, they were simply tacked on to the scheme without any rationalisation. As a consequence, there exists a variety of jobs, job titles and terms and conditions prevalent across the branch structure and in headquarters. In general, the situation could be summarised as follows:

- as far as it is possible to tell, the Society seems to pay average salaries;
- most branches compare themselves to other similar local organisations rather than with each other;
- with the exception of a subsidised mortgage, the Society provides very few benefits and no incentive payments at all; and
- there is no real appraisal system in place and the term 'performance' is not well defined, understood or managed in the organisation.

Karen holds a strong belief that salary levels are not based on any systematic review of what the current jobs actually entail or what it might be 'worth' either inside or outside the organisation. As BRBS branches covered a wide geographical spread, Karen regularly receives requests from branch managers for 'special treatment' in providing everything from exceptional salary increases to special travel allowances for staff in remote, far flung branches. The lack of any sensible, well researched or up to date policies already makes Karen's life difficult. She is convinced that the branch managers find it even more difficult to explain to their staff the rationale for various decisions the Society takes in this area.

Competency framework

BRBS has recently designed and developed a competency framework which supports its training and development initiatives. Karen feels sure that there must be some way of integrating a competency framework into the HR management infrastructure. For example, she has been given a special project by the Personnel Director to review and redesign the performance management system. Karen has also read widely and feels that the Society will also need to consider how it rewards people when they develop their competencies and improve their performance. She has come across the notion of 'contribution' in her reading and professional experience and feels sure that the organisation is far from clear about what contribution each job makes to its business activities.

When Harry tells Karen

Karen knows Harry from her previous company where Harry did some work as a consultant. They meet for lunch one day and Karen takes the opportunity to talk through some of her concerns about her responsibility for reward management and about what she sees as the lack of strategic direction of the personnel function in the Society. Harry is concerned by Karen's assessment of the existing situation and decides to give her some idea of the radical structural and cultural changes proposed by the Board.

Karen is initially angry that George does not seem to have been involved in the process so far, or at least has not communicated the fact that a strategic plan has been formulated and serious people issues have been raised. She calms down as she walks back to her desk after lunch and her mind gets to work on a preliminary assessment of the current situation in relation to reward management. As and when changes are announced, or her advice is sought, she wants to be have analysed the current problems and issues and have some appropriate solutions to propose to George and the Board.

Karen begins to think through her analysis of the current situation. She starts by trying to write down what she believes the organisation thinks and believes about reward management and what it values. This, she believes, will help formulate an appropriate reward strategy. She also reviews her earlier thoughts about pay policy and practice, especially in the branch network.

At the end of the afternoon, her initial thoughts take shape and she sketches out her proposals. The creation of the new customer service centre would provide an ideal testing ground for a new approach to reward management. If the Board could be persuaded to involve the personnel function right from the start, Karen would propose to:

- design the organisation structure from a blank sheet of paper;
- design new 'roles', rather than using the old job descriptions, detailing the purpose of the job, its overall responsibilities, plus the skills and competencies required;
- build in some indication of measures of success for the new roles;
- set up a more coherent performance management scheme; and
- align the payment system to the new system.

She believed that this approach could be piloted in the new customer service centres and, if successful, could be extended across the Society.

Student activities

1. Imagine you are Karen conducting a preliminary analysis of the organisation's current reward management strategy. List the organisation's current values, beliefs about reward and any existing policies and practices you can identify.
2. How would you assess the Society's current business, human resource and reward strategies?
3. Assuming that the Board's proposed plans are implemented, formulate a reward management strategy to match this. How would you propose to implement your proposals?
4. How would you convince the Board that your proposals are sound and should be implemented?

Standard reading

	Armstrong and Murlis	*Armstrong*	*Milkovich and Newman*
Pages	23–52	53–77	18–28

Further reading

IDS (1993) 'Moving to staff status with performance pay – a case study of Co-Steel Sheerness', *Report No. 654*, pp 25–28

IRRS (1996) 'Merit pay and grading at the BBC', *Pay and Benefits Bulletin 396*, March, pp 6–9

Saunier, A and Hawk, E (1994) 'Releasing the potential of teams through team-based rewards', *Compensation and Benefits Review*, July/August, pp 24–33

Smilansky, J (1996) *Improving Human Resource Performance*, Thomson Business Press, London

Case Study 6

With the Woolwich in a Take-over

Part 1 – The problem

Introduction

When re-organisation, re-structurings and take-overs are examined, changes in the reward structure are not normally the first items which come to mind. However, such changes can be a very valuable source of motivating employees to accept the new regime and to reinforce the changed values of the organisation. This case study is a case in point.

Background

In February 1991, Woolwich Property Services, the estate agency arm of the Woolwich Building Society, reached agreement with the Prudential Corporation to take over their 190 estate agency offices in East Anglia, London and the Thames Valley. The Prudential had built up their chain through a series of purchases of small and medium-sized local agencies during the booming 1980s, making millionaires out of a number of small-scale housing entrepreneurs who could not believe the prices that the Prudential was prepared to pay. When the housing boom collapsed in 1989, the chain started making heavy losses and a strategic decision was made to 'get back to the knitting'. A number of other insurance companies followed this pattern, as did some major building societies. The total losses made by these misjudgments has been estimated to run into billions of pounds and the recovery in the estate agency market is only just beginning in the mid-1990s.

The package that landed on the Woolwich's desk was a very mixed one in terms of pay and conditions. The pace of purchases had been so great, extending right up to 1990, as had the apparent growth rate and profitability, that the Prudential had not stopped to rationalise the business, leaving it as a loosely federated set of businesses. Such fundamental decisions as basic rates of pay and bonus systems were more or less left to the local managers, often the previous owner of the business.

This meant that the Woolwich found:

- 14 different systems of basic pay;

- 30 different bonus and commission systems; and
- 25 different benefit systems.

On examining pay details, early indications were that there was little or no rationale explaining the large variations in pay or benefits. Some individuals seemed to be paid way over the industry average and many apparent high performers were under rewarded. For example, there was a difference as high as £15,000 between two managers who had the same job title. Pension variations were substantial, as were the criteria for awarding company cars.

Rationalisation

The Woolwich had two main objectives. Firstly, the principal business objective of rationalising the creaking structure, disposing of branches which competed too closely and creating an operating and marketing image with which the public and the employees could identify. The second objective was to decide on a strategy on pay and conditions which would help to support the new business plan. This included merging the existing Woolwich operation with the new acquisition.

The make-up of employees in the combined organisation was relatively simple:

- 300 branch managers, including trainees and reliefs;
- 780 'negotiators' who were responsible for selling the properties;
- 370 surveyors; and
- 550 clerical staff.

Staff turnover was traditionally high in the estate agency profession, especially with staff being generally younger, who had few expectations to stay in the industry all their life, let alone the organisation. Although the deep recession has set in, there was still the need to attract and retain high quality staff in the right locations.

Student activities – task 1

You are James Tait, Head of human resources for Woolwich Property Services and it is early 1991. You are aware that 50 branches are to be closed and this will involve some 350 job losses. However, given the relatively high staff turnover (28 per cent in 1989-90) you anticipate that compulsory redundancies will be limited.

Your brief is to devise a new reward system covering the range of pay and benefits. Set out the methods by which you would approach the brief, detailing the various problems you would face and the possible solutions. The system must be in place within four months and must be robust and sufficiently flexible to last for four to six years in a variety of economic conditions.

Case Study 6

The Take-over

Part 2 – The Solution

Finding the facts

Before any decisions could be made, the precise details of the situation needed to be ascertained. This included the following for all employees:

- their age, length of service and qualifications;
- the system of pay grading, whether it is based on a formally evaluated scheme and how employees progressed within the grade, if at all;
- the actual basic pay of employees and their expectations of contractual salary progression;
- the details of the various systems of bonus and commission. How much of this was individual and how much calculated by the branch. The actual earnings under these schemes over the past three years;
- any payments made under a form of 'profit-sharing';
- details of any overtime payments;
- the benefits systems, including to whom benefits apply, what the trigger points are and the actual costs. Full details of the company car and pension schemes;
- an evaluation of any problems which could exist in relation to equal pay; and
- the level at which decisions on pay were taken.

Information was also required which compared the existing pay with the market rates in the industry, both locally and nationally in respect of pay, bonus and benefits.

Finally, employees' perception of their pay and benefits needed to be ascertained.

James Tait, carried out the internal analysis with the help of his two personnel staff and two staff hired on contract from an agency. All the staff earnings and benefits information was put onto a computer pay package which produced tables and charts to assist understanding and analysis. The information was used to identify the individual and group problems which would emerge when the new systems were devised.

The market survey was carried out by Wyatt Company who also completed the employee survey.

The market survey showed that, on average, the median pay matched the local pay rates quite well although the standard deviation was quite large. This was reflected in the employee survey where the average response was that their rates compared to the market were satisfactory although a sizable minority felt otherwise. The response to internal equity was another matter. Only 23 per cent viewed their pay as fair compared with others in the same company, compared with the norm of 61 per cent that Wyatt had found in previous surveys in other organisations.

Questions were asked in the survey whether there were strong links between pay and performance and whether this should be so. Only 22 per cent considered any existing connection but 72 per cent gave a preference for some form of performance-based scheme. Not surprisingly, sales staff wanted an individual based scheme whereas managers looked for rewards for the team. There was widespread contempt for the company car arrangements and pay communications were also given a low rating.

The outline of these results were given to all employees in a simple newsletter, without comments, except to say that a new system of pay and benefits would be announced within three months. The company had always taken the view that if the organisation asked employees to take the trouble to complete a survey, it was only courtesy to give them the results as soon as they were available. It also wanted to start to build trust with employees and giving such information quickly showed that the employees' views had at least been listened to rather than collected, filed, then forgotten.

Deciding on the strategy

There were a number of fundamental decisions on pay for the Board at Woolwich to decide.

Firstly, whether there should be a consistent pay policy across the company. This was an easy decision as the days of easy profits and loose control were over. Survival would be based on well-focused, tightly controlled large organisations with wide coverage (leaving niches for fleet of foot small local operators). The pay match had to be one of consistency with a centrally organised system for basic pay and benefits that would allow movement between branches and areas and give an organisational pay orientation.

Secondly, how close should be the link between pay and performance? Again, this was not difficult as the nature of the property market made it critical for each employee to make their contribution felt. Paying for this performance would reinforce the culture of performance orientation. In any case, employees had voted for this in their survey. What was more difficult was deciding the proportion of pay that would be guaranteed and how much would be bonus.

Thirdly, there was the question of the relationship between individual, team and organisational performance and pay. This was more difficult to decide. The Board wanted an element of profit-related pay and employees varied in their views on team against individual pay. Could a scheme be devised which incorporated all these elements, or would different groups have to have different incentive schemes which may cause a divisive effect? The Board considered the norms of the industry which took the path of separate schemes. They also took the advice of Wyatt who said they could set up a global scheme but it would either be so simple that it would not motivate or so fiendishly complicated that it would not be understood. The Board decided on different bonus schemes for different groups of employees.

Fourthly, the resources necessary to fund the new scheme. Due to the nature of the recession and the financial stringencies the unusual decision was taken that the changes would be financially neutral. This implied that there would be losers as well as winners.

Having taken these strategic decisions, the detail could be worked out for basic pay, performance pay and benefits.

Creating a basic pay structure

As the number of job-types was quite small (manager, surveyor, negotiator and a few clerical positions) there was no necessity to embark on a job evaluation exercise. What was required was a meaningful base rate. Again, Wyatt was used to compare the position of branch manager in other sectors and the pay of surveyors. James Tait also used his networking skills to compare results with Wyatt's reports.

A salary range for each job was defined. It was not a wide range (20 per cent from bottom to top) with certain geographical allowances for London and the Home Counties. The position on the range would be established by experience and qualification. For example, the basic rate for a branch manager was established at £15,000 to £18,000. This was lower than most currently received but the change in the bonus arrangements would seek to remedy this.

Paying for performance

The new 'performance culture' meant that, for most employees, there was a sizeable change in their basic/bonus relationship. The new scheme for target groups was as follows:

Table 1.4 *Target groups*

	% On target bonus	How performance measured
Branch manager	50%	Branch profitability/performance
Negotiator	50%	Individual sales/performance
Surveyor	20%	60% by individual performance 40% by branch profitability
Clerical staff	20%	Branch profitability/performance

Branch profitability for managers was essentially a financial calculation of return on capital employed (ROCE) adjusted by one or two special quality measures such as customer satisfaction. (Woolwich used an agency to run an 'anonymous customer' system. This was carefully executed in order to measure all the staff from telephone reception to surveyor punctuality.)

The bonus scheme for negotiators was fairly traditional except that customer and quality satisfaction criteria were again built in rather than being wholly based on the volume of sales.

Competitions for top branches and top performers were set up with one-off prizes for teams and individuals ranging from a week-end abroad to Harrods vouchers. Although this had the potential for divisiveness, the competition element matched the new culture and the professional approach gave a challenge to branches at all levels, not just to those with a chance of winning. Those towards the bottom of the table had a major motivation to improve their performance given the transparent nature of their results.

Benefits

Rationalisation of benefits also took place. All employees were invited to join a central Woolwich pension scheme which was based on final salary. Most took up the offer, except for the under 30s, as many had been on a less than generous personal pension arrangement with their original privately owned estate agency which Prudential had not got round to changing. The company car scheme was revamped and a clear entitlement criteria set out.

A remuneration committee, chaired by James, examined the remaining benefits on a cost/benefit basis and scrapped those that gave little value for money and which had received a lower rating under the original employee survey. A small selection of benefits were awarded to high performers for a two-year period as a reward for performance but which then had to be won again when that period expired.

Administering the new structure

It was necessary to decide on the responsibilities for decision making on pay. Should the branch manager be allowed freedom to change salaries or should they merely recommend increases to human resources, who would have the final say? James saw the benefits of decentralised decision making, particularly as the branches were cost and profit centres. However, he wanted to be careful that the new structure was bedded-in first and managers sufficiently trained to be able to take on these responsibilities. It was therefore agreed that these responsibilities would be delegated after one year's operation and review of the system. This would allow managers sufficient time to understand the revised integrated company culture and new methods of working.

Another major area was what action to take in the case of employees who were currently being paid in excess of their new rates. It was decided that those facing pay cuts should have their pay reduced in stages over three years. The first year they would receive a supplement of 75 per cent of the difference between their old pay and their new pay. The second year, the figure would be 30 per cent and the third year they would receive the new rates. Those employees would, in any case, have the opportunity to earn much higher bonuses to make up the losses. Employees with a non-matching car entitlement would keep their car for two years or until it needed replacement, whichever came first.

Communication

Recognised as a major weakness previously, James was determined that the new structure would be explained properly. Wyatt helped the company to make a video and produced a booklet on the package, ***Working with the Woolwich*** which went into a pack for each employee with a letter explaining the individual's new salary and benefits.

Wyatt and the Woolwich then held a briefing with regional directors and area managers, followed by a two-day session with branch managers, at which they were briefed about their own pay and taught to replicate the event in their branches.

Student activities

1. Estimate the costs involved of using the consultants. You can work on the basis of £800 per consultant per day. Was it worth it?
2. What are the on-going evaluation processes that James needs to put in place?
3. Are there any other ways of dealing with employees who are currently being paid in excess of their revised rates?
4. Draw up a briefing note to managers explaining why it is to their advantage to accept the new arrangements.

Standard reading

	Armstrong and Murlis	*Armstrong*	*Milkovich and Newman*
Pages	441–448	53–96	1–43

Further reading

Industrial Society (1996) *Rewarding Performance*, No. 20 in series of Managing Best Practice, London

Lawler, E (1971) *Pay and Organisational Effectiveness*, New York, McGraw Hill

There are numerous books and articles on change management which should be read in association with this case study including:

Grundy, T (1993) *Implementing Strategic Change*, Kogan Page, London

Kirkbride, P and Duncan, J (1996) *The Managing Change Reader*, Thomson Business Press, London

Leigh, A (1988) *Effective Change*, IPD, London
Obolensky, N (1996) *Practical Business Re-Engineering*, Kogan Page, London
Sadler, P (1996) *Managing Change*, Kogan Page, London

PART 2
DEVELOPING PAY STRUCTURES

Introduction

This short set of cases examines how organisations convert their strategic reward objectives into practice by designing a remuneration framework.

The ideal is a framework which is tailored (the word is important – made to measure, not off the peg) to be consistent with the organisation and to support the way the work gets done. A low-cost, customer-focused strategy similar to Woolworths or McDonalds is more likely to succeed with a pay strategy that generates low labour costs.

In contrast, ICL's business strategy requires constant product innovation and a short product design-to-market cycle time. Therefore, its pay structure needs to reinforce innovation and cross-functional flexibility together with close teamwork across the organisation.

The framework has to incorporate two key factors:

- the requirement for internal consistency so the structure is defensible in terms of logic and fairness; and
- the requirement for external consistency so the needs of the pay market can be met.

Internal consistency

Advocates of equity theory stress that a defensible pay structure needs to establish the concept of equal pay for work of equal worth and pay differentials for work of uneven worth (distributive justice). Just as important, procedural justice deems that there should be a system of pay determination within the structure that is seen as fair by the players (Jacques[1], Folger and Konovsky[2]).

For 30 years or more, job evaluation techniques have been used to meet these requirements, setting up hierarchical structures consistent with the belief in the way that the employer is motivated to recognise differences in the employees' skills and responsibilities and to encourage employees to bid for promotion to a higher graded job through a permanent, fair and transparent system. A higher job, a higher grade, a bigger salary, nothing could be simpler or fairer.

Case Study 8 describes how a typical medium-sized organisation, the Strand Housing Association, carried out a traditional job evaluation exercise to attempt to produce a fairer pay structure. The story is continued in Case Study 9 where the organisation runs into difficulties in converting the outcomes of the job evaluation into a salary structure.

One of the major difficulties associated with such schemes is that they can encourage employees to adopt a rigid approach to their job, expressing such views as:

> My job has been described closely, it has been fixed at a particular grade therefore that is the job I am paid for. I am not prepared to do anything new or extra outside the job description unless I am paid more for it.

In this situation, employees think of themselves, or describe others, in terms of their grades. In one large engineering company I visited recently, I asked what job a particular employee did, 'Oh, she's a grade 5' was the reply, as if that explained everything! In this respect, the system has a de-humanising element.

Today, the environment has changed considerably. Promotions are now far fewer as organisations have de-layered, reducing greatly the number of management and supervisory positions. Employees need to be far more flexible, willing to change their roles and learn more skills to meet the needs of the quickly changing national and international market place. Case Study 7 describes the actions taken by Merck & Co to move away from a more confined structure to one that is more likely to match the quick-moving, responsive culture required in both the manufacturing and service industries.

Broad-banding, with its association with decentralized, empowered, de-layered, flexible work teams, has made enormous inroads in the last ten years on both sides of the Atlantic. Even the Treasury have been convinced of its efficacy (IDS[3]). Proponents argue that it fits very well the contemporary business requirements. There have, however, been some recent words of warning on the following counts:

1. Indications are that it could prove expensive. Under narrow grades, employees came to the top of their grade and realised they had to stay there unless promoted. Under broad bands, most employees see an almost unlimited opportunity to make continuing salary progress and this puts an additional onus on the line manager to control his costs. HR departments will give advice on restraint and train managers on appropriate courses of action, but the reality is that some will perform better than others and pay leakages could be considerable.

2. Employees may be demotivated if they meet the criteria for increased salary but the line manager's budget prevents the justified increase. Under conventional job evaluation schemes, budget restrictions would not stop a successful re-grading being implemented.
3. The flexibility of a broad-banded scheme has led to the criticism that it is a backward step to the days where managers took salary decisions on the basis of subjectivity and favouritism which led employees to demand a job evaluated scheme in the first place. Unless the criteria for salary progress are robust, well-understood and operated fairly, then the system may become self-defeating in terms of motivation.

External consistency

Case Study 7 also examines the broad approach by a market-leader to research the pay market and the considerable effort made to ensure their data was verified. Practitioners will be aware how important is such research before entering the market place in a recruitment exercise. There are three major problems to overcome:

- is your summary of information comprehensive enough to be correct? Surveys may come out with biased results (Cook[4], Rynes and Milkovich[5]) and the shelf life for published data is weeks, if not days;
- there is an inflationary danger if all the leading players decide to pay at the upper quartile, as statisticians will confirm. One survey contributor will see from the result that they are paying at only the 60 per cent mark and increase their pay accordingly. This will have the immediate result of moving up the mean and upper quartile and result in the other players following suit; and
- if the level of salaries is so important, should the information be so freely exchanged? There is a narrow line here between providing information for the mutual benefit of participants and giving away highly confidential information.

Balancing internal and external consistencies

Bringing together these two factors into a balanced salary structure is no light task. Sometimes differences occur because a shortage of a particular skill has driven up the market rate. Or it could occur because of the internal power of a group of employees who drive a rate up well beyond the market rate for that job.

This is where broad-banded structures win out as their inherent flexibility allows them to be far more responsive to market rate changes at either end of the scale. In many organisations, there is no longer a fixed rate for graduate recruits – the rate is an individual one depending on the applicant's marketable skills. Broad bands can allow a range of several thousands of pounds, as today's graduates know all too well.

References

1 Jacques, E (1961) *Equitable Payment*, John Wiley, New York

2 Folger, R and Konovsky, M (1989) 'Effects of procedural and distributive justice on reactions to pay raise decisions', *Academy of Management Journal*, March, pp 115–130

3 IDS (1996) 'Case study – HM Treasury', *Report 719*, August pp 29–32

4 Cook, F (1994) 'Compensation surveys are biased', *Compensation and Benefits Review*, September–October, pp 19–22

5 Rynes, S and Milkovich, G (1986) 'Wage surveys: dispelling some myths about the market wage', *Personnel Psychology*, Spring, pp 71–90

Case Study 7

Movement to Broad Banding at MSD

Background

Merck, Sharp and Dohme (MSD) is a wholly-owned subsidiary of the US based Merck & Co Inc, which is one of the world's leading pharmaceutical companies operating in every major market throughout the world, with its headquarters in New Jersey, USA. There are around 1500 UK employees in a number of sites with the UK headquarters in Hoddesdon in Hertfordshire. It is not unionised although joint consultative committees discuss points of mutual interest.

Employee reward and benefit programmes, together with training and development, are seen by Merck as underpinning the philosophies they wish to promote. Consequently, Merck has always regarded reward systems as key areas of human resources and has put them at the heart of their integrated corporate systems. Employee appraisal, job evaluation and pay determination mechanisms are established at the US headquarters and cascaded through the various subsidiaries world-wide. This supports Merck's international operations with some employees moving from country to country. Therefore, managers operating in, say, Australia will be appraised and rewarded under the same system as in the UK.

The Hay job evaluation scheme has played a central and successful part in the overall pay system for over 20 years for managerial and senior technical staff. Each and every position has been carefully evaluated: Hay points have been allocated and the employee's basic salary determined by the Hay system on a range of 80 per cent to 125 per cent around the salary control point. This control point was carefully researched in relation to the market place through extensive and continuing market surveys and generally represented a point around the upper quartile of market rates. This degree of direct salary reflection of Hay points meant that it was never considered necessary to establish grades as such.

The responsibility for determining the Hay points lay with specialists in the HR department who were extensively trained in the Hay process and kept very close liaison with Hay staff on market developments. Most managers knew how many Hay points had been allocated to their job although they generally knew little of the scheme's details and were unsure of how the precise points total had resulted. This was even less well known at lower levels.

Pointers for change

As part of their close relationship, Hay carried out a regular audit of the scheme's operation on an international basis. In 1992 their audit showed that difficulties related to the application of the scheme had begun to surface. There were two main problems. Firstly, it was becoming increasingly difficult to align the scheme successfully across America and Europe. During the 1990s, the economic circumstances in America had been markedly different from Europe. Their recession had been earlier and was not so deep as that occurring in Europe. Even within Europe at that time, economic circumstances varied greatly between, say, Britain, where unemployment had been rising steeply for two years and Germany, where their steep rise had yet to begin. These differences, accentuated by currency fluctuations, were reflected in the job market and the salaries required to attract the right calibre individuals. It was becoming impossible to encompass all of these varying cases in one all-embracing scheme.

In addition, a fully maintained Hay evaluation system was extremely time consuming. Increasingly, Merck's business was demanding a more responsive and flexible approach to grading to support issues of high productivity and cost containment.

The final problem was the growing difficulties of switching jobs. The era of de-layering had started (although on a low-key basis) and some employees whose jobs had been re-defined or re-engineered, were being offered alternative jobs. More commonly, employees developing their careers were considering and being offered jobs seen as 'lateral' moves by the company. In a number of cases, employees were refusing jobs that carried fewer Hay points (say, from 588 to 571) even though the salary and other benefits were identical or even better. The rigidity of the Hay scheme became a barrier. Problems with international transfers came into the same category.

Designing a new scheme

It took two years of deliberation from the 1992 Audit to the launching of the revised system as part of a world-wide compensation re-design programme sponsored by the US Corporate Head Office.

The principal feature was the establishment of graded salary structures. The first global system was for professional staff (called Hay grades) and had seven grades from graduate entry to senior management. The second local system was for administrative and operative staff and was specific to the UK. These were called 'Jones' grades, after the consultant who designed the structure.

An extensive mapping operation took place to fit the existing jobs into the Hay grades. The know-how element of Hay evaluation was retained as the principal measure and the grades fell roughly into line with one step of know-how.

The salaries established against the grades were a more tricky problem. The intention was to establish a grade range that encompassed all of the jobs and the current job-holders' salaries. As in all salary re-organisations, not everybody fitted into the structure. Moreover, the US Head Office preferred bands that were not too wide, probably with a range of 50 per cent from bottom to top. This was felt to be too narrow by the UK HR department and lengthy persuasion was necessary to allow the scheme to have bands of around 75 per cent for grades one to five and 125 per cent for the senior management grades six and seven. Examples of the new salary bands were:

£14,500–£27,000
£17,000–£30,000
£22,000–£40,000

To overcome the difficulties of some current employees having salaries over the maximum of the grade, the grade-band limits were set as parameters for guidance to line managers who, in special circumstances, were allowed to set a salary above the limit if market forces dictated this necessity. The overlap of grades was in the order of 15 per cent which facilitated movement between grades.

The process of slotting employees into grades was achieved by the normal process of establishing a series of benchmark positions and then comparing all other jobs with those benchmarks. The HR staff carried out this exercise, liaising with line management to confirm straightforward decisions and consulting over the five per cent or so that did not naturally fit. It provided the opportunity to remedy perceived distortions where the Hay system had not adequately recognised a complex and sometimes unique role.

A similar grading structure has been set up in the UK for administrative and operational staff (Jones grades) which has five grades and a 60 per cent width for each grade.

Market information

Decisions on salary movements have always been heavily influenced by the market information provided by the HR department. This information is generated from four main sources, predominantly from within the pharmaceutical industry.

1. Exchange groups – MSD has joined together with other top companies in the industry to exchange information on compensation and benefits. These groups meet at least twice a year and provide detailed breakdowns of crucial salary movements and any innovations in benefits or incentives. They have a high value to participants in that the information is focused, the service is free, up-to-date and accurate. Participants can follow up particular areas of interest on an informal one-to-one or small group basis.
2. Jones survey – Alan Jones, based in Monmouth, established the pharmaceutical pay survey more than 15 years ago and now has 100

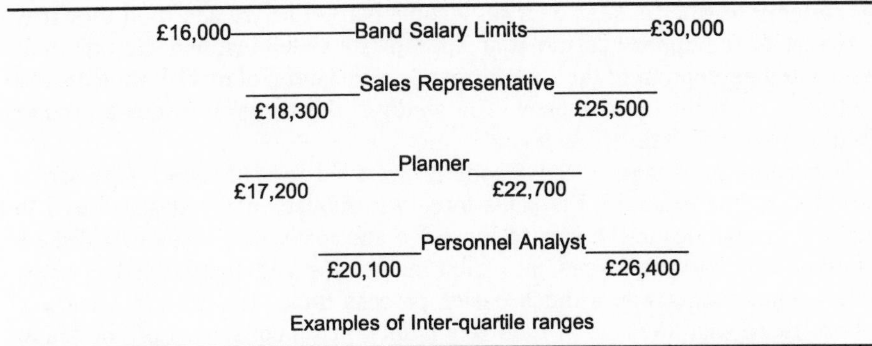

Figure 2.1 *Example of market information for line managers*

participating pharmaceutical companies in the UK. The company has around 1000 client companies in over 40 surveys covering particular employment sections, including one for secretarial and clerical staff in the South East. A conference is organised once a year for the pharmaceutical group to consider the findings in their surveys and discuss wider issues. The information is important for monitoring pay across the full range of professional roles and in the Jones grades, and to consider any areas where special skills shortages are developing, demonstrated by exceptional pay inflation.

3. Hay survey – this is a very substantial and wide-ranging survey of organisations that regularly use the Hay evaluation scheme. It provides very useful checking information to confirm exchange group data and to compare pharmaceutical management and technical salary data with other industries.
4. Local surveys – MSD takes part in local salary surveys for locally recruited jobs such as accounting and clerical staff, storekeepers and security staff. This is, in effect, a local exchange group. It is free, with the information very focused.

Figure 2.1 provides an example of information on market trends provided to line management. They are also provided with a Salary Guide Matrix for management grades based on market data terciles.

In total, the budget set aside for gaining market information works out at about £4.00 per employee plus the cost of half a person to collate and process the information into regular internal reports.

Salary determination

The authority for determining initial basic salaries and for movement within the salary band still lies with line management. The comprehensive market information provides them with a more precise tool with which to make these decisions. Rather than the rigid Hay progression system of moving steadily between 80 per cent to 125 per cent of the control point, employees are now recruited into what is seen as a reasonable market salary and then they may progress to the upper quartile at an appropriate speed justified through their manager's perception of their performance, acquisition of market-valued skills and their value to the company. The width of the bands provides a greater flexibility than before.

A second advantage is the flexibility provided for changing organisation structures. For example, the sales force was fundamentally re-structured in 1994 with significant changes to job roles and many new roles established. Slotting existing employees into their new roles and managing the many salary adjustments was a much easier process under the grading structure where there was no issue of total Hay points, just a consensus on the know-how factor and a continuing discussion on individual progression through the grade. The degree of precision necessary has been much reduced.

Performance management

The final part of the basic salary determination jigsaw is the performance management system. Currently, this is a corporation-wide system with a fixed distribution of designations in particular groups depending on divisional performance. The first group are 'TF' (in the top five per cent), the next 'TQ' (top quintile) and the next group are 'Outstanding', with 'Very Good' and 'Good' being the next categories. LF (lower five per cent) brings up the rear and this category leads usually to no pay rise, bonus or stock option for the recipient. As with all other PM systems, difficulties arise when employees drop a notch, being 'TQ' one year and only 'Outstanding' the next – in this instance, being compounded by the technology.

The PM system, which is also the basis for the payment of incentives and stock options, takes place in December/January with decisions on bonuses taken in February and paid in March before the end of the tax year, while salary changes are implemented from April lst.

Incentive arrangements

Two incentive schemes play a major part in the remuneration system: the Annual Incentive Plan Bonus and Stock Option Scheme.

Annual incentive plan (AIP) bonus

Each year, Merck sets aside a sum of money for bonus payments, depending primarily upon the overall performance of Merck & Co Inc. This sum is divided between the subsidiary companies and their divisions, depending on their results. Each division then decides how to allocate the AIP awards, according to its business needs and the contribution of its people. In general, it is awarded only to those employees who are rated 'Outstanding' or higher although the decision is left to the divisional directors. The MSD *Employee Guide* states:

> The precise way that your division defines 'excellent performance' may be different from that of another division, because each one has different business requirements and priorities.

In 1994, for example, bonuses were awarded, on average, to the top 35 per cent of employees by performance although one division with outstanding results paid all their staff a bonus. It was made clear in 1994 that the emphasis for the payments became focused on performance rather than being determined by status or job title. Previously, there were some jobs which carried an automatic bonus but there are no such guarantees under AIP. This scheme applies to all staff, except sales staff, who still retain their own bonus scheme.

Stock option scheme

This incentive is also used to recognise strong performance and contribution and provides employees with an opportunity to build ownership in Merck & Co Inc. Its major purpose is to reward performance over a longer period of time and it is rarely awarded to new employees. The organisation believes that stock options make special sense in their case because of the long-term nature of the pharmaceutical industry, inviting the employee to extend their vision beyond the immediate horizon and to encourage them to stay with the organisation. The Stock Option scheme works on the same basis as similar schemes (see Case Study 25 for a further example) usually providing an exercise date five years hence at an option price fixed at the date of the award. The total amount set aside for stock options is controlled centrally and cascaded down the organisation based on performance in the same way as the AIP Bonus.

Summing up the total package

In moving towards the broad-banding system, MSD do not regard the change as revolutionary, more an evolutionary process reflecting the faster nature of the changing world and the need for a greater degree of flexibility. The operation of the incentive schemes encourages that degree of flexibility as set out in the MSD *Employee Guide.*

Your manager might decide to:

- provide more of your total reward by increasing your base salary, if you are paid low in your defined job range and provide only a modest AIP Bonus;
- limit your salary increase because your base salary is right where it should be, relative to the market, but provide a larger AIP Bonus because you have made an outstanding contribution in the last year; or
- combine an AIP Bonus, which rewards current contribution and performance, with a stock option grant, which can have future value and emphasises long-term reward, to deliver total compensation that reflects the nature of your contribution.

The scheme has been well received by employees to date. The somewhat tortuous process of appeals against total Hay points has been abolished and the new arrangements have led to no formal appeals under the company grievance procedure.

Further evolutionary progress may come through systems of team-based pay and 360 degree appraisal, both of which are currently being evaluated but, like any new pharmaceutical product, they need to be tested with extreme care before being marketed to employees.

Student activities

1. You are a line manager working under a scheme similar to Merck & Co's. Detail the factors which would influence your decision on a basic salary increase for a member of your staff at the time of the annual review.
2. Place all the factors you have listed in order of importance. You have 50 points altogether – distribute them between the factors.
3. Taking an employee's viewpoint, what do you see as the main advantages and disadvantages of the new scheme?
4. Analyse the necessary communication processes which need to operate under the scheme. What should be their strengths?

Standard reading

	Armstrong and Murlis	*Armstrong*	*Milkovich and Newman*
Pages	151–204 and 127–150	224–238	156–157, 208–242, 282–286

Further reading

Armstrong, M and Ryden, O (1996) *The IPD Guide to Broadbanding*, IPD, London

Barringer, M and Milkovich, G (1995) *Changing Employment Contracts: The Relative Effects of Proposed Changes in Compensation, Benefits and Job Security on Employment Outcomes*, Cornell Centre for Advanced Human Resource Studies, Working Paper 95–14

Hewitt Associates (1994) *Broadbanding – The Challenge of a New Approach*, St. Albans

Sable, R (1990) 'Job content salary surveys design and selection features', *Compensation and Benefits Review*, May/June, pp 14–18

Appendix A

Alan Jones and Associates

Alan Jones and Associates is a firm of management consultants specialising in salary and benefit surveys with around 1000 client companies taking part in the surveys in the UK. There are regional surveys now covering the whole of the UK mainland for locally recruited jobs (up to junior management level). A large number of surveys are UK-wide and are open to any industry/sector, eg managerial and professional, executives and PC network. These surveys are strictly confidential and are participant only. They are paid for by subscription.

The company also produces a series of surveys of HR policies. The subjects are generally suggested by salary survey clients and the results are normally available free of charge to those who contribute information. Unlike the salary surveys, these policy surveys are sold on to non-participants. Recent subjects include: company cars, shifts and overtime, redundancy, flexible benefits, flexible working and employee attitude surveys. The policy surveys highlight best practice and provide companies with a means of sharing problems and experiences.

Alan Jones and Associates can be contacted at:

Apex House, Wonastow Road, Monmouth, Gwent NP5 4YE.
Tel: 01600 715521.

Case Study 8

Devising a New Job Evaluation Scheme at Strand Housing Association

Introduction

Reward management takes on different guises at varying stages of an organisation's development. As it grows, the freedom offered by cosy, personal informality is overtaken by the need for consistency, equity and transparency. This case study looks at how the need for a job evaluation exercise was analysed and the resultant system agreed and completed.

Background

The Strand Housing Association faced 1994 with a huge challenge. It had grown from a small, voluntary group of like-minded liberals running two new housing developments for old people in one area in 1980 to a 600 strong housing association managing 20 units spread over the South-East, made up of:

- 10 ex-local authority council housing estates;
- 3 ex-local authority old peoples' homes; and
- 7 new purpose-built housing developments for special needs, mostly sheltered housing for old people and handicapped groups.

The basis of the expansion had been Compulsory Competitive Tendering (CCT) where local authorities had been forced by Thatcherite legislation since the late 1980s to put into the tendering process the managing of their estates and homes. Strand had been a highly respected operator for sheltered housing and was an obvious candidate to be accepted onto the tender lists from the earliest stage of the process. Contracts had been won by a combination of processes. On some occasions it was a competitive quote in the tender and in others it was a majority vote by the tenants following open, honest and convincing communication with tenant groups.

Strand was led by a dynamic and inspirational manager, James Packer (later named as Chief Executive) whose previous experience in the Royal Navy had bolted efficient administration onto a long standing commitment to public service. The Chairman and other leading lay members of the Association had given long and worthy service, supporting the expansion programme and giving many unpaid hours to help the Association through its growing pains.

Public service, unpaid service, trust and openness had ensured that there was a strong cultural element permeating the organisation. No redundancies were ever made when contracts were taken over and a great deal of local autonomy was given to the appointed managers.

By 1994, the number of employees had risen to 610, made up of:

Table 2.1 *Number of employees*

	Head Office	Units	Total
Board	5		5
Managers	10	20	30
Supervisors	15	50	65
Maintenance		80	80
Operational		80	80
Auxiliary		100	100
Nursing		80	80
Office Staff	80	90	170
Total	110	500	610

Due to the rapid growth, terms and conditions of employment were inconsistent. Head Office employees were paid on spot rates with a general cost of living increase once and occasionally twice a year. For employees in the units, some came under continuing national agreements arising from their previous employment under the Transfer of Undertakings Regulations. This meant that not only was the level of pay different but hours of work, shift payments and holidays all varied. The working week at head office was 37 hours but varied between 37 and 42 hours in the units. The range of holidays spread from 20 to 27 days, some relating to service. There was also a variety of shift payments in the units ranging from zero for some nursing and auxiliary staff, to time plus 60 per cent in the London borough units. Due to the informal management approach, no attempt had been made so far to introduce an integrated payment structure. Personnel matters were dealt with from Head Office by the Association's accountant and company secretary, but he concentrated mostly on practical issues such as payroll, selection procedures (especially references in units dealing with special needs) and terminations. There had been only one claim for unfair dismissal (an unsuccessful and difficult unit manager) and this had been settled through ACAS conciliation at an early stage.

Most employees, especially those who had worked for the Association from the early days, were generally well motivated and both liked and respected the management style, feeling no need to join a trade union. However, some recently won contracts from London boroughs contained a high penetration of the Public Workers Union. Although not hostile in any way to the organisation, the Union had demanded and obtained continuing recognition for bargaining purposes in the existing units and attempted to spread these rights to other units. They had achieved a modicum of success in that membership had grown from 18 per cent to 30 per cent over a two-year period. No other union was recognised.

Regular meetings had been agreed with the union and the issue of the variety of terms and conditions had been raised on more than one occasion. The union had pointed out that some members, having heard of the salaries in other units, had become dissatisfied and wanted action to be taken. An informal request had been made for a proper salary structure based on some form of job evaluation and the Association had agreed to consider this seriously over the next 12 months, although they had no clear idea which road to take.

The appointment

In 1994, the governing board of the Association considered the issue of the need for a personnel department. Not only were there the questions of trade union recognition and pay and conditions but a number of other difficulties had arisen. Decentralising decision making to the units had considerable advantages but many managers were unprepared for the full responsibility and this had shown in recent years in areas such as poor selection and the training of new staff. A project to identify their own training needs and deliver the necessary training programme was sorely needed. Informal recruitment procedures was beginning to produce an unbalanced and stereotypical employee pattern, so issues of equal opportunity needed addressing. Finally, a blueprint for the usually confused process of taking over contracts needed drawing up, particularly in relation to employment issues.

In September 1994, Sarah Jones was appointed as Personnel Executive. She was 28, a sociology graduate and had two previous positions. From college, she had spent three years at IBM, specialising in recruitment and pay matters and then had moved to a trust hospital where she had been a generalist, deputising for the trust personnel director.

Her experience had demonstrated the benefits and difficulties of union and non-union cultures. IBM's firm non-union stance had worked well during their extraordinary growth period as they could afford to be genuinely people-oriented and provide the best in terms and conditions. There was freedom to be innovative and flexible on pay and conditions and she assisted in introducing some novel benefit systems. However, by the end of the 1980s, IBM were going through a much less comfortable patch where redundancies had commenced, bonuses were far less forthcoming, some benefits were scrapped and employees had become much more insecure. Some employees even started considering union representation.

In the trust hospital, on the other hand, unions had 80 per cent membership and most changes of any substance needed to be negotiated, which had often proved to be long, drawn out and ultimately, on occasions, fruitless. She had watched her manager carefully treading in the minefields of inter-union rivalries and wanted to avoid such a situation at all costs.

In the early weeks, she concentrated her activities on examining the existing terms and conditions of all staff and the role, responsibilities and rewards of the unit managers. She found a very confused picture. Not only were there ten different payment systems in the 20 units but the rewards for the unit managers did not correlate with her perception of their responsibilities, taking into account the size and location of the contracts, and special care issues. She came to the conclusion that it would be inevitable that major problems of morale and motivation would arise unless some type of revised pay and conditions system was introduced over the next 18 months. If the Association continued to grow, then these problems would be more severe.

The issues

Sarah had experience of working within two job-evaluated salary structures and had assisted in several re-evaluations when major job changes had occurred. The system in the trust hospital was very formal with strict and detailed re-evaluation and appeals procedures which always involved the union. It often took as long as six months from the date of the appeal to the final decision. In IBM it was less formal, quicker and easier to resolve using an adapted proprietary system similar to Hay. She had never, however, started a system from scratch. She consulted colleagues in the network and drew up a list of the issues involved. After discussions with the Chief Executive, she wrote a report to the governing body setting out these issues and possible avenues for action.

The issues were as follows:

(a) Is job evaluation really necessary?

Option 1 – solve the problem by an informal process of evaluation, eliminating the glaring anomalies and dealing with those employees who had complained through a re-defined grievance procedure. Keep the union closely informed as to progress but exclude them in any way from the decision making process.

This would ensure that the process was fully in the management's control and no aberrant decisions should therefore result. It could also take place in the time-scale desired. It would avoid the need to closely define jobs which sometimes led to a rigidity in the work process ('I can't do that job – it is not in my job description' syndrome). However, the results would not necessarily be perceived as fair by either the union or the workforce as a whole. Where employees work on different sites and they and their work are not personally known to each other, it is more likely for dissatisfaction to arise by comparisons arising from rumour and innuendo. Nor would it establish a robust structure for future developments and appointments.

Option 2 – set up a formal job evaluation process leading to a formal salary structure. Involve the union and employees in the process.

Involvement would give support to the culture of trust in the organisation and a formal salary structure arising from the process should be seen as fair and justifiable, both immediately and for the future.

On the other hand, other colleagues' experience had shown Sarah this was a long and time-consuming activity which raised expectations that could not always be met. The total rationalising of the salary structure would add between six per cent and 16 per cent to salary costs and although some of this could be phased-in, it still represented a substantial cost for a people-intensive sector.

(b) Which groups of employees should it include?

Option 1 – all employees. Of the 610 employees, there were about 120 separately defined jobs, 70 of them at head office. It would seem logical to produce an integrated salary system which encouraged the 'one company' concept. To start excluding groups of employees from the process would encourage suspicion and drive a wedge between, say, head office and unit employees. When the jobs were looked at in detail, it was thought possible to reduce the number by grouping together similar jobs and encouraging the flexibility issues by widening the job descriptions.

Such a path of action would have considerable time consequences, tying up managers and employees alike in the somewhat bureaucratic process. It would need an experienced and dedicated facilitator to keep it on track.

Option 2 –a first stage of managers and supervisors only. Given the similarity of managing a number of units, there would be only 40 jobs among the 95 or so employees involved. This was manageable on a part-time basis and could be achieved within a few months. It would also give the organisation experience of operating a job evaluation scheme and dealing with the inevitable mistakes that would be made. It would make sure that the key employees were correctly rewarded within a clear framework.

It would not satisfy the union, however, as they had few members in those groups and it may send the wrong message about the way the organisation operated.

(c) What sort of job evaluation scheme should be used?

Option 1 – proprietorial. Using a well tried and tested scheme meant that there were few arguments relating to the comparative fairness in general. A scheme like Hay, that was operating in 7000 organisations around the world, or Price Waterhouse's profile methodology which has been used in both blue- and white-collar environments, must be fundamentally robust and suitable for every kind of organisation. It would be validated for 'equal-value' claims and, if necessary, computerised easily. Moreover, the links to a database of market rate comparisons would help determine the salary structure. The wheel did not need to be re-invented.

Sarah's experience of a proprietorial scheme was mixed. Firstly, she knew it was a relatively expensive operation either through a licensing arrangement or using the advice of a consultant. Secondly, she recognised that Strand really was a unique type of organisation whose values differed from all commercial and most public sector organisations.

Option 2 –a tailor-made scheme. It was not a large organisation and devising a scheme to fit was not out of the question. It could be simple and easy to understand. The process could also come about through consultation which should mean that there should be greater commitment to the final product from all sides.

If it proved unsuccessful, there would be severe repercussions as the organisation would be regarded as incompetent, or at least, guilty of making a bad judgment.

(d) What type of scheme – conventional points factor or competence-based?

Having revisited the academic viewpoint of scheme choices, Sarah had eliminated the non-analytical systems as too simplistic and the factor comparison method as too production-oriented. Of the mainstream methods, this left two to consider. Firstly, the conventional points-factor rating and, secondly, competence-based evaluation which was a much more modern development.

Option 1 – points-factor schemes. Having operated under a points-factor scheme and knowing the advantages and pitfalls, Sarah was initially tempted to offer only this alternative as the tried and tested way. It could easily cover all the range of jobs, was easy to understand, had the firm appearance of being analytical, thorough and fair and could be translated into a proposed salary structure without too much difficulty. Once, that was, one obtained agreement and understanding of the relationship between points and factors which was not always so easy.

There was also a tendency for a mechanistic viewpoint to develop where points had to be awarded due to the factor descriptions, even though the actual job may work out different in practice. For example, just as many points can be awarded for 'contacts' to receptionists as to project managers unless the definition is carefully prepared. Arguments could subsequently arise, once salary scales were announced, where employees just missed out on a higher grade due to one lower rating on one factor. Appeals could take up considerable time in these circumstances where a few points extra could lead to a sizable pay increase in the higher grade.

Option 2 – competence-based schemes. Linked very closely to the subsequent salary structure, these schemes had attraction to Sarah who recognised the organisation as one that was very 'people' oriented and where the performance of individuals was probably more important than their job title. Although a relatively new concept, she could see the immediate advantage of a scheme that led easily into a pay progression system where employees' pay increased as they became more competent in the job. This would eliminate some of the problems of initial disappointment at the results as employees could become more competent and increase their pay without having to go through lengthy appeals for re-grading.

To get such a scheme going would need a substantial amount of preparation to develop a competence framework, including defining the core competencies of the organisation and proving that the achievement of these competencies would lead to improved organisational performance. This was no small task and must involve external experts so there was a sizable cost element. As the idea was new, there would also be an additional training cost.

The decision

Sarah put together a report on these main options. She argued forcefully the need for a well defined pay system for all employees that would be based on a credible, fairly evaluated scheme, one that would take the Association through the next phase of expansion. She was less certain as to which type of scheme to use and therefore whether to recommend a proprietorial or tailor-made one. She worked out some basic costing which showed that the competence scheme would cost a minimum of £60,000 more than the conventional scheme, taking into account the need for external consultants and additional training. Talking these options over with the Chief Executive, it became clear that he was not altogether committed to the competence approach generally (partly, he admitted, through a lack of thorough understanding and because he had recently read a report that rubbished NVQs because they only looked at today's needs and were very bureaucratic). He would find it difficult to give 100 per cent support to Sarah if she pressed for a project to define a complete competence framework for the organisation and the additional cost was off-putting.

Sarah thought the situation through again and came up with a compromise. She would work out a draft conventional points-factor scheme but it would be linked to a separate initiative where the organisation would give greater emphasis to certain key values which would be built into the scheme. She suggested:

- high quality customer care;
- improved trust through keeping promises (repairs, etc);
- effective communication; and
- value for money.

She put the proposal to the Board in October 1994 who accepted the need for a scheme to cover all employees below Board level and were happy at the compromise proposal. They decided that the initiative would cover the first two suggestions and set up a project group, chaired by Sarah, to get this underway. This initiative would be launched within two months and the time-scale for the complete job evaluation would be 12 months so that a new salary system could be announced by the time of the annual review in January 1996.

Getting the evaluation going

Immediately a steering committee was set up whose function was to:

- agree the nature of the scheme and its details;
- agree on the composition of the job evaluation team;
- set the time-scale; and
- monitor the expenditure against the budget.

The Steering Committee was chaired by a George, a part-time Board member and consisted of Sarah, a head office manager, a unit manager, a union representative (who was based in a unit) and an employee from head office (Doreen, a senior clerk). Sarah realised the difficulties of having a union representative involved in the key decision making body but she knew the scheme would never achieve acceptance without employees being committed to the scheme from the start. Without commitment to the scheme, employees would be able to dismiss any of the ultimate decisions as 'management's mistakes'.

Sarah acted as Secretary to the committee, determining the agenda and working closely with George behind the scenes. The time-scale was agreed quickly enough and a chart prepared (see Appendix C). Next, she put forward a rough outline plan for the scheme. This was to have five key factors:

- responsibility for customers;
- responsibility for staff;
- accountability;
- knowledge, skills and physical effort required (including educational requirements); and
- flexibility.

This was accepted by the committee. Sarah then had a separate meeting with each committee member in turn, discussing the details including the number of levels for each factor and the number of points at each level. Not surprisingly, there were a number of disagreements. For example, the managers wanted more levels and points for staff responsibility and accountability; the union, more points for physical effort. She brought to the next committee meeting a draft proposal which incorporated most of their views but allowed for last minute compromises. By being able to point out to members how their specific proposals were put into the scheme, she and George were able to get total agreement on a final version at the end of a long meeting after a number of last minute changes to accommodate everybody. Each factor would be on a six-point scale ranging from 50 points to 300 points. Examples of the scales for responsibility for customers and flexibility are at Appendix A. It was not entirely the scheme that Sarah wanted, but it did keep to the fundamentals and it now had the name of all stakeholders stamped on it.

The job description forms and questionnaires needed for each job were agreed more quickly. These were sent out immediately to managers for consultation with their employees and completion within 15 days.

The next decision was to set up the job evaluation committee that would actually carry out the evaluation work and reach long-lasting decisions. Sarah believed firmly that it had to be small and balanced between management and employees so that decisions made would be mutual ones. She pressed for a committee of four, including herself, a unit manager, a union representative and a head office employee. She managed to get this accepted despite the scepticism of the rest of the steering committee who, for different reasons, doubted that it would work. The unit manager, David, was a young graduate with considerable potential who had made a great success of a new housing estate contract in an inner London borough and who needed a new challenge. The head office employee was Doreen, who was reliable, sensible, but unambitious and had no strong views on trade unions either way. She was happy enough to work with Arthur, the union representative.

Subsequently, the steering committee met once every two months for a progress report and to monitor the costs. Sarah drafted a newsletter to make sure all employees were informed of the progress and the method by which the evaluation would take place.

The job evaluation

Sarah had arranged, for training purposes, a full day with an experienced consultant who took the job evaluation committee all together through the job evaluation process in general and gave them some practical examples of evaluating jobs from job descriptions and interviews, with the consultant playing various roles. This proved hilarious at times and the committee agreed that it was both enjoyable and worthwhile. It helped to bond the committee members at this early stage.

The job evaluation committee next decided their order of evaluation. There were 120 jobs to evaluate over six months. Given that a short meeting would take place with each job holder, or a representative if there were a number, this would take 20 meetings a month. It was agreed that the committee would split into two for these meetings (a manager and an employee/union rep) who would then report back when the evaluation took place. This reduced the number to ten a month. Given the split nature of the job locations, careful planning was required to ensure that three such meetings could take place in a morning or afternoon on one site. The committee members were thus committed to roughly four half-days a month on meetings with job holders. It was agreed that about the same amount of time was necessary for reporting back and agreeing on the evaluation itself. There was also the procedure to agree should the committee fail to be unanimous on an evaluation. In this situation, a majority vote would prevail. However, if it was split two against two and this could not be resolved at the subsequent meeting, then ACAS would be brought in for binding arbitration. The programme was then published ensuring that holidays were taken into account.

It was agreed that decisions by the committee would be published all together on 1 October. The committee needed complete trust to maintain complete confidentiality during the period. No details of the discussions (ie who voted which way) would ever be disclosed. Not even the steering committee would be told any of these details.

The first jobs to be evaluated were the *benchmark* jobs, numbering four in total. Examples of these were rent collector, nursing auxiliary and accounts supervisor, each with a number of job holders whose rank and position in any job evaluated structure would be crucial. The committee agreed that, in these cases, the whole committee would carry out the these meetings to ensure consistency in subsequent separate meetings. Sarah spent considerable time with David to ensure that they had a firm, concerted policy on where they wanted the result to finish up on these jobs. Mistakes made here could be a cause of continuing problems throughout the evaluation. She even went as far as to check their consensus views with the Chief Executive.

The preparation for these meetings proved essential. David and Sarah were able to guide the discussions unobtrusively so that the job holders, with their managers, were able to identify their jobs in general with the particular rating levels that David and Sarah felt appropriate. On occasions, it took searching questions about the reality of their jobs for this to happen. For example, the rent collector's concept of knowledge and skills was far higher than anticipated and it needed careful and sensitive discussion to bring this down to earth. The distinction of the knowledge of customers (rated under responsibility for customers) and knowledge and skills in general had to be emphasised. Sometimes it was the job holder's manager who attempted to enhance the job excessively. Sometimes it was a question of reconciling the different views between the manager and the job holder.

When it came to the subsequent meeting of the job evaluation committee, the copious notes which Sarah had taken also proved useful in the few areas where there was disagreement. She could point to details of their jobs and items of discussion to support her case. This was one area where compromise was not possible. At the end of a very long meeting, the benchmark ratings finally agreed coincided with David and Sarah's objectives (see Appendix B).

The remaining evaluations proved far easier, although there were a number of long and drawn out meetings. Unanimity between David and Sarah was no longer a prerequisite where certain jobs were comparatively unrelated to the mainstream activities such as a purchasing clerk at head office and part-time clerical support at the sheltered housing. Here the decisions taken were vital for the job holders but a higher or lower evaluation would not undermine the credibility of the final result. In these situations, they felt they could act in their proper role as independent job evaluators rather than representatives of management and there were a number of examples of one or the other being out voted. This gave increased credibility to the committee in the eyes of the union.

Only in one case, that of a senior maintenance craftsman, was there a split vote. The actual job responsibilities were no different to that of any other maintenance craftsman but his service was long and he was a very reliable and efficient employee. He had been 'promoted' some years back. Deadlock was reached and Sarah arranged for an ACAS arbitration which took place in September.

After hearing all the evidence, the ACAS official took a conciliatory line that if the job holder had a number of other relatively minor responsibilities added to his job, (such as monitoring YTS trainees and involvement in the induction process) which would differentiate him from the standard maintenance job, then his rating could be enhanced. This was subsequently arranged with his unit manager.

As the committee became more experienced, then the evaluation of each job took less time. They were able to compare each job with the original benchmarked jobs and positions they had subsequently rated to ensure they were truly comparable and consistent. Also a degree of fatigue occurred so that committee members in the minority often concurred without too much of a struggle. A disaster loomed when Doreen caught the flu (no substitutes were allowed) but, luckily, it was of short duration and the committee managed to get back to their tight deadlines.

Publication

By the middle of September, the committee met for the last time to look at the full list and to examine for any final anomalies. Two jobs had been changed since being evaluated and they considered these revisions as detailed to them. One rating was changed, the other remained the same. They went back over some old ground where individuals had been out voted (especially Arthur) and agreed one last concession which did not appear to create instability. The list was then finalised (see Appendix B).

It was published in every location at 3.30 pm on October 1st. There had been a discussion as to whether the list should contain just the final total or the individual constituent factor marks. The concept of trust and openness directed full disclosure although it was recognised that this could provoke more strong reactions.

To prepare employees for this publication, Sarah's newsletter explained that no system was perfect. The committee had listened carefully to employees and their manager and had attempted to come to a fair decision taking all the detailed factors into account. It was realised that the result would not please everybody. The appeal system, and the short time-scale allowed, was explained. It was pointed out that the exact number of points would not necessarily exactly relate to an individual's salary in the coming 1996 salary review. No decisions had yet been made here.

On the day of publication, there were a number of very unhappy employees. Some of these who were unionised gave Arthur a number of difficult sessions. At one point, he considered disassociating himself from the result but Sarah had prepared for this eventuality and made sure that she counselled him thoroughly. Within a week, the fuss had died down. Appeals took place in the case of three jobs involving five employees. One of these proved successful, chiefly because there had been some minor changes in the job and it was one where the evaluation had been rushed at the end of a long afternoon.

The stage was now set for the final and most important activity, the preparation of the new salary structure.

Student activities

1. What are the cost implications involved in carrying out a job evaluation exercise?
2. Explain some of the difficulties in having a union representative on both the steering committee and the job evaluation committee.
3. Choose four of your class to act as the job evaluation committee, one to act as the housing maintenance craftsman and one to act as his manager. Role play the meeting where the job is discussed and the subsequent meeting of the job evaluation committee when the job is rated.
4. Did Sarah make the right decision to advise on a points-factor scheme? What are the practical benefits of a competence-based scheme and how could she have justified it as the preferred option?
5. Work out a points-factor scale for 'accountability' and 'knowledge', 'skills' and 'physical effort required'.
6. Explain the steps needed for Sarah to integrate the initiative on 'high quality customer care' and 'improved trust' with the job evaluation scheme.

Standard reading

	Armstrong and Murlis	*Armstrong*	*Milkovich and Newman*
Pages	95–126	97–141	123–174

Further reading

Armstrong, M and Baron, A (1995) *The Job Evaluation Handbook*, IPD, London

Barrett, G and Doverspike, D (1989) 'Another defence of points-factor job evaluation', *Personnel*, March, pp 33–36

Hillage, J (1994) *The Role of Job Evaluation*, The Institute of Employment Studies, Brighton

McHale, P (1990) 'Putting competencies to work: competency-based job evaluation' *Competency*, Summer, pp 39–40

Neathey, F (1994) *Job Evaluation in the 1990s*, Industrial Relations Services, London

Appendix A – examples of point-factor scale

Responsibility for customers

Level 1	50 points	Little or no contact with customers. Responsibilities towards customers well defined and authority to act only within these guidelines.
Level 2	100 points	Occasional contact with customers. Responsibilities towards customers well defined and authority to act only within these guidelines.
Level 3	150 points	Regular contact with customers on a day-to-day basis. Responsibilities towards customers well defined and authority to act only within these guidelines.
Level 4	200 points	Occasional contact with customers. Wide responsibilities and authority for solving customer problems.
Level 5	250 points	Regular contact with customers on a day-to-day basis. Wide responsibilities and authority for solving customer problems.
Level 6	300 points	Responsibility for defining guidelines and objectives relating to customer care and for ensuring these are carried out. Regular dealings with difficult customer situations.

Flexibility

(*Note*: Temporal flexibility means working flexible hours including shifts, weekends and overtime at short notice plus on-call situations. Occupational flexibility refers to the variety of jobs that the jobholder can be called on to carry out after training.)

Level 1	50 points	Occupational flexibility required very small and no temporal flexibility.
Level 2	100 points	Limited occupational flexibility. Work may involve occasional temporal flexibility.
Level 3	150 points	Limited occupational flexibility. Regular temporal flexibility.
Level 4	200 points	Reasonable level of occupational flexibility (at least 4–6 jobs to learn) with occasional temporal flexibility.
Level 5	250 points	Reasonable level of occupational flexibility (at least 4–6 jobs to learn) with regular temporal flexibility.
Level 6	300 points	Position where flexibility is at a premium and where a wide range of jobs have to be learnt and applied. Regular temporal flexibility.

Appendix B – results of job evaluation exercise

	Responsibility for customers	Responsibility for staff	Accountability	Knowledge skills and effort	Flexibility	Total
Benchmarks						
Rent Collector	150	0	150	100	150	550
Accounts Sup.	100	100	250	200	200	850
Unit Manager	250	300	300	250	250	1350
Auxiliary	150	0	50	50	150	400
Other Jobs						
Housing MS	250	100	200	250	250	1050
Maintenance Op	150	0	150	250	250	800
Unit Administrator	200	0	150	200	200	750
Housing Labourer	100	0	50	100	150	400
Sen Nursing Sister	200	100	250	250	200	1000
Nurse	150	0	200	200	200	750
Purchasing Clerk	100	0	150	150	100	500
Accounts Clerk	100	0	150	100	100	450
Receptionist	150	0	200	150	100	600
Purchase Ledger Clerk	100	0	200	200	100	600
Tender Supervisor	100	100	250	200	200	850
Manager, Tendering	150	150	300	250	200	1050
Sen Maintenance Craftsman	200	50	150	250	250	900
Wages Clerk	100	0	200	150	100	550
Personnel Clerk	100	0	150	150	100	500

Appendix C – time-scale

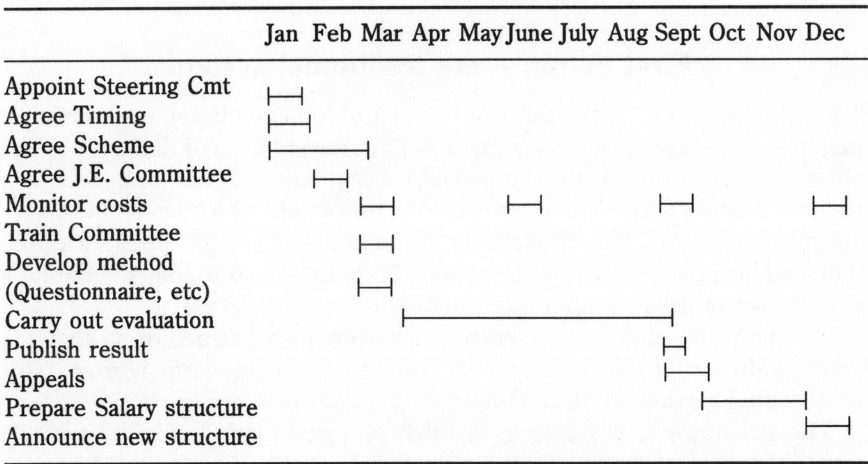

Case Study 9

From Job Evaluation to Salary Structure at Strand Housing Association

Introduction

In Case Study 8, the Strand Housing Association had carried out a job evaluation exercise for the 120 jobs covering the 610 employees. This case study continues the story, describing how a salary structure was developed from the results of the job evaluation exercise and the difficulties which resulted.

Sarah was very pleased that the job evaluation had been completed within time and with full agreement of the parties involved, including the union. It had been a long haul and taken up far more of her time than she had expected but she felt that it had been worth it. There was now a sense of expectation in the organisation – a mixture of hope blended with apprehension – as employees waited for the announcement of the revised salary structures.

Although the process of evaluation had been a success, Sarah knew that creating a salary structure was laden with booby traps. Time was short – only two months to prepare – and the consultations this time would be very limited to avoid too many rumours breaking out. She had to get it right first time.

First option – the traditional system

The first task was to list all the jobs in order of total points and the number of employees in these jobs. (See Table 2.4 – this covers most of the key jobs and about 70 per cent of the personnel.) From here, Sarah first took the traditional approach, dividing up the jobs into strata which would become a six-grade structure. The division was made at suitable break points with the four middle grade-widths being either 100 points or 200 points. Thirdly, a suitable set of salary ranges was constructed for each grade.

The first selection was to have a non-overlapping structure so that the grade widths of £2000 for grades three to six were quite narrow. This represented a grade-width of around 20 per cent in these grades.

The advantage of this system was that promotion up a grade immediately gave a salary increase so there was a pecuniary advantage for employees to aim for in promotion. It was also a very tidy and logical system and easy to defend.

There were a number of disadvantages, though. For those employees in jobs on the boundary, there could be dissatisfaction that one small decision of 50 points on one of the factors could make quite a sizeable salary difference. With no salary overlap, employees were on one side of the fence or the other. The scheme would also work against flexibility. For example, the accounts clerks and the purchase ledger clerks often helped out each other in the Finance department. Would they be so willing to do so when one job was graded higher than the other and with higher salaries?

Problems of overpay

The most significant difficulty related to employees' current salaries and the salary range for their grade. In the majority of cases, there was no problem as current salaries coincided with the proposed grade salary. However, in a significant minority of cases, this was not so. In the case of rent collectors, 18 of the 40 job holders were above the maximum and there was a total of 70 employees in this situation.

On investigation, Sarah found that these situations of apparent overpay had arisen from a variety of causes with some employees coming under more than one category:

- the largest number of these cases (42) applied to employees who worked in the London borough units;
- a second factor appeared to be connected with length of service – 29 employees had service in excess of 15 years;
- seven employees had been demoted or moved sideways within the last few years, but their salaries had been protected and they had continued to receive the annual increments; and
- there were five cases where special responsibilities had not been reflected in the evaluation exercise. Three of the unit managers had particularly large contracts and two other employees were involved in special tendering work where particular market rates applied.

Sarah set about trying to solve these problems.

London allowance

It would be straightforward to insert a London allowance into the salary structure. At £1000 pa this would dispose of 28 of the 42 problem cases. If the figure was £2000 then all but five of the cases would be covered. Alternatively, the allowance could be pitched at a percentage of salary, say ten per cent, which would give greater protection for the better paid. At this level, this would cover 33 employees. However, a complication was that the payment would have to be built into the salary of all 90 employees working in the London borough contracts, whether apparently overpaid or not. This would involve some cost increases.

Table 2.2 *Effect of London allowance*

Grade min and max	Current payment	New basic	London Allowance	Total	Cost
£10,000–14,000	£14,500	£13,500	£1000	£14,500	–
£10,000–14,000	£10,000	£10,000	£1000	£11,000	£1000

Table 2.2 shows two examples: the first shows an employee over the maximum for the grade where the payment of the allowance brings the basic pay back inside the grade; the second where an employee entitled to the London allowance would receive an additional £1000 to remain above the minimum of the grade.

In the first example, it would appear that there is no additional cost involved, merely a re-adjustment of the components of the salary. A purist may argue that, in paying this allowance, the opportunity is wasted to save costs through reducing the salary of overpaid employees. These continuing costs could be as high as:

£1000 fixed sum	–	£90,000 pa
£2000 fixed sum	–	£180,000 pa
10% salary supplement	–	£120,000 pa

Sarah was not prepared to accept this argument. A London allowance was paid in most London companies and it would be difficult to conclude a fair settlement (or avoid a future claim) without the inclusion of this allowance.

Length of service

A number of employees had been transferred from previous contract holders whose salary progression system had been more generous with a longer set of increments. Transfer of Undertakings Regulations (TUPE) had insisted that the employees' terms had to be transferred intact and no action had been taken to remedy the situation to date. Sarah considered the possibility of adding a grade supplement for service in excess of 15 years. At £500, 12 of the employees would be covered and £1000 would include all but four of the 29 employees. However, as with the London allowance, there would be added costs of paying the allowance to another 40 employees in the organisation with this length of service.

Sarah also considered other alternatives including paying only those with 20 years of service but protect the salary of those who had 15 years as the problem would be resolved within a few years. To pay only for 20 years' service would mean that the payment would apply to a further 24 employees with knock-on costs of only £12,000.

Demotion

Protecting employees who have been demoted usually arises from individual circumstances. In this example, there were two cases arising from the return to work following extended illness, both maintenance supervisors, one of whom who became a unit administrator and the other a craftsman. Three other cases arose from the employee finding the existing job too much due to the caring responsibilities arising from poor health of a close relative. These were cases where two nurses became auxiliaries with limited shifts and a unit manager became a supervisor. An older employee may find difficulty in coping because of technological developments so they were shuffled to a less demanding job. This happened in the case of two accounts supervisors who became accounts clerks.

In all these situations, it is the benevolent employer who protects the salary of those employees concerned. However, following a job evaluation exercise, the situation can no longer be hidden. Sarah knew that, unless their salaries were reduced, then the organisation could have easily become liable for an equal pay claim. The 'red circle' defence has been tested at equal pay tribunals in recent years and the gate has been progressively narrowed, especially in the *Snoxell* v. *Vauxhall Motors* 1977 ICR 700 EAT case.

All such cases should have an end in sight, either through looming retirement or through a progressive reduction in the salary excess. In three of these cases, employees would retire in the next five years but the other four cases were more difficult to solve. Each would need to be counselled as to their future plans but this needed to be carried out sympathetically, particularly where care responsibilities were involved. Some form of payment could have been involved through voluntary retirement but these would be difficult to quantify. The situation could not be left to stand.

Special responsibilities

This had an easy solution for the unit managers where additional payments could be made in respect of contracts in excess of £2 million pa. Four other unit managers would also come into this category and the knock-on costs would be £6000. For the tendering staff, Sarah believed that a supplement of £2000 would be generally acceptable, at a cost of £3000.

Problems of underpay

59 employees were below the minimum salary for their grade. To bring them up to the minimum level immediately would cost £89,000. Another solution was to phase this in over two years by employees being paid half the difference in the first year. This would save a one off payment of £40,000. The long-term costs, however, would be the same either way. Most employees would probably be prepared to wait the extra year.

Summing-up

Sarah drew up a cost statement for the implementation of the scheme, choosing a mid-position costing for the London allowance and service awards. This is shown in Table 2.3.

Table 2.3 *Costs of implementing a narrow band scheme*

Extra Payments	Employees	Ist Year	2nd Year
London allowance	8	£12,000	£12,000
Service payment	5	£9,000	£9,000
Special jobs	7	£9,000	£9,000
Underpay	59	£49,000	£89,000
Total		£79,000	£119,000

This was a substantial cost, representing two per cent of payroll. The other options, which were not so clear cut and defensible, needed examining.

Second option – overlapping grades

In this structure (see Table 2.4) the same grading system is used but the grades have a much wider salary scale. For example, grades three to five now have a width of £4000, double their previous width. However, the top of grade five overlaps grade six to the tune of £2000.

Implications

There were still 24 employees over the top of the salary maximum and 16 employees below the minimum. By dealing with these issues in the same way as with the narrow grade system all but a handful of problems could be solved. The additional costs were substantially less (see Table 2.5) so the scheme appeared to have considerable merit. Moreover, in terms of flexibility, it made the interchanging of jobs far easier. Purchase ledger clerks and accounts clerks could do each other's jobs without quite so much immediate concern with the salary implications.

In terms of equity, Sarah could see that it may produce some disappointments. A nurse, on mid-scale at £12,500 would be on lower pay than a rent collector on the top of their scale at £13,000 although she was on a higher grade. An employee might be promoted to a higher grade but not necessarily receive a higher rate of pay. This made the structure more difficult to justify and it was not so clear cut.

Movement within the grades

What became crucial was the decision on what salary level within their grade new employees would start and how existing employees would move up their pay grade. For new employees, they could start at the base of their grade scale, but this would not always be realistic in recruiting experienced employees into the organisation; or they could be taken on at an appropriate level depending on their age, experience and the current market situation which could present some difficulties if new employees were recruited on rates higher than existing, experienced employees.

Table 2.4 *Comparison of Option 1 and Option 2*

SELECTION OF JOBS					Option 1 – Discrete Grades				Option 2 – Overlapping Grades			
Grade	Job	Actual points	grade points range	nos staff	suggested grade salary range (£K)	Existing salary range £K	Nos over max.	Nos under min.	Suggested Grade Salary £K	Existing Salary £K	Nos over Max.	Nos under Min.
1	Unit Manager	1350	1201 +	20	19–24	17-30	4	3	17–26	15–30	2	1
	Manager, Tendering	1050	1001–	1		19	1	–	15–20	19	–	–
2	Housing Maintenance		1200									
	Supervisor	1050		13	16–19	14–22	3	3		14–22	1	1
	Senior Nursing Sister	1000		3		13–15	–	1		13–15	–	–
	Senior Maintenance											
	Craftsman	900	801–	25	14–16	12–17	3	6	13–17	12–17	–	2
	Accounts Supervisor	850	1000	3		11–15	–	2		11–15	–	1
3	Supervisor, Tendering	850		1		17	1	–		17	–	–
	Maintenance Operator	800	601–	40		11–19	10	4		11–19	2	3
	Unit Administrator	750	800	50	12–14	9–15	2	14	11–15	9–15	–	5
4	Nurse	750		60		11–15	3	4		11–15	–	–
	Receptionist	600		2		11–12	–	–		11–12	–	–
	Purchase Ledger Clerk	600	501–	6	10–12	9–11	–	1	9–13	9–11	–	–
	Rent Collector	550	600	40		10–15	18	–		10–15	8	–
5	Wages Clerk	550		2		10–12	–	–		10–12	–	–
	Personnel Clerk	500		1		8	–	–		8	–	–
	Purchasing Clerk	500	under	3		9–10	–	–		9–10	–	–
	Accounts Clerk	450	500	7	8–10	7–13	2	1	7–11	7–13	2	–
	Housing labourer	400		40		9–14	5	–		9–14	4	–
6	Auxiliary	400		100		6–12	18	20		6–12	5	3
	TOTAL			417			70	59			24	16
		(Out of total of 610 employees)										

Table 2.5 *Costs of implementing an overlapping bands scheme*

Extra Payments	Employees	Ist Year	2nd Year
London allowance	3	£5000	£5000
Service payment	1	£2000	£2000
Special jobs	3	£4000	£2000
Underpay	16	£19,000	£40,000
Total		£30,000	£49,000

Movement within the grade was an even more complex issue. Under the previous informal regime, salary increases were arbitrary, isolated and individual, causing a general sense of injustice. The new structure had to have a central, well-defined mechanism and this could come about in at least four different ways:

1. By service, so that each grade would have a set of four to eight increments. Employees would move up the scale by receiving an increment each year so they reached the top in four to eight years. This would take no account of the performance of the employee. It was certainly clear and straightforward but Sarah felt that ignoring performance made it too mechanistic and it did not match the growing awareness of the customer-led culture of the organisation.
2. By performance, whereby employees would be assessed each year by a form of appraisal which would determine how far up the scale they would move, if any. In other words, a form of merit pay or performance-related pay.
3. Thirdly, by acquiring competencies, so their behaviour would be assessed against the ideal type of behaviour required in that job and for the organisation. Employees who demonstrated that they had become more competent would move their way up the scale (competence-based pay).
4. Fourthly, by acquiring skills, chiefly measurable skills which could be accredited to some qualification (skills-based pay).

The latter three options involved a huge amount of work and could not be brought on stream for at least a year. Length of service could be chosen as an interim measure but this could become difficult to move away from to a more progressive method.

Option 3 – broad-banding

The last option Sarah considered involved taking overlapping grades a stage further by simplifying the grading structure to three broad bands, as set out in Table 2.6. The first would cover managerial positions, the second supervisory and technical positions and the third clerical, administrative and operational positions. Putting all the jobs into these three bands would ensure that there were no employees over the top of their band and only a small handful below the minimum.

Sarah could see that the idea had a number of advantages:

- the scheme would add only around £10,000 in additional salary costs;
- flexibility was built into the scheme. New employees could be recruited on a wider salary frame and new jobs and processes could be introduced without worrying too much about employees' narrowly defined jobs, and the resulting grading appeals;
- most existing employees would be able to work towards higher salary levels than on the narrow-banded schemes and this should provide an additional incentive; and
- internal sideways moves would be easier to implement.

But there were also some disadvantages:

- control of salary movements becomes very important. When the bands are wide and the apparent opportunities for salary increases are inviting, then there is a risk that employees have higher expectations and salaries drift upwards. This can be an expensive process. Control could be through the HR department or by 'empowering' managers but this would need to be introduced with considerable care and training; and
- after all the effort of the job evaluation exercise, some employees may be deflated by the scheme that puts them into a grade with employees on much lower points.

The solution

Sarah put the three proposals to the Board in a summarised form. The Broad-banding proposal appealed to the head of finance but was ruled out by the Chief Executive as it would be unlikely to match the expectations of employees. Option two became the preferred solution and Sarah was instructed to put forward the detailed proposal for discussion with senior managers and the union in late November.

Her briefing document gave a fair and balanced summary of the advantages and difficulties of the scheme and why it was the preferred solution. For the ten employees still above the maximum for their grade, the following two options were put forward.

Firstly, that they remained at the same salary until the salary reviews each year increased the grade maximum up to the point where they fell back within the grade. For example, an employee in grade three on a salary of £18,700 where the existing grade maximum was £17,000, would have to stay on £18,700 until the salary reviews increased the grade maximum by ten per cent, which would probably take three years.

Secondly, that the employee accepted a buy-out of a year's 'excess' paid as an immediate one-off taxable, non-pensionable lump sum. In the case above, this would be a payment of £1700.

Table 2.6 *Option 3 – broad bands*

SELECTION OF JOBS Grade	Job	Actual points	Grade points range	Nos staff	Suggested grade salary range (£K)	Existing salary range £K	Nos over max.	Nos under min.
1	Unit Manager	1350		20		17–30	–	–
	Manager, Tendering	1050	1000+	1	14–30	19	–	–
	Housing Maintenance Supervisor	1050		13		14–22	–	–
	Senior Nursing Sister	1000		3		13–15	–	–
	Senior Maintenance Craftsman	900		25		12–17	–	–
	Accounts Supervisor	850	601–	3		11–15	–	–
2	Supervisor, Tendering	850	1000	1	10–17	17	–	–
	Maintenance Operator	800		40		11–19	2	–
	Unit Administrator	750		50		9–15	–	2
	Nurse	750		60		11–15	–	–
	Receptionist	600		2		11–12	–	–
	Purchase Ledger Clerk	600		6		9–11	–	–
	Rent Collector	550		40		10–15	3	–
	Wages Clerk	550		2		10–12	–	–
3	Personnel Clerk	500		1		8	–	–
	Purchasing Clerk	500	under	3	7–13	9–10	–	–
	Accounts Clerk	450	600	7		7–13	–	–
	Housing labourer	400		40		9–14	1	–
	Auxiliary	400		100		6–12	–	3
	TOTAL			417			6	5

(Out of total of 610 employees)

Consultation

The response of the senior managers was positive with only minor details to confirm. The situation was more difficult with the union. They did not like either of the solutions for those employees above the maximum and wanted them to continue to receive salary increases based on their existing salaries. The equal pay implications could not dissuade them of this point. They also wanted a reasonable pay increase effective from January 1st. Their final request was to enter into discussion on the detail of the proposed grading and salary structure before it was announced.

The Board could not countenance more than a cost-of-living salary increase, given the costs involved in introducing the scheme. Sarah advised that they stand firm on the solutions offered on employees above the maximum, considering that the small numbers involved would not stop the arrangement going through. On the final point, she had difficulty in refusing to discuss the detail of the scheme and advised that an extra session with the union could be fitted in before the end of the year. The Board accepted both these pieces of advice.

The union committee was therefore given the proposed scheme details and a further meeting arranged the next day. By the middle of that meeting, Sarah realised she had made a mistake. The committee representatives wanted to make so many detailed changes to the proposal to accommodate their various members' interests that she knew that she had opened a can of worms. Some of the committee's proposals were contradictory and it appeared that it would take many meetings of the committee itself to sort out their own final proposal. Then there would have to be several meetings with the management to agree a final revised version. This was not what the Board had in mind. There was not time for this process if the new scheme was to be implemented in January, nor did the Board relish a complete re-think.

Sarah argued that the decision to release the new scheme could not be reversed without severe difficulties developing. After a stormy meeting with the Board, she proposed that a deadline of mid-January be imposed where agreement had to be reached or the scheme would be implemented as it was. The Board reluctantly agreed to this proposal, as did the union committee and this was communicated to all the staff. The union also agreed to keep the proposal in confidence but Sarah knew that details would leak out.

A very hectic four-week period followed. Sarah tried to work closely with Arthur, the union chair, but Arthur was having considerable problems pulling together the conflicting interests of his committee members. He said, on one occasion, that he wished that Sarah had not released this information and caused these problems. By the mid-January deadline, a small number of adjustments had been made to accommodate special pleading which involved an additional expenditure of £6,000. However, there were still two or three more substantial issues on salary limits where agreement could not be reached. After the final session ended at 10.00pm, the parties admitted defeat.

At a final meeting with the Board, Sarah pressed for one last concession but the Board relied on the agreement reached with the union to revert to the original scheme and this was published, together with a cost-of-living pay increase.

The publication of the new scheme led to the expected mixture of disappointment and disillusion from a substantial minority of staff. There were also difficult relations with the union for some time thereafter. A number of employees subsequently applied for re-grading when their jobs changed very slightly as they saw the opportunity to move to the next salary band. This took up a considerable amount of Sarah's time and they were difficult decisions as success for one would lead to the chance of further claims being laid.

Sarah reflected that what had seemed, at one point, to be a hard-won and successful enterprise had turned to ashes in a very short period of time.

Student activities

1. Identify the employee relations strategy which would have had a better chance of achieving a smoother introduction to the scheme.
2. How important are the cost issues? Is there an alternative process which could be used to carry out a realistic cost of the alternatives?
3. Draw up Sarah's briefing document for introducing the new scheme.
4. Write Sarah's proposal to the Board either for or against the broad band proposal.

Standard reading

	Armstrong and Murlis	*Armstrong*	*Milkovich and Newman*
Pages	151–204	195–238	282–286

Further reading

Hill, S (1993) 'Get off the broad-band wagon', *Journal of Compensation and Benefits*, Jan–Feb, pp 25–29

Le Blanc, P (1992) 'Banding – the new pay structure for the transformed organisation', *ACA Perspectives*, March, pp 1–6

Murlis, H (1996) *Pay at the Crossroads*, IPD, London

Weightman, J (1994) *Competencies in Action*, IPD, London

Appendix A

Advice for practitioners on broad-banding

Hewitt Associates advise that broad-banding is not an approach which necessarily suits every organisation. Their research shows that the organisations which derive maximum benefit from broad-banding share certain common characteristics. These are:

- they have a large proportion of knowledge workers;
- they are planning to de-layer or have already done so;
- status consciousness is not a feature encouraged by the organisation's culture;
- they want more scope to reward individual differences; and
- they take a pragmatic approach and can live with flexible systems.

An organisational questionnaire has been devised to help focus on these key issues. More information is available from:

Hewitt Associates
Romeland House
Romeland Hill
St Albans
Herts, AL3 4EZ.
Tel: 01727 866233

PART 3

PAYING FOR PERFORMANCE

Introduction

More articles have been written about the issue of performance pay than any other reward topic and it still continues to generate heated debate. When we are asked whether the high performing employee should be paid more than the low performing employee doing the same job, then nearly all of us would say 'yes', because we see that as equitable treatment and because it reflects the market economy in which 85 per cent of us work. We may also be influenced by the fact that we generally regard ourselves as a high performer!

There remains, however, a minority view that the high performers should be rewarded but not in pay terms. They should have intrinsic rewards – personal satisfaction, more authority on the way that the work is carried out, acknowledgment by the powers-that-be in public and in writing, a greater chance of promotion and more freedom and flexibility in their personal terms and conditions. This view holds that we should make every effort to raise the performance of the low performer through training and counselling (but, please, no incentives).

Alfie Kohn[1] is such a proponent, believing that once you pay more money for higher performance, employees change their behaviour and centre their activities only to win those rewards, narrowing their focus and shortening their horizons. In the process, the intrinsic rewards are destroyed.

These views are shared by many academics, (Thompson[2], Kessler[3], Heery[4]) and most trade unionists (Edmunds[5]). They view the endless experiments as alchemy, juggling with the consultant's latest base metals in a doomed search to find the elixir of life.

Despite these weighty views, they remain in a minority. Increasingly, all organisations – public, private and voluntary – are attempting to develop a high performance culture with the expressed support of their employees. In this situation, pay as a motivator is one of the preferred vehicles. Differential payments are seen as both motivators/incentives and as rewards.

Changing nature of performance pay

It has a long history. It used to be called piece work or a productivity scheme. It was purely individual or sectional and limited to one measure (usually sales or output). It had little or no relationship with the overall performance of the organisation and the customer rarely came into the equation.

The history of such schemes is littered with the remnants of inter-sectional disputes, over-payments to ingenious employees who managed to circumvent the system and a wide range of dysfunctional behaviour due to a narrow focus – poor quality, late delivery and contempt for customer preferences being just a few examples.

In recent years, it has been approached more intelligently. It has a much wider focus and tries to cover large areas of the organisation's aims and objectives. Serious attempts are made to involve employees in the whole process from initial consultation to wide evaluation after the event. Usually, most employees are included in the scheme. The judgment of performance is often based on a sophisticated performance management scheme. Even so, there remains evidence that many schemes fail to reach their objectives, notably in motivating employees (Marsden and Richardson[6]).

Reasons for failure have been registered by many commentators. Murlis[7] lists 15 issues causing concern, including the over-emphasis on individual achievement (the 'back-stabbers' charter'), poor or misunderstood communication about what the whole process involved and how annual reporting or appraisal procedures did not relate logically and defensibly to eventual performance rewards. Lewis[8] dismisses the rhetoric surrounding PRP as it applies to the education sector, pointing out, amongst his nine lessons, that the management prerogatives do not sit easily with the more democratic structures in the public sector.

PRP in practice

In practice, it is not all gloom. In Case Study 10, a whole raft of HRM initiatives took place at Associated Telecommunications alongside the payment changes, leading to an integrated approach to employment and reward. Here, the scheme received a much greater amount of employee support and has proved successful in leading to higher performance levels by individuals and the company as a whole. In Case Study 14, the concept has been centred on one small group of employees in a crucial and growing area – those dealing with the telephone sale/service environment. Case Study 13, on the other hand, looks at the planning process leading to the introduction of PRP based on the job-families concept.

There is no doubt the system of PRP must be made to fit the culture of the organisation. This either means that the existing culture can be receptive to the competitive and individual elements of PRP or the culture has to be changed. PRP can be used as part of the change process but, on its own, it is unlikely to be powerful enough to prove successful.

This is demonstrated in two of the studies. In Case Studies 11 and 12, the introduction of PRP into the police service and into a local authority has not been a success. The initiatives have not been accompanied by other supportive measures and their isolation has helped to lead to their apparent downfall.

It is amongst the sales force that the concept more naturally feels at home. The psyche of most sales forces is aligned with the individualistic, competitive and incentive driven characteristics familiar in PRP. Case Studies 15 and 16 cover two extremes. Case Study 15 shows a traditional bank moving into the modern sales environment and looking at the incentive options for staff who are not altogether used to sales motivation. Case Study 16 describes a sales contest for very experienced self-employed sales people and all the razzmatazz that accompanies it with a huge variety of cash and non-cash rewards.

PRP – a judgement?

The question is often asked, does PRP work? Conclusions are difficult in all management issues where scientific experiment using control groups is practically impossible and PRP is no exception. Most US experience is that greater use of performance pay results in improved organisational performance as measured by return on capital employed, particularly when applied to managerial pay (Wagner et al[9], Gerhart and Milkovich[10], Abowd[11]). In the UK, the few studies have been largely negative or inconclusive.

In a recent Industrial Society[12] report, 43 per cent of employers said their schemes were effective or very effective in rewarding performance compared to 26 per cent who thought them ineffective or worse.

Finally, all research has confirmed that employees regard positively the concept of PRP but deny quite strongly that it acts as a motivator for them in practice, and are mostly critical of the resulting procedural and distributive justice. We may conclude that employees may work harder, in a more focused way and get better results through a PRP system which is underpinned by a robust performance management scheme but employees may do this through a mixture of necessity and fear, rather than a genuine desire to do so.

References

1. Kohn, A (1993) *Punished By Rewards*, Houghton Mifflin, New York
2. Thompson, M (1993) 'Pay and performance – the employee experience', IMS Report No. 258, Brighton
3. Kessler, I (1994) 'PRP – contrasting approaches', *Industrial Relations Journal*, Vol. 25, No. 2, pp 122–135
4. Heery, E (1995) 'A return to contract? The causes and effects of PRP in the public service', Paper presented at conference 'Organising Employment for High Performance' Cardiff Business School, September 4–5th
5. Edmunds, J (1996) Keynote talk at Open University Conference – 'HRM, the real story', April 3, Milton Keynes
6. Marsden, D and Richardson, R (1992) *Motivation and Pay in the Public Sector: A*

Case Study of the Inland Revenue, Discussion Paper No. 75, Centre for Economic Performance, London School of Economics

7. Murlis, H (1992) 'The search for performance improvement', *Public Finance and Accounting*, 28 February, pp 14–15.
8. Lewis, P (1993) 'PRP in higher education – nine lessons ... but no songs of praise', *Education and Training*, Vol. 35, No 2, pp 11–15
9. Wagner, J, Rubin, P and Callaghan, T (1988) 'Incentive payment and non-managerial productivity: an interrupted time series analysis of magnitude and trend', *Organisational Behaviour and Human Decision Processes*, Vol. 42, pp 47–74
10. Gerhart, B and Milkovich, G (1990) 'Organisational differences in managerial compensation and financial performance', *Academy of Management Journal*, Vol. 33, pp 663–691
11. Abowd, J (1990) 'Does performance-based managerial compensation affect corporate performance?', *Industrial and Labor Relations Review*, Vol. 43, pp 52–73
12. Industrial Society (1996) *Rewarding Performance*, Managing Best Practice No.20, London

Case Study 10

Introducing Performance Pay at Associated Telecommunication Ltd

Background

The Swiss-owned company in this study is a major player in the sales and service of communication technology, including telephone, fax, voice data and video conferencing both in the UK and abroad dealing with around 40,000 customers. 1200 staff are employed throughout the UK with the head office in Manchester. The Company was formed as a result of a number of mergers over the last ten years and, by 1994, had the experience and expertise of a number of companies brought under one name but with very different styles and cultures. The company at that time recognised that morale amongst employees was low. This came about for a number of reasons:

- resulting from the mergers was a series of redundancy exercises, some of which were compulsory, leaving a strong element of survivor syndrome;
- in 1993, the company appointed a new managing director who implemented a number of significant strategic directional changes, unsettling employees, particularly those with long service;
- the recession had taken its toll in the business area, resulting in the company posting a loss in 1992 and 1993. Pay increases in these years were minimal; and
- during the period of the mergers, there had been some informal and unpredictable rationalising of terms and conditions where some long-standing benefits had been removed in what was regarded as an arbitrary fashion.

Change was necessary and they were in a position where there were a number of levers of change (see Figure 3.1). Recognising this situation, the Board instituted a set of fundamental changes in the human resources area, enshrined in a new set of values easily recognisable in HRM terms:

- the customer comes first;
- total commitment to quality;
- empowerment and responsibility;

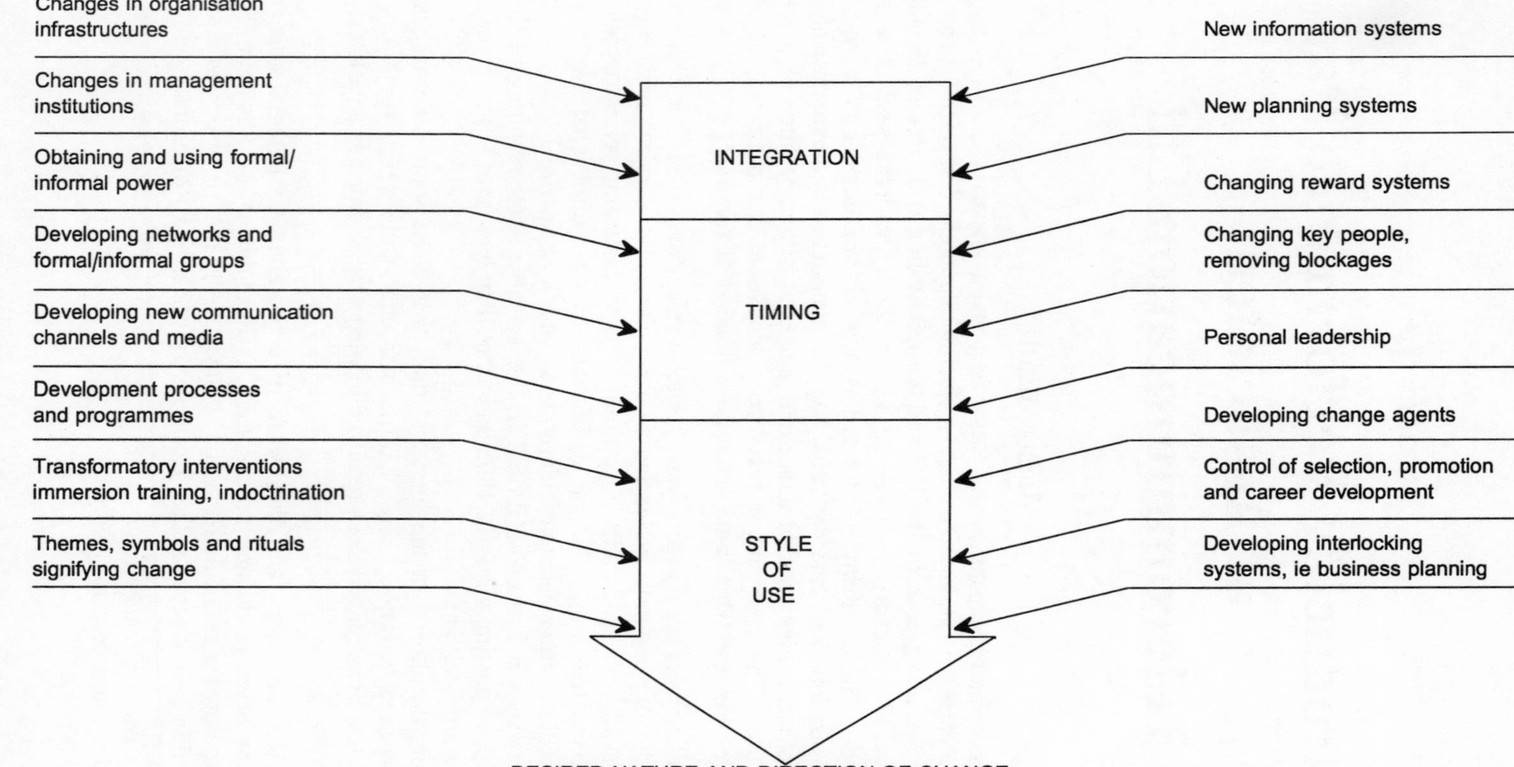
Changes in organisation infrastructures
Changes in management institutions
Obtaining and using formal/ informal power
Developing networks and formal/informal groups
Developing new communication channels and media
Development processes and programmes
Transformatory interventions immersion training, indoctrination
Themes, symbols and rituals signifying change
INTEGRATION
TIMING
STYLE OF USE
New information systems
New planning systems
Changing reward systems
Changing key people, removing blockages
Personal leadership
Developing change agents
Control of selection, promotion and career development
Developing interlocking systems, ie business planning
DESIRED NATURE AND DIRECTION OF CHANGE

Figure 3.1 *Levers for change*

- teamwork makes a winning team;
- communication is open and honest; and
- recognition and reward for individual merit.

To drive these values home, a number of initiatives were implemented: customer care courses were undertaken for all staff; sales and service support staff were interchanged so a mutual understanding of their needs were achieved; BS5700 accreditation company-wide was achieved; company communications were overhauled to improve the system of direct communication; employee attitude surveys were instigated and a further reduction in managerial/supervisory jobs took place, associated with the creation of empowered work-teams who would take over some of the planning and quality roles previously undertaken by managers and supervisors.

In view of the losses incurred in previous years and the increasingly global, competitive nature of their business, the overall improvement in employee performance was seen as the most major priority. An effective pay system was seen as the reinforcer of this concept which would need at its heart, firstly, a re-vamped job evaluation scheme encompassing all employees; secondly, a revised and robust performance management scheme based on the new values; finally, the introduction of performance-related pay.

The job evaluation process took place during the early part of 1994 and integrated a set of overlapping and contradictory grading structures in the pre-merged companies into one broad-banded nine-grade structure covering all employees below Board level. Allowing for appeals (which were few) this was introduced by the middle of 1994 with general acceptance.

The objectives that the executive management team (including the head of human resources) set themselves for the performance management system and PRP are set out in Figure 3.2.

- to distribute pay increases in line with employee contribution;
- to increase employee morale and commitment;
- to motivate the work force by letting them have influence over their achievement of targets and thereby having an influence on their financial rewards;
- to instill a positive message about performance expectations and the achievement of company objectives for the good of all thereby making employees feel more secure with the company;
- to focus attention on increased Company results and profits; and
- to offer a competitive salary and benefits package in comparison with rival companies in order to reduce staff turnover and attract a higher calibre of staff.

Figure 3.2 *Objectives for a performance management system and PRP*

Performance management

It was recognised that improving employee performance comes first and PRP is a mechanism for stimulating and reinforcing this performance improvement. So any PRP scheme is heavily dependent upon a robust performance management scheme.

Before defining the new performance management scheme, the following list of issues were drawn up:

- what groups of employees would take part?
- what role would individual objectives have in the scheme and how could they be integrated into the Company objectives?
- would individual competencies be part of the scheme and how could they be assessed?
- how could team work be encouraged?
- could managers be empowered to run the scheme so they had a larger commitment to it without the organisation losing control?
- would it be a 'top-down' scheme or could employees themselves take a part in the design and implementation?
- would the assessment take place all at one time or staged during the year?
- what would be the format for feedback?
- would there need to be an appeal system?

It was decided to include all employees in the new scheme except those already working under an individual incentive scheme, which covered sales staff.

Performance management schemes usually fall into one of three camps: they are either those based on the achievement of a set of objectives, measurable or subjective or, alternatively, they are behaviourally based, measuring competencies. The third camp is a combination of these two, dealing with both. The scheme chosen aimed to incorporate the best of both types of scheme. This was developed into a model (see Figure 3.3).

Concerning objectives, all employees agreed a set of objectives (maximum of five) with their managers prior to the start of the review period based on required performance improvement or revenue targets. (These are sometimes referred to as 'hard targets'.) Some of the objectives may refer to team results. (See Figures 3.4 and 3.5 for an example of the form used.) This meant that employees could have a part in implementing the scheme and that teamwork was encouraged. It was the responsibility of the management of each unit to ensure that all objectives were complementary both in terms of the unit's targets but also in relation to the target of any other unit where there was an operational or support link. At the end of the review period, achievement of the objectives were measured and a percentage rating produced indicating the extent to which objectives were achieved.

Concerning competencies, the scheme established a mechanism to measure an employee's contribution, (often referred to as the 'soft targets') based on five of the set of values, namely those referring to the customers' needs, quality, empowerment, teamwork and communication. Examples of the rating system (see Figures 3.6 to 3.10) set out the series of definitions which indicate the possible performance levels that can be achieved. The manager decided which series best describes the employee concerned on the scale of one to five. The rating from the five values is totalled and then multiplied by four to give a rating out of a maximum 100.

It was recognised that the achievement of objectives is vital in higher graded positions and less so in lower grades. For this reason, there is a weighting between the two measures, shown in Figure 3.11.

Feedback

There were three formal stages where feedback was given:

- at the start of the review period, a discussion with each employee must be held to agree the objectives and ensure they are formalised and clearly understood;
- at approximately the half year point, a full staff dialogue meeting took place, where progress against objectives was reviewed and a plan established for any actions necessary to assist in improving results;
- at the end of the review period and when all measurement and assessment has been concluded, the immediate manager discussed the outcomes with the individual, giving reasons for the ratings achieved; and
- employees had the right of appeal under the newly devised grievance procedure.

The scheme begins

Consultation with the unions took place in July 1994 and managers were briefed shortly after. All managers were given a refresher course in Effective Objective Setting. They were responsible for briefing their own staff by October 1st with the use of a briefing pack. The period of operation of the scheme began in August 1994 and the implementation of the first payment under PRP took place in April 1995.

Salary determination in the first year of operation took effect through the Salary Review Matrix (Figure 3.12) where salary increases ranged from zero (low performers) to eight per cent for high performers on the lower 25 per cent of their pay band. For the second year onwards, the period of operation will be one year.

Evaluation

Independent research was carried out to identify the strengths and weaknesses of the scheme. A questionnaire was issued when the scheme was introduced and the same questionnaire was issued at the end of the first year of operation. Employees' attitudes towards the scheme upon introduction was very mixed, probably due to the low morale and the many changes

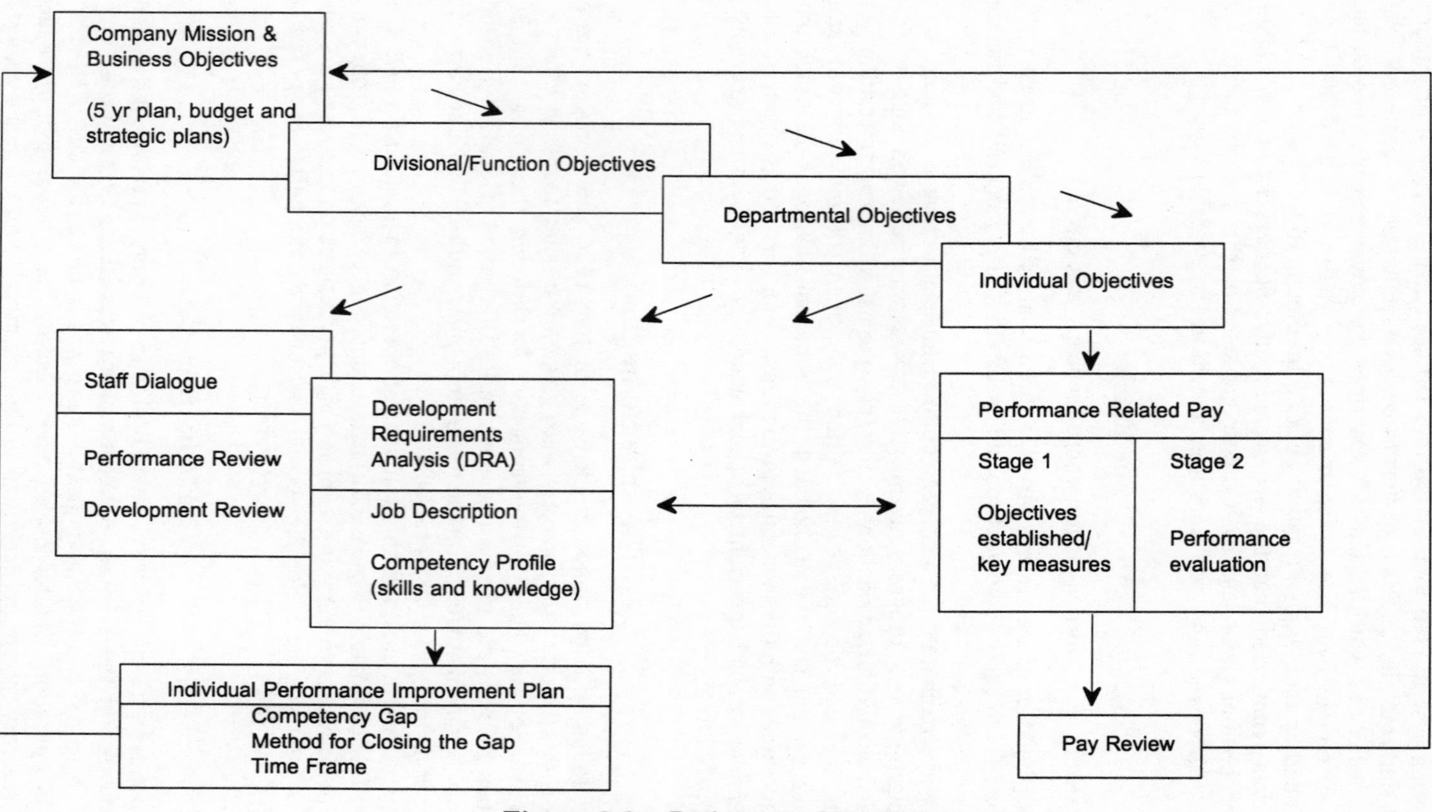

Figure 3.3 *Performance Management*

OBJECTIVE SETTING AND REVIEW

Name: ____________ Dept: __________ Job Title ________________ Period from: ___/ ___/___ to: ___/ ___/___

No	Statement of Objective	Completion date	Maximum points	Achieved points
1				
2				
3				
4				
5				

Agreed Date: ____________________	Reviewed Date: __________________
Job holder: ____________________	Job holder: ____________________
Manager: ____________________	Manager: ____________________
Approved: ____________________	Approved: ____________________

Figure 3.4 *Objective Setting and review*

DEPARTMENTAL SUMMARY SHEET

DEPARTMENT.. DEPARTMENT NO............................

NAME	ID NUMBER	OBJECTIVE RATING	CONTRIBUTION RATING

Immediate Manager: Name .... Signed ....

Approved By: Name .... Signed ....

Figure 3.5 *Departmental summary sheet*

COMMUNICATION IS OPEN AND HONEST

Level					
5	Always prepared to give and seek feedback in order to develop continuously. Feedback given is valued by those in receipt.	Always clear, concise and confident when talking to others, whether face to face or by telephone.	Accurate, concise and unambiguous in written communications – letters, memos, reports, quotes etc.	Effectively sells ideas and plans and persuades others to take a particular course of action.	Exceptional personal credibility, trust and respect from all customers and colleagues.
4	Regularly accepts and gives constructive feedback. Views feedback positively and acts upon it accordingly.	Capable communicator both orally and in writing, able to express self accurately and appropriately.	Usually sells ideas to others and gains commitment to act.	High level of personal credibility from colleagues and customers.	
3	Accepts and responds to constructive feedback. Gives constructive feedback when asked.	Ideas put forward are normally well received and frequently able to gain agreement to act.	Competent communicator in all media. Well respected by colleagues/customers.		
2	Accepts and responds to constructive feedback.	Confident in some matters and can convince others in these. Normally satisfactory standard of communication.			
1	Lacks confidence in ability to communicate and possesses only basic skills.				

Oral Communication
Written Communication
Interpersonal Relationships
Giving and Receiving Feedback

Figure 3.6 *'Communication is open and honest'*

TEAMWORK MAKES A WINNING TEAM

5	Sought by others, within own team and elsewhere, as an expert. Willingly gives advice and guidance.	Promotes team objectives and spirit to act together to achieve Department and Company goals.	Always contributes own ideas and opinions for the team good. Regularly gains team backing for suggestions made.	Seeks to assist other team members to develop. Motivates others to want to improve.	A major contributor to team success. Fully participates and encourages all other members of the team.
4	Shares information and expertise with the team. Seeks to build on contributions from others.	Encourages others to contribute more in order to improve team success.	Able to put forward own ideas and opinions and positively influence acceptance of the team.	Willingly advises others and gives feedback to develop the team.	
3	Exchanges information with colleagues clearly and concisely. Participates as a full member of the team.	Supports colleagues when possible/able. Trusted by team members.	Prepared to work with the team to develop overall success and advancement.		
2	Normally joins in with the team to achieve departmental goals.	Seeks advice from other team members and occasionally puts own ideas forward.			
1	Works independently. Does not share information or seek opinions of other team members				

Support

Team Membership

Contribution to Team Success

Contribution to Team Development

Figure 3.7 *Teamwork makes a winning team*

EMPOWERMENT AND RESPONSIBILITY

Level					
5	Influences views and opinions of others to optimise solutions and results.	Operates effectively in a changing environment. Welcomes change and adds value to it.	Always anticipates problems and personally instigates solutions. Not limited by the parameters of the job.	Takes whatever action is necessary to achieve goals and objectives within and outside of own area of responsibility.	Actively looks for challenges outside the normal requirements of the job.
4	Influences the actions of others to generate improved results.	Positively accepts change–able to maintain effectiveness in a changing environment.	Anticipates problems and assumes ownership until resolution is reached. Prepared to go beyond the job description if needed.	Achieves goals and objectives within the job and seeks opportunities for further development.	
3	Completes the requirements of the job on time, within budget and to the necessary standards.	Prepared to undertake tasks outside the basic job description if requested. Able to adapt to change.	Anticipates problems, takes immediate action to resolve or prevent and sometimes proposes longer-term solutions.		
2	Understands the basic requirements of the job and performs all aspects of it satisfactorily.	Accepts ownership of problems encountered in the course of the job, taking advice where needed.			
1	Does the minimum. Does not see self as accountable for own performance and results.				

Initiative

Self Motivation

Ideas Implementation

Responsibility for Personal Results

Figure 3.8 *Empowerment and responsibility*

THE CUSTOMER COMES FIRST

Level					
5	Anticipates customer requirements. Works with the customer to develop the business relationship.	Sets customer expectations at a high but achievable level. Win–win situations sought between self and customer.	Seen by customer as a partner.	Always listens to the customer and suggests improvements to their wants.	An ambassador.
4	Seeks to anticipate customer requirements. Listens to customers and influences customers' views.	Asks customers for feed-back and follows customer comments through.	Sought by customers as an adviser.	Performs in ways that enhance both personal and image.	
3	Reacts to customer requirements. Understands customers' viewpoint.	Accepts ownership of customer problems and complaints. Adds value to the business relationship.	Customers satisfied. Performs in line with reputation and image.		
2	Performs own job without proper regard for customer opinion. Needs constant reminding about customer skills.	Customers sometimes dissatisfied. Falls short of Customer First value.			
1	Limited awareness of customer needs or the effect of own actions. Adds no value to the relationship.				

Co-operation

Responsiveness

Customer Relationships

Identifying Customer Needs

Figure 3.9 *The customer comes first*

A TOTAL COMMITMENT TO QUALITY

Level					
5	Explores ways of dealing with problems to produce lasting improvements.	Encourages others to work more effectively through quality practices, focused on the customer.	Symbolises and promotes Company Mission and Values. A role model for others to aspire to.	Consistently meets and sometimes exceeds all business needs and standards.	Right first time, every time.
4	Looks for and recommends improvements to own role and departmental procedures.	Consistently meets all departmental needs and standards.	Sets an example for others to follow through own behaviour, achievement and personal application of values.	Right first time most times.	
3	Aware of Company Mission, Values and strategy. Seeks to improve conduct of and results of own role.	Well organised, understands priorities and always satisfies the detail requirements for the job.	Sets a good example to colleagues. Usually right first time.		
2	Aware of Company Mission and Values. Understands own job and complies with required procedures.	Makes effective use of time and resources. Mostly right first time.			
1	Little understanding of Company, Mission and Values. Rarely right first time.				

Reliability

Judgement

Attention to Detail

The Right Things Right First Time

Figure 3.10 *A total commitment to quality*

WEIGHTING OF ASSESSMENT RATINGS

GRADE	OBJECTIVE RATING	OVERALL CONTRIBUTION RATING
1,2,3	25%	75%
4,5,6	75%	25%
7,8,9	85%	15%

The above percentages are guidelines indicating the minimum weightings to be applied to the Objective ratings in normal circumstances. Variations to the above will need approval of the Departmental Manager.

Figure 3.11 *Weighting of assessment ratings*

SALARY REVIEW MATRIX

RATING	0–25%	25%–50%	50%–75%	75%–100%
86–100	8%–6%	6%–4%	4%–2%	Note 1
71–85	6%–4%	4%–2%	2%–0%	NIL
56–70	4%–2%	2%–0%	NIL	
41–55	2%–0%	NIL		
0–40	NIL			

NOTES:

1. High performing employees in this performance rating range will receive an increase equal to the average percentage cost of the review.
2. The percentage figures above are for illustration purposes only and do not indicate any actual salary review to be applied at any time.

Figure 3.12 *Salary review matrix*

that had occurred over the previous four years. The second questionnaire showed a much higher level of satisfaction with the scheme with some positive suggestions as to how it could be improved. Interesting points that emerged from this survey were:

- a large majority of employees agreed with the principle of PRP and gave approval to the design of the scheme and the way it integrated the competency and objectives-based approaches;
- there were a number of criticisms of the practical operation of the scheme related to the way objectives were set and reviewed together with the assessment of the competencies. Most of the suggestions centred upon these areas together with the need to improve the communication processes attached to the scheme;
- a similarly large majority believed that it did not motivate them to work harder or improve the quality of their work;
- there was uncertainty whether it went far in improving morale in the organisation or assisted in the cultural change process; and
- with all its faults, employees did not want to return to the old scheme.

Conclusion

The scheme has had a number of minor changes for the subsequent period, particularly related to target setting, and a more in-depth training course has been devised for all managers and supervisors involved in this area.

In management terms, it has been successful with a perception of a more focused and motivated work force which has coincided with a better all-round set of financial results. In turn, this allows the annual pay round to be more generous in terms of performance-based rewards.

Student activities

1. How far has the scheme gone to meet the issues and objectives detailed on Figure 3.2? Comment on those which have not been addressed and suggest ways that these gaps could be filled.
2. Give a critique on the scheme in general, commenting on its strengths and weaknesses.
3. What would be the major roles that the HR department would play in the designing and implementation of this scheme?
4. How important is the communication process in the successful implementation of such a scheme?

Standard reading

	Armstrong and Murlis	*Armstrong*	*Milkovich and Newman*
Pages	247–278	239–270	299–360

Further reading

Geary, J (1992) 'Pay control and commitment – linking appraisal and reward', *Human Resource Management Journal*, Vol. 2, No. 4

Kessler, S and Purcell, I (1992) 'Performance-related pay – objectives and application, *Human Resource Management Journal*, Vol. 2, No. 3

Marsden, D and Richardson, R (1992) *Motivation and PRP in the Public Sector*, LSE Centre for Economic Performance Paper No. 75, London

Mason, B and Terry, M (1990) *Trends in Incentive Payment Systems*, University of Strathclyde

Thompson, M (1993) *Pay and Performance – the Employee Experience*, Institute of Manpower Studies Report No. 258, Brighton

Appendix A

Paying for performance – advice to practitioners

In their standard work, *Reward Management*, Michael Armstrong and Helen Murlis analyse the requirements to encourage performance pay to act as a motivator. Here are ten of them:

- fair and consistent means are available for measuring performance. Unless you can measure performance, you cannot pay for it;
- the reward follows as closely as possible the accomplishment which generates it;
- the reward is clearly and closely linked and proportionate to the effort of the individual or team;
- employees should be able to track performance against their targets and standards throughout the period over which performance is being assessed;
- there is a reasonable amount of stability in work methods and flows;
- constraints are built into individual schemes which ensure that employees cannot receive inflated rewards which are not related to their own performance;
- employees covered by the scheme are involved in its development and operation and in making needed modifications;
- managers have the people skills required to obtain the maximum benefit from the scheme;
- the scheme is properly designed, installed, maintained and adapted to meet changing circumstances; and
- determined and continuing efforts are made by the organisation to communicate to employees the rationale of the scheme and how they can benefit from it.

Case Study 11

No Panacea – a Failed PRP System at Midland Shire Council

Introduction

During the 1980s and early 1990s, many local authorities started to carefully examine their long-standing systems of pay and conditions. This was in response to a number of internal and external tensions:

1. The growing shortage of skilled professional staff in areas such as accounting, computing and law brought about by the rapid economic boom from 1985 to 1989 which substantially raised pay levels for these professions in the private sector.
2. Pressure increasingly came from the Thatcher government for local authorities to produce 'value for money'. This pressure came in various forms. Firstly, the Audit Commission was set up to investigate and compare performance between authorities and to highlight areas of waste and inefficiency leading to poor performance. Early reports purported to identify better management control methods which eventually led to the creation of performance indicators. Secondly, Compulsory Competitive Tendering (CCT) ensured that in-house units had to get their act together and improve efficiency and performance if they were to win contracts and stay in business. Finally, as part of the government's attempt to rein back public spending, local authorities had their funding increasingly squeezed and authorities had their spending capped if they exceeded the Secretary of State's estimate of what they ought to spend (the basis of this calculation, one must add, changed almost every year!).
3. Political influences also occurred within the authority as conservative-controlled councils moved to the right and looked to the private sector for successful operating innovations. These included de-centralising decision making and local accountability together with the desire to provide a better customer service.
4. Pay rates were generally determined by national negotiations under various National Joint Councils and these were rigid, inflexible and did not take into account the variations in the living costs in different parts of the country. Increasingly, this was perceived as crude and unfair and

unlikely to motivate employees to support the changes towards improved performance that were on the agenda.

The move towards a greater emphasis on performance led to a large number of PRP schemes being introduced in this period. Not all of them have proved successful or durable. This case study is one in question.

Background

Midland Shire Council, an authority with 20,000 employees, was faced by all the issues raised above. In particular, salaries for section managers (fourth tier) and team managers and senior professionals (fifth tier) had been placed on the same salary bands in 1980 regardless of professional qualifications and the differing times it took to obtain them. There were many professional vacancies and the list was growing. Moreover, the national scheme was one of narrow bands which meant that the maxima were achieved in six years or less, with the result that most staff in these jobs were on the top of the scale.

The price of housing in the area had risen substantially and the level of temporary assistance allowed by the NJC rules was nowhere near sufficient to cover the costs of the move.

The revised scheme

The authority had the choice to leave entirely the NJCs, as did some Home Counties' authorities (notably Kent), or to adapt part of the structure to resolve the immediate problem concerning the fourth and fifth tier staff. The second option was chosen and a new scheme was devised with the help of Hay consultants, leaving the greater part of the old structure unaltered.

In a number of ways, the scheme remained unaltered as four salary bands were retained with seven incremental points in each band. There were, however, a number of significant changes as follows:

- the midpoints of the new bands were substantially above the old ones, in one case by £1700 to take account of the higher market rates;
- progression through the band was wholly performance-driven and there was a provision for down-rating in the case of inefficiency; and
- those joining the scheme renounced their right of appeal under the NJC grievance procedure and the grievance procedure became a local and much shortened affair.

There was considerable debate within the authority as to how wide the cover of the new scheme should be and whether the principle of moving up the scale by performance alone should be extended to staff at lower levels. Should the scheme apply only where recruitment and retention problems applied or should it be part of the cultural change towards a performance-oriented culture? Should special cases be made of professional staff or should equity considerations apply and equal opportunities be given to high performers at all levels to move more swiftly up the scale?

The decision was made to take a broad view of the scheme. As unemployment continued to fall sharply in 1987, it was forecast that retention problems would, in any case, spread throughout the authority and the demographic time-bomb was just down the road. This decision, although ensuring equal treatment of staff, would be more likely to increase the cost of implementing the new system.

Appraisal scheme

Underpinning the PRP scheme was a revised appraisal scheme which incorporated a quarterly appraisal. Ratings were based on points awarded under a set of up to 12 performance measures. These measures included the attainment of 'goals' which were reset each year and 'accountabilities' with the remainder being reflections of the different qualities expected of the appraisee – clarity of expression, depth of thought, ability to work under pressure, etc. Due to the differences between each job, a 'gearing' system was instituted so that the indicators had a different value at each grade level with differential weightings applied between five per cent and 25 per cent. The points that were awarded at each level of performance (excellent, good, etc) against the gearing for that indicator is set out in Table 3.1.

Table 3.1 *Rating x % weighting*

From the table below, enter against each job factor in the appraisal form, the points score which corresponds with the factor and weighting and the rating assigned to that factor.

Points Score

% Gearing	Outstanding 6	Excellent 5	Good 4	Satis-factory 3	Less than Satisfactory 2	Unsatis-factory 1
25%	150	125	100	75	50	25
20%	120	100	80	60	40	20
15%	90	75	60	45	30	15
10%	60	50	40	30	20	10
5%	30	25	20	15	10	5

The appraisal was carried out by the employee's immediate supervisor who would award the points on each indicator and provide a total. The resultant ratings arising from the total scores are set out in Table 3.2.

Employees whose ratings were either satisfactory or good would receive one increment on their scale. Those below satisfactory would not receive any increment and those who were 'very poor ' would be disciplined. Those in the 'excellent' and 'outstanding' categories could receive an additional increment.

For those on the top of their grade who could not be in receipt of a further incremental increase, a further incentive was introduced two years after the initial PRP scheme. This gave one-off bonuses where employees continued to

Table 3.2 *Overall performance ratings and rewards*

Total Score – All Job Factors	Equivalent Overall Rating	Scale Points	Subject to the Following Maximum in the 7 Point Scale
Above 550	Outstanding	To any Scale Point	7th Point
Above 450 To 550	Excellent	2	7th Point
Above 350 To 450	Good	1	7th Point
Above 250 To 350	Satisfactory	1	5th Point
Above 150 To 250	Less than Satisfactory	0	Assimilation/ Appointment Scale Point
Below 150	Unsatisfactory	0	

be rated 'excellent' or 'outstanding'. A caveat had been inserted at the start explaining that funds would need to be available for additional increments or bonuses to be implemented.

Difficulties with the scheme

Construction of goals

It was made clear at an early stage that goals had to be seen as over and above an employee's main duties in their jobs. To complete an audit on time could not be a goal – that was a normal duty of the job and extra increments could not be earned by simply doing your job. Defining that narrow channel between what was a normal duty and what was an extra goal became very controversial. It was difficult enough for those staff with comparatively routine and predictable management positions, such as in accounting or public service areas, to agree what were definable goals. For those in project-based areas, such as planning and development, where their job normally involved a set of goals for each project in any case, constructing and agreeing the 'extra' goals became almost impossible.

Working the system

It did not take too long for a proportion of the staff to work out what they needed to concentrate on to achieve higher ratings. Firstly, they could ignore those indicators which carried low gearings. For example, goals that had a gearing of five could be ignored. No matter how good or bad their achievements for these goals, it would make no difference to their final rating. The same point applied to those accountabilities with low gearings. Indicators which were ignored became marginalised and merely added to the bureaucratic process. Staff concentrated their effort on indicators which had a significant influence on the final result. Now, it is possible that this could have positive results for an organisation. Creating priorities (giving indicators a high gearing) could focus staff's attention on those areas which are crucial to the authority's performance at the expense of areas which have received too much attention and contribute little to the authority's success. What tended to happen, however, was that there was too much focus on large value goals at the expense of important routine activities particularly those that served the public.

Assessment processes

Not unexpectedly, the difficulty arose with applying quantitative judgments to qualitative indicators, ie when the question is not 'how many does she do?' but 'how well does she do them?'. The same appraisee may be rated a good verbal communicator by manager X, wordy and verbose by manager Y. There were also large variations between the amount of work assessed. Some conscientious managers examined every goal, assessed every accountability and judged each personal quality for each of the staff under their control. This took place every quarter. Others recognised that they could not be expected to spend over 20 per cent of their time on this activity and cut their cloth accordingly. Another difficulty was the reluctance of assessors to allow a final rating to finish on the three lowest grades or the higher ones which meant that most employees finished up in the satisfactory or good grades. These may be intrinsically satisfying but carried no additional increment.

The major fault here was lack of training for the assessors. Not only would it have helped the managers concerned to gain confidence and experience in this most difficult of skills, but it would also have ensured a reasonable degree of consistency in the process. As it was, the recipients became progressively confused and angry at their unequal treatment which ranged between the cavalier and the deadly serious.

Individual versus team

The entire system was set up to allow increased rewards for individuals justified by their high performance. Unfortunately, this encouraged some individuals to concentrate on improving their own performance at the expense of the team with whom they worked. If there was a choice between furthering their own goals or helping out the team then the choice was an easy one. Teamwork, therefore, had little encouragement from this scheme.

Employees' perception of the scheme

The scheme had been introduced as a major break from the traditional pay system which was based on service only and unrelated to performance. Although the initial pay increases when the scheme was introduced were welcomed, the on-going results left most employees feeling that the scheme had barely changed. The number of additional increments awarded was fairly small in the first year of operation and fell in each successive year so that, by 1994, no additional increments were awarded at all. It seemed to employees at all levels that a great deal of administrative work in terms of appraisals, measures and indicators was being carried out four times a year to achieve little or nothing.

Union opposition

The scheme was opposed by the union who saw acceptance as employees signing their rights away. In the end, however, all but the Branch Secretary accepted and signed up to the new arrangement.

Funding difficulties

The final and most crucial difficulty was that related to the funding of the scheme. When it was begun, there was a genuine belief that it would be self-funding. This would be through the general expansion of business and services in the community which would generate higher local and national funding together with efficiency savings and through the withholding of increments to poor performers.

The reality was that the recession at the start of the 1990s cut back income from all sources and the efficiency savings had to go towards funding these shortfalls in income. Moreover, the number of withheld increments was very small providing little or no extra income sources.

Conclusion

In 1994, the authority decided to abandon the scheme, using the argument that it could not be funded. By that time, it no longer served any useful purpose. With hindsight, it can be seen that it carried the seeds of its own destruction. It was conceived as a method of salary enhancement and it ran out of steam as soon as problems of recruitment and retention disappeared.

Unfortunately, this coincided with additional pressure from the government for authorities to implement John Major's Citizen's Charter. In setting out the need for all areas of the public domain to improve their service to their clients, the government implied strongly that authorities should use performance pay to reward employees who contributed to authorities meeting their service targets. Midshires were faced with another dilemma. Given the demise of the PRP scheme, it would be more than difficult to resurrect a new performance pay scheme with any degree of conviction and it would be met with a large degree of cynicism. The issue may be unresolved nationally where numerous schemes survive in various forms but in Midland Shires, pay has reverted to the NJC scales and PRP is no longer on the agenda.

Student activities

1. Define the necessary conditions for performance-related pay to operate successfully in the public sector.
2. Read Littlechild's article in *People Management*. Put forward arguments for and against the trend set out in the article.
3. Is there any foolproof way of working towards achieving consistent appraisal assessment judgements across a range of line managers? If not, how do you improve results in this difficult area?

4. How would you distinguish between 'achieving a goal' and simply carrying out your normal job under a PRP scheme?

Standard reading

	Armstrong and Murlis	*Armstrong*	*Milkovich and Newman*
Pages	247–278	239–270	321–415

Further reading

Arkin, A (1994) 'Paying the price of performance', *Personnel Management*, June, pp 24–27

Audit Commission (1995) *Paying the Piper – People and Pay Management in Local Government*, HMSO, London

Audit Commission (1995) *Calling the Tune – Performance Management in Local Government*, HMSO, London

Brignall, S (1995) 'Performance management and change in local government', *Public Money and Management*, Oct–Dec, pp 23–36

Henemen, R (1985) *Pay for Performance: Exploring the Merit System*, Work in American Institute Studies in Productivity No. 38, Pergamon Press, Elsford, New York

Labour Research Department (1990) *Performance Appraisal and Merit Pay*, London

Littlechild, D (1996) 'Councils swop PRP for staff development', *People Management*, 26 September, pp 15

Spence, P (1990) 'The effects of performance management', *Local Government Studies*, July/August, pp 3–6

Case Study 12

Piloting Appraisal-related Pay in the Police Service

By Sharon Mavin Taylor
Senior Lecturer, Newcastle Business School, University of Northumbria

Background

The police service is in a time of crisis. It faces falling public confidence and internal ambiguity about its role and direction. Self-confidence and self-esteem are wavering at the same time as severe police problems threaten society. However, it is now the turn of the UK police service to experience government reform.

The service is now experiencing a number of decentralization initiatives, changes to working hours, shift patterns, a reduction of benefits and a demand for increased public accountability. Private sector management practices are being introduced to the service as a means of improving performance, reforming police management and controlling expenditure. As a result of this reform, the UK police service of the future is perceived to have fewer officers, less opportunity to achieve rank, more decisions made at a lower level and an increased work load for officers left within this now commercial institution. To support government reform, HRM approaches are currently seen to have strategic importance to the police service. The perception that performance-related pay (PRP) is a vital mechanism for achieving commercial or managerial attitude in the public services has prompted the government to demand that the police service develop a performance management approach. This has translated into the proposed appraisal-related pay scheme (ARP) which has been piloted in 13 forces.

The proposed ARP scheme has arrived as a result of the government's 'Inquiry into police responsibilities and rewards' (Sheehy[1]). The Inquiry offered the following recommendations on which the proposed ARP scheme is based: reward jobs according to their size; encourage sustained good performance; provide a basis for individuals to be rewarded for their contribution other than through promotion and develop local flexibility so as to recognise exceptional individual or team performance through the award of additional increments or bonuses.

Introduction

Research was conducted into an individual force appraisal system in 1993/4. The aims of this pilot research exercise were to obtain a thorough understanding of the systems of appraisal and career development operating within a chosen police force, to investigate these against the aims and objectives and to examine the systems in the light of policy, practice and organisational culture. The chosen force is in the North-East of England and at the time of the research had an establishment of approximately 3600 police officers and 1500 civilians. The force had recently introduced a new appraisal and career development system as a direct response to the Home Office Circulars Nos. 12/1987 and 104/91, which sought to regulate appraisal and career development in the police service.

At this point it is important to recognise the hazards of research in the police. Young[2] comments that even serving officers who have attempted constructive criticism in the police risk being labelled as traitors and put their promotion prospects in jeopardy. If internal criticism is unwelcome, the views of outsiders are more likely to be seen as hostile and derogatory. The difficulty in acquiring accurate data from the police service is compounded by the covert character of policing and the sourcing of officers to contribute to the research was a difficult task. Qualitative research methods were chosen to investigate the human resource systems: these methods allowed the examination of the impact of policy and illustrated the effects of implementation on every-day activities.

A sample of police officers from a particular division were identified in order to control for gender, varying lengths of service and past experience, different experiences of specialist departments and varying ranks and qualifications gained through promotion exams. In addition, officers still in their probation period were also interviewed. This sample allowed different perceptions of the appraisal and career development systems and conveyed the perceptions of both the appraiser and the appraisee. One acknowledges the limitations to the research findings that arise from problems of access and restricted population, however, there is no reason to believe that the sample is unrepresentative.

A number of conclusions were drawn which highlight various issues regarding appraisal within the police service. These have become increasingly important due to the external pressures to introduce appraisal-related pay to all officers within the service by 1996.

The existing appraisal system

The scheme was established with a number of objectives on top of those set out in the Sheey Inquiry. These included:

- it must be acceptable to the officer being appraised, who must have confidence that it is fair;
- it must be acceptable to the appraiser who must have confidence that they can deliver it to an acceptable standard;
- it must be acceptable to the organisation, which must have confidence that it can afford it and that it will not damage morale; and
- it must be acceptable to the public, who must have confidence that it will not encourage unethical conduct (Nelson and Golding[3]).

The principles of the proposed ARP scheme were: openness, shared responsibility and fairness (National Police Training[4]). Currently officers are awarded an annual pay rise plus an increment for each year of service, regardless of performance or contribution to the job. The three-tier grading system of the proposed ARP scheme was:

- 'unsatisfactory' – withholding of any pay increments;
- 'satisfactory' – award of any pay increment; and
- 'outstanding' – award of PRP enhancement.

Unsatisfactory and outstanding grades have to be endorsed by a second line manager and should be based on overwhelming evidence provided by both the appraiser and the appraisee. Satisfactory grades could cover performance which is barely satisfactory or very good and extremely competent but not truly outstanding. An appeal procedure is in place for officers who disagree with the overall grading.

The ARP scheme has seven stages:

Stage 1 – agreeing the role requirement and relevance of core skills, reaching a common understanding of what is to be appraised during the coming year;
Stages 2/3 – collecting and pooling the evidence, on which extra payments or with held increments will be based;
Stage 4 – the ARP interview, making pay recommendations;
Stage 5 – endorsement of extreme appraisal-related pay gradings;
Stage 6 – the career development appraisal to encourage and achieve the best performance possible from individual police officers; and
Stage 7 – reviewing role requirement, evaluating its success against the originally agreed role requirement.

Research conclusions

A number of conclusions were drawn from the research and these have become increasingly important due to the external pressures to introduce appraisal-related pay to all officers within the service. These can be set out in a number of headings which relate to the wider use of ARP or PRP systems.

Strategic link to business policy

Although the written policy did appear to be strategically linked to the business policy, in practice this system had little organisational value in the opinions of those who operated it. It was not a scheme that emerged from the workforce but one imposed by the government and seen as such.

Communication

The aims of the system were to measure quality of performance and to promote performance critical to the success of the business plan. The research concluded that the force had failed to communicate the policy's aims and objectives and as a result this affected officers' perceptions of the system in practice, as they were not aware of the aims of the process nor were they able to recognise any links between their own work objectives and the force business strategy (Mavin[5]).

Training implications

A general concern of officers interviewed was that appraisers are not given sufficient training in management issues and that as a result, they felt that there was a lack of commitment from the top with regards to appraisal: 'Police officers are promoted to sergeant on the basis of their policing abilities and their perceived management abilities and are afforded little training in this area. Therefore how can you ensure a standard performance from all appraisers?' Police Officer B (Mavin[6]). This has serious financial implications for the proposed ARP scheme. The scheme has provided the 13 pilot forces with two days' training for every appraiser and a half-day briefing, plus a distance learning pack for all appraisees. This will be supported by a workshop which will 'clear up' any questions from the pack. Experience throughout private and public sector organisations has shown how important it is to ensure that before implementation the design of any PRP system is thoroughly researched and that adequate preparation is made for its delivery. An estimate of 129,000 days has been offered as the minimum training cost of implementing the ARP scheme (Nelson[7]). The training implications are horrendous and the amount of work implementing it won't produce the benefits needed to justify it (Mackenzie[8]). Details of further proposed appraisal training to supplement this is unknown at this time.

If officers feel that appraisers are not thoroughly trained, then there may be a substantial number of grievances in the event that pay awards are affected by a lack of the necessary skills to conduct appraisals. The Federation and some Superintendent Association members are allegedly concerned about the training implications of the proposed ARP scheme. The Federation warn of the considerable numbers of appeals and grievances likely to follow in the event that appropriate training is not provided. This is also important in such a low-trust environment where a straight superior/subordinate performance review may not feel very safe, especially if the appraiser has the feedback skills of Genghis Khan (Murlis[9]). The police service will have to place a strong emphasis on appraiser training for ARP. Fowler[10] comments with regards to appraisal and the appraiser, that even with an extensive training programme there are few mechanisms to help the appraiser cope with a lack of confidence in the ability to appraise. He also points out that most managers are reluctant to give assessments which reduce their subordinates' standard of living and which upset working life and relationships. This may be exacerbated by the nature of policing, whereby the appraiser could then be placed in a life or death situation with someone directly affected by the assessment of their performance.

Logistical problems

Some officers who contributed to the research, reported that their appraiser had begun the appraisal process, having worked at the sub-division for only three weeks and therefore had not had the opportunity to work with the appraisees (Mavin[11]). Even if the previous appraiser is consulted, an objective appraisal cannot take place and the turnover of appraisers has negative implications for consistency in the appraisal process. Dale[12] reports that even those sergeants who have worked at sub-divisions for a considerable length of time experience problems assessing officers' performance.

Relationships

Dissatisfaction with the appraisal system was reported by all officers who contributed to the research. All mentioned their concern with the preparation for and delivery of appraisal. The subjectiveness of the relationship with the appraiser was highlighted as an area for further research as the force was perceived to have been unsuccessful in overcoming traditional problems associated with these issues. Objectivity within the appraisal may be impossible as an individual has little control over variables which may influence performance: positive or negative factors external to the formal appraisal event can exert overriding influences on both appraiser and appraisee alike; both are influenced by territorial and political considerations, ideologies and coalition of rules, interest and power positions (Barlow[13]).

The fact that the appraisal system was based upon the assessment of an officer by one superior and the second line manager (perceived as simply 'rubber stamping' this assessment) was a major factor contributing to the officers' dissatisfaction. Officers reported that the grades allocated in an appraisal interview were affected by their relationship with the appraiser. 'You can tinker around with appraisal as much as you like, but if the appraiser does not like you then you've had it' Police Officer A. (Mavin[14]). Two officers reported that they had been downgraded in specific areas because of isolated incidents, where they had been in conflict with their appraiser. Unless there is mutual trust and understanding, the appraisee is likely to view appraisal discussions with apprehension and suspicion. The appraiser in turn is likely to view appraisal time as a daunting experience where employee hostility and resistance are likely to emerge (Anderson[15]).

Evidence

One would have expected the police force to be fastidious in the collecting of evidence for the appraisal. It could have been, of course, that the problems associated with the high standards of evidence required by the court acted as a barrier to collecting appraisal evidence because of the time and effort necessary. Whatever the cause, the ineffective collection of evidence by the appraiser to underpin grades awarded was also seen as problematic. The resulting perceived subjectiveness of the appraisal system was shown to challenge the basic assumptions of openness, fairness and consistency on which the system was based.

Team versus individual appraisal

It is often asserted that individual-appraisal-linked pay can harm the working relationships of teams (Thompson[16]). In the police force, the constables are encouraged to work effectively as a team and the current challenge within the police service is to further develop team working at all levels. Team work is perceived to be at the heart of future improvements in productivity within the police service (Butler[17]). The development of teams encourages the sharing of information, support, co-operation, mutual trust and complementary team roles. This is believed to be the way forward for the police service, ensuring that the business strategy can be achieved. It was felt keenly in this research that the appraisal activities cut across this important objective.

ARP may lead to individuals avoiding team work and keeping information to themselves, simply for financial reasons. ARP introduces competition between officers when what the service wants is co-operation and team spirit (Mackenzie[18]). How will the established teams of officers cope when one member receives a bonus payment for outstanding performance or when another is graded as 'unsatisfactory' and loses the normal pay award? How will teams be affected by role requirement, when officers choose not to perform certain duties because they are not within the appraisal remit and therefore the appraiser will not be 'monitoring' this performance? To be successful any appraisal scheme has to reflect the current needs and skills of the appraiser, appraisee and the organisation. This is not easy as there are invariably many different expressions of needs and skills and the vested interest of groups and individuals colour perceptions. It may be that the introduction of such an individualistic process will do more harm than good to the performance of police officers who are working in teams.

Cultural problems

The police service has developed a culture necessary to cope with and adjust to the pressures and tensions which confront the police. This has resulted in a bureaucratic, power and control based culture, which adheres strongly to the chain of command. This culture is socially generated: a response to a unique combination of facets of the police role, danger and authority, which should be interpreted in the light of a constant pressure to appear efficient. Policing is not just a job, it is a way of life: a sect, like a religion! (Reiner[19]). Officers who contributed to the research exercise appeared defensive when discussing culture: it was as if they had been asked to break a rule of silence. Police Officer C summed up the organisational culture by commenting, 'It's a siege mentality – as a shift you have to pull together because you are constantly taking shit from the street, so you have to build walls around yourself and don't let anyone in – you have your own team and you defend it against another shift or another department and other divisions and then as a force against other forces and then as a whole against external influences or attack' (Mavin[20]). This defensive team culture necessary for the type of situations officers have to deal with has to be taken into consideration when proposing ARP.

Behaviour

The problems of this relationship is exacerbated when employee reward is added. Appraisal then represents the very personalised applications of power and in doing so deliberately reinforces the role of the manager. Townley[21] states that performance appraisal is inherently self-defeating in the long run because it is based on a reward punishment psychology which serves to intensify pressure on the individual. Managers often perceive their appraisal of others as a hostile, aggressive act which unconsciously is felt to be hurting or destroying the other person.

Linking pay to appraisal raises a number of further issues, as Lawler[22] points out, when pay and performance appraisal are linked the pay issue may overshadow all other purposes of appraisal. There may be a tendency for employees to withhold information about performance, leading to a less frank discussion. Employees may try to influence the appraiser in seeking to lower, more conservative goals. Employees may adopt behaviour to target on receiving good ratings and therefore monetary reward, rather than genuinely improving overall performance. Managers also find it difficult to combine the roles of judge and counsellor. There was reported evidence of all these behaviours in the research findings.

Safety scoring

The ARP scheme has three gradings (shown previously), the middle grade assesses officers as 'satisfactory', awarding the normal pay increment. If awarded this grade then there would be no change to an officer's reward. However, this is still based on an exchange of subjective perceptions of performance by two individuals and the fact that the Service expects that this will be the majority, means that problems associated with the subjectivity of performance appraisal maybe exacerbated. A safeguard introduced by the ARP scheme is that in the event of the absence of evidence of extreme performance, officers will be graded as 'satisfactory' and will therefore receive the annual increment Evidence from the Civil Service shows a tendency to give the vast majority satisfactory grades (Marsden and Richardson[23]) and a similar grading pattern in the police service would allow appraisers to allocate officers normal rewards without actually monitoring performance and therefore undermining the process. If an officer is graded as 'unsatisfactory' or 'outstanding' then overwhelming evidence must be provided under the proposed ARP scheme because these grades would either remove the normal increment or give an additional performance bonus.

Conclusion

In most organisations the adoption of performance management seems to have come about largely as a reaction to external pressures rather than as a proactive process of examining and changing the values of the organisation (Fletcher and Williams[24]). There has never been so much upheaval in the Service and most of it has been driven by outside pressures. At a time when the pressures upon the police are greater than ever before, the Service appears to be introducing a management system to appease the government's pressure for performance management. The system does not appear to fit a culture which consists, not only of a bureaucratic hierarchy, but which has a steep hierarchical structure, is rule-bound and is concerned with power and control. The police service is historically inflexible to environmental change: concerned more with organisational survival than meeting externally derived goals. However, it is proposing to introduce PRP by 'adding on' to an appraisal system which is undeniably one of the most difficult activities to carry out successfully in any environment, without the unique variables affecting the police service Acknowledging this and the fact that appraisals do not operate in isolation – they are affected by the culture and the operational requirements of the organisation – the Service has to consider the existing attitudes to appraisal before adding on PRP.

Young[25] points out that the police can never really be geared to incorporate structural challenges to their existing concepts of order and control because they are set up to maintain the symbols and practice which sustain their status. It would be paradoxical for them to be in the vanguard of social change because they are there to preserve the structure and to uphold the *status quo*. Of more fundamental importance is the possibility that the individualism associated with PRP, if not handled properly, may become divisive and inconsistent with team working. With a number of industrial firms moving away from PRP schemes, other public service organisations such as the NHS have been warned that they should be clear why they want to introduce PRP.

The police service should also be examining its own motives for the introduction of ARP. The transition from what has been described as a command organisation to an empowered organisation will require the development of a more sophisticated adoption of team structures and performance management systems which are seen by staff as being driven by the needs of the task, rather than as a means of satisfying some external body (Butler[26]). Organisations must be aware of the risks and issues involved before linking pay and reward to performance appraisal. The advantages of PRP all presuppose that a valid performance appraisal system operates. If invalid data emerge from the appraisal system then the damaging effects in terms of loss of motivation and feelings of employee grievance could be substantial. The success of performance appraisal depends on the system's homogeneity with the culture of the organisation, previous experience of the appraisal in operation and the effectiveness of training and publicity during implementation. Independent evaluation of the existing appraisal systems operating in all forces should therefore take place before the additional complexity of pay is added. This evaluation should consider the fact that the traditional performance appraisal system is undergoing a slow conversion, as organisations are now asking for performance feedback from the employee's team members, managers and customers (both internal and external) and when applying this information are now calling it 360 degree feedback or appraisal. The traditional monolithic appraisal system may no longer be appropriate considering the current business aims of improved service, public accountability and the focus on developing team structures.

The Home Office, the Sheehy Inquiry and a number of other bodies have all been scrutinising the Service and coming up with solutions. The last people to be asked are the men and women who actually do the job! It is of great concern that officers themselves are not committed to the ARP process. As performance appraisal is a central part of the management process it is of vital importance that all employees in the organisation should have feelings of ownership regarding the appraisal scheme and should recognise that their whole hearted involvement is central to its success (Anderson[27]). Failure to consult, lack of commitment, unequal standards, over-elaborate paperwork and inadequate feedback are seen as some of the reasons why appraisal systems fail. One quote from the research sums up the general attitude of the officers interviewed, 'I don't think appraisal has much value in that it just tells me what I already know, it is just how one person perceives my performance; it is totally subjective. If I hadn't had the appraisal it wouldn't have made any difference to me at all!' Police Officer D. (Mavin[28]).

The police service is now proposing to add the complexity of employee reward. Even as a member of the steering committee overseeing the implementation of appraisal-related pay, the President of the Superintendents' Association is concerned about the proposed system. He is far from convinced of the worth of the ARP scheme and is not sure that the pain is worth the gain or that the scheme sits comfortably with policing (Mackenzie[29]). PRP and performance appraisal is likely to be effective only in organisations where jobs are designed in such a way that allow individual performance to be measured. In situations characterised by high interaction amongst jobs in achieving results, group-related pay systems may be more appropriate (Anderson[30]). Individual based PRP is currently being removed from the agendas of many private and public sector organisations: should the proposed ARP scheme be implemented and then withdrawn, it may leave devastation and destruction in its wake and the performance record of the police service may fall below any level it has achieved to date.

Student activities

1. Read *Employee Reward*, by Michael Armstrong, p 261. How does the ARP scheme compare with Armstrong's defined list of performance management attributes?
2. Evaluate this case study against the favourable and unfavourable conditions necessary for the success of PRP in private sector organisations.
3. What changes would the police force have to make to their scheme to successfully introduce the appraisal-related pay scheme?
4. Design an alternative reward system which would suit the police service and the aims of the reforms needed by the government.

Standard reading

	Armstrong and Murlis	*Armstrong*	*Milkovich and Newman*
Pages	205–247	260–270	321–415

References

1. Sheehy, P (1993) *Inquiry into Police Responsibilities and Rewards: Executive Summary*, HMSO
2. Young, M (1991) *An Inside Job*, Oxford University Press, Oxford
3. Nelson, W and Golding, R (1994) Working Paper, ACPO Autumn Conference, Warwick
4. National Police Training (1994) 'Appraisal: the facts and guidance notes', *Police Central Planning and Training Unit*, Harrogate
5. Mavin, S A (1994) *Appraisal and career development: An investigation into the career development systems of a police force in the North of England, University of Newcastle upon Tyne*, School of Business Management
6. *ibid*
7. Nelson, W (1994) Assistant Chief Constable: Project Team Leader, 'Appraisal Related Pay, Report of the Project Team', Volume 1, March
8. Mackenzie (1995) President of Superintendents' Association, 'Closing ranks', *Police Review*, 24 March
9. Murlis, H (1994) 'The myths about PRP', *Personnel Management*, August
10. Fowler, A (1988) 'New Directions in Performance Related Pay', *Personnel Management*, November
11. Mavin, op. cit.
12. Dale, A J (1991) from *An Inside Job*, M Young, Oxford University Press, Oxford
13. Barlow, G (1989) 'Deficiencies and the perpetuation of power – latent functions in management appraisal', *Journal of Management Studies*, Vol. 26, No. 5, September
14. Mavin, op. cit.
15. Anderson, G (1992) 'Performance appraisal', *HRM in Action: The Handbook of HRM*, edited by Brian Towers, Chapter 10, Blackwell, Oxford
16. Thompson, M (1995) *Team Working and Pay*, Institute of Employment Studies, Report No. 281, Brighton

17. Butler, A J P, (1994) Chief Constable Gloucestershire Constabulary 'Pruning the rank structure', *Policing*, Vol. 10, No. 1, Spring
18. Mackenzie, op.cit.
19. Reiner, R (1992) *The Politics of the Police*, 2nd Edition, Harvester Wheatsheaf
20. Mavin, op.cit.
21. Townley, B (1989) 'Selection and appraisal – reconstituting social relations', *New Perspectives on Human Resource Management*, Storey, Routledge, London
22. Lawler, E (1981) *Pay and Organisational Development*, Addison-Wesley, Reading
23. Marsden and Richardson (1992) 'Motivation and PRP in the public sector. A case study of the Inland Revenue', Discussion Paper: 75, *Centre for Economic Performance*, London School of Economics, ESRC, London
24. Fletcher, C and Williams, R (1992) 'The Route to Performance Management', *Personnel Management*, October
25. Young, op.cit.
26. Butler, op.sit.
27. Anderson, op.cit.
28. Mavin, op.cit.
29. Mackenzie, op.cit.
30. Anderson, op.cit.

Further reading

Association of Chief Police Officers (1993) Response to Sheehy, Vol. 1, para. 5.20, September

Sheehy P (1993) 'The Sheehy Report: Inquiry into police responsibilities and rewards', *Police Review*, July

Case Study 13

Performance-related Pay in Action at Barland Bank

By Sarah Kelly
Senior Lecturer, Bristol Business School

Background

Barland Bank is a large retail bank operating in the UK and overseas. Its head office in based in Birmingham, but it runs an extensive national network which covers the whole of England and Scotland. It is one of the top five retail banks in the country and has approximately 45,000 employees. The Bank has segmented its UK market according to the size of its clients and customers and operates in several units including the corporate, commercial, personal and private banking business divisions.

The corporate banking division is based in the City of London and private banking operates predominantly from the Channel Islands. However, the personal and commercial services operate from the national network and by the far the majority of employees work in these two business divisions. Like many other retail financial institutions, Barland's competitive market place is developing rapidly. The Bank faces significant competition in the sector from other banks as well as building societies and insurance companies.

There have been some significant innovations in the sector over the past ten years and this trend looks set to continue. Enabled by recent developments in the use of information technology, other financial services retailers have introduced direct telephone banking services with great success. The most innovative organisations in the sector are constantly looking for new ways to harness the power of technology for competitive advantage. Many of Barland's competitors have diversified to offer an increasingly large range of products and services. Others have acquired estate agency, insurance or other related financial services businesses.

Barland Bank operates, therefore, in a rapidly changing and competitive sector. The Banks' Executive Board are being forced to review their operating structure, culture, and practices. This is not a straightforward task for a large, somewhat bureaucratic institution, and causes some soul searching amongst senior executives of the Bank. Their chief concern is the maximisation of return on investment for shareholders – banks have always been such a safe investment for shareholders in the past – and they have been forced to try to think differently about the ways in which people work. Whereas competitors are introducing new services and products, the Bank has decided to stick with its traditional services, but must offer either a cheaper or a better service in order to compete. Eager to keep its shareholders happy, Barland has decided to focus on improving the overall performance of the Bank.

Human resource strategy

In recognition of the pressures and challenges facing the business, the Bank's HR team have undertaken a fundamental review of their personnel policies and strategies. The team has decided that the Bank must concentrate on getting more out of the people it employs. They also realise that, in many cases, advances in technology will mean that additional skills will be needed by the Bank's employees in the network. The focus on providing good customer service will also prove to be an issue for the Bank where competition for customers is so fierce. At the same time, the Bank must retain and encourage technical lending expertise as it cannot afford to lose money on bad debts in the rush to get new customers' business. Credit and risk assessment skills will continue to be vital in the future but customer service and relationship management competencies will also be crucial.

The HR team has therefore undertaken a major project that will affect each and every business unit in due course. A team of HR consultants working in the central personnel function have called the project 'Introducing job families into Barland Bank'. The job families initiative has been a major programme for the Bank and for the project team. Business by business, the team have analysed the work taking place and have redefined work in terms of what is important to the future success of the Bank. The HR project team have decided to use a competency framework to underpin all their policies and practices. This decision has been made in light of the Bank's need to get more out of people and focus on what 'good performance' entails in Bank terms. Twenty-seven competencies have been defined and put in to a framework designed to describe all the attributes that will be needed by the Bank if it is to perform successfully.

Changing reward systems

Prior to the project being launched, the focus of reward management at Barland was based on a traditional model of pay. Concerned about potential equal value claims, the Bank had undertaken a massive job evaluation programme fifteen years earlier. The legacy of this exercise was that each job had a very detailed job description so there was a proliferation of different job descriptions. The HR department had inherited from this time a whole department of job evaluators, who were constantly involved in evaluation, grading and re-grading claims. The only way to get more money in the Bank was to be promoted. This was difficult to achieve given the large number of clerical positions and relatively few management posts following a business process re-engineering exercise two years earlier. Too much time was spent by management on behalf of their staff in trying to get their jobs upgraded. The HR team had come to realise, however, that it was no longer the job description which mattered, it was the skills and competencies brought to the role together with the level of individual performance which would make the difference in terms of overall organisational performance.

The Bank's pay arrangements were based on a traditional view that it was the job you did that mattered, not how you performed it. Where jobs used to involve routine clerical operations, this was an appropriate approach. However, where customer or client contact was becoming increasingly important or where new skills and competencies were to be developed, this approach was no longer adequate. The pay scales were based on the original job evaluation exercise which had resulted in a very large number of job descriptions being translated into a very large number of narrow grades. With hindsight, it was easy to see that the grading structure was very difficult to manage effectively as people became obsessed about the detail of their job description and not what they were actually producing in terms of quality of work.

There were also a very large number of employees in the Bank who were at the top of their grade and incremental pay scale but who were far from being the organisation's top performers. At times, it seemed to employees that they were part of a large bureaucracy with little incentive to do other than turn up each day to their jobs.

Often closely involved in individual grading claims in the past, the banking and finance union, BIFU, had done reasonably well in terms of attracting and retaining members from within the Bank. The Bank's relationship with the union was a reasonably cordial but not very constructive one.

Management positions

Management jobs and positions had always been viewed as very separate and different jobs. Once in the management positions, promotions were equally difficult to achieve as the common view was that an individual needed to spend three to five years in a post before being eligible for promotion. There was a great deal of frustration as well as competition in the management ranks as it often seemed that good performance and contribution to the Bank's financial achievements went unrecognised and unrewarded. The Bank tried hard to develop its own 'home grown' talent and operated a management training scheme, predominantly fed by its graduate recruitment programme. Whilst there were career progression opportunities for graduate trainees, it was also recognised that it could take many years to reach the top.

Other financial institutions such as the merchant and investment banks seemed to offer many more opportunities and inducements to carry out commercial and corporate business in a much more dynamic environment.

Barland ran an annual appraisal scheme for all its management cadre, and special interviews or boards were held for those considered eligible for the senior management grades. The appraisal scheme tended to concentrate on identifying potential for promotion or training and development needs. The Bank had a good reputation for its management training, but this was not open to general demand and rather restricted to those who were identified and selected as having potential for promotion.

Job families initiative

The job families initiative has been a major programme for the Bank and for the project team and was based on the realisation that the Bank must concentrate on getting more out of the people it employs. The aim of the programme has been to look at all of the Bank's HR policies and practices and link them altogether to enable the organisation to get greater commitment and performance out of its employees. However, as a consequence of this approach, the HR team also want to identify a wider variety of career opportunities for high-performing staff as well as providing a greater incentive to individuals to improve and develop themselves. The team believes that the Bank's HR strategy needs to be overhauled to improve recruitment, training, development, career management, succession planning, performance management and reward management policies.

This initiative also provided an important opportunity for the organisation to start thinking differently about how to define and describe work and jobs in the Bank. The old style job descriptions and grading structure were doing nothing to help the Bank achieve its objectives of improved performance through greater flexibility and less demarcation. Without losing some of the benefits of having undertaken a job evaluation scheme, the HR project team began to review and re-define the work of each of the major business units. They drew together representatives from each of the businesses and encouraged the teams to re-define the work it carried out in terms of role rather than job descriptions.

Role descriptions were compiled for each area of work and included a set of overall responsibilities or expected outputs for each role, together with the competencies required to perform the role successfully. In addition, specialist technical skills were listed for each of the groups or families of work (see Figure 3.13). The project team then reviewed all of the roles created and compared roles across each family and between families. They were then able to note linkages between similar roles in each of the various families and divisions. The team were then able to identify a number of career progression routes through all of the Bank's business operations. Specialist families were also derived from analysis of work in the finance, IT and personnel areas. The initiative provided the foundation from which to review all HR policies and competencies were used to help to describe and articulate the type of performance needed as well as the links between roles, families and business divisions in the organisation.

ROLE SPECIFICATION
ROLE TITLE:
FAMILY: REPORTS TO: *Definition of role* *Core responsibilities* *Competencies* *Skills & knowledge* *Suggested performance measures*

Figure 3.13 *Role specification template*

Performance-related pay

As a result of the creation of job families and role definitions, the HR team's pay unit reviewed the Bank's pay structure. A number of guiding principles became apparent as the unit reviewed the old system and considered what would be required by a new approach to pay. First and foremost, it was obvious to the pay specialists that assisting the Bank to achieve a strong financial performance was to be a critical success factor. The team knew, therefore, that any new pay arrangement should not incur additional cost to the Bank (not on a permanent basis at least) but would also need to focus on getting more out of each employee. The pay team also realised that the culture of the Bank as typified by the Executive Committee was very 'risk averse'. This would mean that any changes to the remuneration system would need to be very thoroughly assessed, costs closely calculated and changes recommended which would be sure to be a success.

The Executive Committee were notoriously difficult to influence and would do nothing that would risk upsetting the favourable opinions of shareholders and city analysts. The pay team knew that to be successful in practice, any new pay scheme would have to be easy to explain and easy to operate from a manager's perspective. Many thousands of employees would need to understand what was happening to their pay arrangements and managers out in the branches would be instrumental in launching and using a new scheme. Special attention would need to be paid to communicating the changes throughout the Bank's extensive network.

The pay team felt that, in the past, changes such as these had not been well communicated. It was feared that, unless all employees were kept up to date and well informed, rumours would circulate and create undue cause for concern. The team were unsure as to whether or not to include union representatives in the communication process. The parameters for redesigning the reward management process were constrained by the strong culture, structure and operating procedures of the organisation.

The pay team's strategy was to base pay and benefits in the Bank more closely on progression within and through the roles identified in the job family project. They also wanted to produce the ability to reward good performance through basic pay increases: what they called 'producing a more flexible pay response to performance'. In other words, the strategy would be to encourage and reward good performance and provide clearer criteria for progression through the job family structure. The team's philosophy was based on the notion that people need to understand what is required of them in order to perform well. The job family structure and role definitions clarified what would be needed for each role in terms of skills and competencies, and also outlined how success in the role might be measured.

Additionally, the pay team wanted to ensure that salary rates would be competitive with the outside market so that the Bank could reward employees fairly in relation to similar work being performed in other financial services organisations. The pay team therefore decided to evaluate the new role descriptions under the existing evaluation scheme to ensure that the job family structure had assessed the value of the roles created on a consistent and fair basis within the Bank. They then created a broad pay band structure against the family structure. Movement through the pay range associated with each band would be dependent on performance in the role (under the existing performance rating categories outlined in Figure 3.14 below). Given the importance of cost control to the Bank, the roles were evaluated using the Bank's existing job evaluation scheme and compared to similar positions and jobs in the retail financial services sector. This process ensured that the pay ranges allocated to the roles within the broad bands were competitive in the market place.

A	Outstanding performance in all respects
B	Superior performance, significantly above requirements
C	Good performance which meets requirements
D	Performance does not meet standards
E	Unacceptable, well below reasonable standards

Figure 3.14 *Performance ratings*

In order to provide more flexibility in the pay arrangements, the pay team recommended the introduction of a variable pay matrix (see Figure 3.15). Put simply, the central pay unit would issue a matrix providing guidelines to

	Position in Range				
Performance Rating	85–91%	92–97%	98–102%	103–108%	109–115%
A	8–12%	7–11%	6–10%	5–9%	4–8%
B	5–9%	4–8%	3–7%	2–6%	1–5%
C	2–6%	1–5%	0–4%	0–3%	0–2%
D	0–2%	0–1%	0	0	0
E	0	0	0	0	0

Figure 3.15 *Variable pay matrix*

managers on what range of increase they would be able to award to their staff. This would be based on research which would establish the overall competitiveness of the Bank, its projected profit and the market rate for each of the job families.

The matrix would be provided to managers in advance of the annual salary planning exercise to help them to decide how the overall pot of money should be allocated in their department or team. The available increase would also be dependent on where the individual was currently positioned in the pay range. Those who were already at the top of the pay range and who performed well could still receive an increase. However, it would not be in the same order of magnitude as someone in the same role performing to the same standard but who was at a lower point in the range.

As an example, an employee currently paid at the midpoint of the grade (100 per cent) and given a B rating, would receive a pay increase in the range of three to seven per cent. The actual amount would depend on the ratings achieved by all the other staff in the department and the size of the budget. A computer programme had been written so that the department manager could input the ratings for each staff and the programme would produce the best fit of salary increases.

Implementation

The team realised that the success of the new scheme would depend on a number of factors. Their first challenge would be to persuade the Executive Committee that the approach and detailed working of the scheme would incur no unnecessary risk or additional costs. This would mean presenting a tightly argued case which would need to demonstrate that the benefits of such a scheme would outweigh any costs. The pay team felt that the Executive team would respond to competitive pressures in the market place and that the idea of focusing on goal and objective setting for all employees would appeal to the senior committee.

Secondly, assuming the approach was accepted at senior levels, communicating the changes to all the staff would pose a significant problem. Making the transition from the old scheme to the new would mean much careful planning and explanation. Finally, the success of the scheme would depend heavily on the managers' abilities to manage performance effectively and to make informed and sensible decisions about pay awards using the new variable matrix.

Student activities

1. How far does the pay team's approach to reward fit with the Bank's strategic and HR objectives?
2. Assess and comment on the Bank's approach to performance management. How does the old system compare to the proposed approach?
3. Assess the pay proposals put forward by the team:
   - what other options to reward performance could have been considered?
   - will the proposals achieve the Bank's objectives?
   - will the approach motivate individuals?
4. What would you do to persuade the Executive Committee that these proposals will work?
5. What operating difficulties can you foresee? How would you plan to implement the proposed approach successfully?

Standard reading

	Armstrong and Murlis	*Armstrong*	*Milkovich and Newman*
Pages	53–59	53–78	43–69

Further reading

Heneman, R (1990) 'Merit pay research', *Research in Personnel and Human Resource Management*, JAI Press, New Jersey, Vol. 8, pp 203–263

Industrial Society (1996) 'Rewarding performance', *Managing Best Practice* No. 20, London, February

Kelly, A and Monks, K (1996) 'Contracts and contradictions in performance-related pay', paper presented at Open University Conference HRM – the Inside Story, April

Milkovich, G (1992) 'Strengthening the pay/performance relationship, *Compensation and Benefits Review*, Vol. 24, No. 6, pp 53–62

Pritchard, D and Murlis, H (1992) *Jobs, Role and People: The New World of Job Evaluation*, Nicholas Brealey, London

Case Study 14

Incentives for Teleservicing Staff at Welton Insurance

Introduction

Welton Insurance was formed as a result of a set of mergers and acquisitions of general insurers in the 1980s, mostly established in the provinces. The eventual union became partly owned by a large foreign insurer in 1990. The early 1990s saw a spate of re-organisations as the company re-positioned itself in the general insurance field and centred its administrative head office in the Midlands with satellite offices in Yorkshire and Reading. By 1995, a total of 3000 staff were employed compared with a combined workforce of around 4000 before the mergers.

Of all the external influences on an organisation, technology is the most influential and deep-seated. As British industry found in the 1980s and the finance world in the 1990s, computer developments cannot be reversed. At worse, they must be accommodated and, at best, accepted enthusiastically as the main factor to create a competitive advantage for the organisation.

In the case of the finance world, computer-driven telecommunication developments had brought a new player into the staid world of finance and insurance. There had been a number of attempts to introduce a 24-hour telephone banking service since the late 1980s, with First Direct (part of Midland Bank) the most successful. A much greater impact was made by the astounding success of Direct Line Insurance, launched only in 1984 and capturing four per cent of the market within ten years.

Insurance companies sold their products either through high street brokers or through direct selling. Prudential, for example, carried out all their business directly but this was through personal contact (a call at home from the man from the Prudential). Brokers and insurance agents were seen by the public as serious, qualified people who knew all about insurance and could give reasoned advice. Nobody had considered it feasible for the public to buy insurance over the phone from a young lady living 200 miles away.

It was a mountain to climb and Direct Line had the right climbing equipment. Firstly, the technology ensured that callers did not wait through the introduction of ACD systems (Auto-Call Distribution) and that all calls could be thoroughly monitored and analysed. The computer system would also provide the quotation immediately. Secondly, they used systematic recruitment and selection processes, including a batch of proven psychometric tests. Thirdly, extensive telephone skills training was given of a type pioneered by Thomson Newspapers in the 1960s to sell small-ads which revolutionised local and regional newspaper finances. Finally, they used that red phone on wheels.

Their instant success meant that the competition, including Welton, had to follow quickly or their market share would start to decline.

The Welton initiative

A decision was made to start a direct selling telephone sales unit in May 1994 to commence operating in January 1995. The unit was small at first, a total of 40 staff, of which 24 would be at the sharp end of providing telephone quotations and closing the sales. They were organised into two teams of 12. The unit grew rapidly so that, within six months, there were seven teams totalling 70 staff.

The teams were recruited from a number of sources. The majority transferred from internal sources, including paper processing sections and customer service sections. A number, including one of the managers, came from a well-known competitor who had re-organised in recent months and had made some redundancies. Detailed testing was carried out using a batch of Saville and Holdsworth tests, including OPQ.

Terms and conditions also altered with hours of working staggered into shifts covering the period 8.00 am to 8.00 pm and Saturdays. The teams recruited were mostly young with a mix of roughly 60 per cent to 40 per cent males to females. 20 per cent of the staff were part-time employees on mornings only or evenings/weekends.

The training programme was run by a communications consultant who had worked with First Direct. Training areas included improving vocabulary, voice projection, rapport, mirror imaging and ideals. These subjects related particularly to telephone sales and lasted three weeks for the introductory course and a further week's follow-up after three months.

Team leaders were paid between £11,000 and £15,000 and received additional external supervisory training. The salary scale for sales staff was a wide one from £7000 up to £12,000, which allowed staff to progress through to the top of the scale through a competency matrix. This was assessed every four months under the performance management scheme.

Performance management

Every four months, employees are rated by the team leader under six headings:

1. Accuracy

This is judged under two headings. Firstly, by measuring the accuracy of input for new and revised business. Errors come to light by checking the difference between what is on the policy print out and what was actually said by the caller on the phone using a taped call. Secondly, by how closely the employee follows the call scripts which they have used in training and which are the constant reference. A rating is achieved by measuring the deviations on both counts. At least two calls a week should be monitored for these measures and the results detailed on the appropriate sheets.

2. Attitude/Application

This subjective measure does not carry a rating but is used to identify strengths and weaknesses. An ideal definition has been set out:

> An employee should show flexibility to change within their working environment, they should be able to move within their team and their day-to-day responsibilities with the least disruption, being open and willing to change. Enthusiasm should be shown in all areas, flexibility will enable a person to communicate in a warm and friendly manner on a one-to-one basis and within the team to build a rapport and make a sale. General interaction within the team members and management is also important, aiding the development of good working relationships and offering a strong sense of the team. Another important factor is initiative with a sense of willingness to make their own decisions.

3. Sickness and timekeeping

A rating is made on the following basis per four-month period as set out on Table 3.3.

Table 3.3 *Ratings on sickness and timekeeping*

Rating	Sickness	Timekeeping/Lateness
1	no occasions	no occasions
2	1–2 occasions	1 occasion
3	3 occasions	2 occasions
4	4 or more occasions	3 or more occasions

4. Teamwork

No ratings here, just an assessment of strengths and weaknesses looking at the following areas:

- Flexibility – working additional hours;
  taking rest days to suit the team;
  swapping shifts to help the department;
  being prepared to help other teams;
  taking on team leader's role; and
  contributing to working parties.

- Help and interaction – helping new staff;
  helping to share tasks;
  being pleasant and sociable, not moody;
  leaving home problems at home and not gossiping;
  maintaining confidentiality; and
  projecting a positive attitude.

5. Communication skills

Table 3.4 is utilised to measure communication skills.

Table 3.4 *Measuring communication skills*

Advisor.................... Checkpoint			Rating	Date..........
How did the advisor sound?	1	2	3	4
How did the advisor pace the conversation?	1	2	3	4
Was the pitch appropriate?	1	2	3	4
Did the advisor listen to what was said?	1	2	3	4
Did the advisor maintain control of the conversation?	1	2	3	4
Did the advisor personalise the call?	1	2	3	4
How well did the advisor overcome objections?	1	2	3	4
How well did the advisor set the context during the call?	1	2	3	4
Total points......................	Team leader...................			

6. Sales targets, conversion rates, etc

Performance relating to the achievement of sales targets and conversion rates are assessed each month. These are numerical targets.

These factors are combined onto a summary review sheet. Before the review meeting takes place, the advisor completes their own perceived rating. The team leader will take the advisor through the results, discussing both subjective and objective measures. An action plan is then agreed for areas which need attention and development opportunities. This completed form is used as a basis for salary reviews.

Incentives

The design team had a number of choices in the area of incentives for staff and they considered three main areas:

Option 1 – no financial incentives

The consultants who helped design the system recommended that there be no direct financial incentives for staff. The competence matrix allowing staff to gain regular basic salary increases should be sufficient for motivational purposes and the controls in place should be sufficient to monitor performance.

There were clear advantages in simplicity in this arrangement but it was an operation that depended on the energy and enthusiasm of its staff on a day-to-day basis and there was no strong conviction that a long-term incentive of a salary increase would be sufficient to motivate employees. After all, the psychological tests used identified staff with the identities and characteristics of typical sales people (drive, determination, tenacity, etc) and the typical incentive they expected were short-term ones.

Option 2 – team-based performance reward

A scheme was put forward to encourage the formation of teamwork and to support the values built into the competency matrix. In this proposal, there are two measures:

1. Availability of a team member for taking calls – it records the efficiency of the adviser in dealing and wrapping up a call and also measures the length of time they are not available to take a call. The benchmark here would be set at 85 per cent and the team average would be calculated and the team with the highest average would receive an award, as long as it exceeded 85 per cent.
2. Quality control measures – through a sampling of staff calls, an assessment would be made with points for greeting, energy in the voice, good articulation, accuracy, energy maintenance and referring methods. The benchmark would be 75 points, the team average would be calculated and that team with the highest average would receive an award as long as it exceeded 75 points.

The prize for the winning team each month would be £200 or roughly £25 per employee, shared equally. The annual cost overall would be £2400 plus a small administration charge. As the prizes are a taxable benefit, the company would also bear the employees' tax liability. The awards would not be cash. They would be music tokens, gift tokens, meals out for the team, team excursions, cinema tickets or points towards weekend breaks.

The advantages of this proposal was that it encouraged and rewarded the team ethos which would include behaviour such as co-operation, peer pressure to perform, covering through absence and working for the team. On the other hand, the high performers may feel unhappy at supporting the rest of the team and the prizes may not suit individuals who would prefer cash. Moreover, the amount of bonus could be considered slight in relation to the average basic wage, working out at less than four per cent on average.

Option 3 – individual incentives

The final option was straightforward sales incentives relating to the volume of sales. A target would be set and a bonus awarded for sales above that target, incremented in bands above this figure. The bonus per sale would also vary according to the media code that attracted the business. For example, business obtained through *Yellow Pages* would not warrant the same incentive. There would also be a team target and team leaders would receive 20p for every sale in their team over the target.

This type of incentive would encourage high performers with no limit on the amount of bonus that could be earnt. However, it would need tight quality controls to insure against rogue selling and the concept of the team would need to be encouraged by the team leader in the absence of financial team incentives.

Actual events

All three methods were used during the first 18 months of operation. During the first seven months, no incentives were used but sales did not develop as quickly as the organisation required. It was agreed that sales stimulation was necessary and, during the latter part of 1995, a series of team incentives were put in place including those detailed in Option 2.

At a review of progress at the end of 1995, the teams reported that the incentives were pleasant but the prizes were simply not big enough to support substantial efforts from all the team members. A majority, including all the high performers, preferred the introduction of individual bonuses based on sales. As this was also the view of management, these were introduced in 1996. Sales have grown steadily since that date, as have the bonus payments. The top earners have regularly been paid over £100 a month and the overall sales per employee have increased by 50 per cent. The bonus scheme has been easily self-financing.

There have been a few detrimental effects. Firstly, there has been a noticeable switch away from co-operation and this has been demonstrated by a number of pointers:

- the lack of willingness to train and support new staff unless some compensation has been offered;
- competitive spirit among the high performers, particularly in aspects of the contests when the rewards have a limit so that if one gains benefit, the others must lose;
- competitive banter has emerged which has been occasionally hurtful; and
- there is far less willingness to switch rest days to help each other.

A second effect has been an increased turnover of staff. A number of new staff who have appeared at recruitment to fit the character profile of a successful salesperson, have left within six months of joining. Exit interviews have failed to pinpoint the main reason but there have been hints that the atmosphere has been too competitive and that there is insufficient sympathy when mistakes are made.

A final problem has been an increase in absenteeism. This has occurred across all levels of performers and has been a cause of concern. There is some evidence that a few of the high performers reach their own self-set target towards the end of the month and then have a day or two off for 'stress'. The rest of team suffer through having to cover and a degree of bad feeling permeates the group. The difficulty is the dilemma of whether to attempt to discipline those individuals who meet or exceed their targets. If action is not taken, then other employees who are not high performers start to copy the attendance pattern and the culture slides towards one of low attendance.

A further review was due at the end of 1996.

Student activities

1. Do the incentive options available relate in any way to the new cultural values of the organisation?
2. How would you tackle the growing absenteeism problem? Suggest options and set out their benefits and difficulties in practice.
3. Although this is a case study about rewards, in what ways does it reflect the changing patterns of working?
4. As a potential customer, what would be your views on dealing with insurance sales staff working partly or wholly on individual incentives?
5. Give a reasoned critique of the performance management scheme in this study. What are its strengths and what areas could give the most difficulties in terms of implementation in practice?

Standard reading

	Armstrong and Murlis	*Armstrong*	*Milkovich and Newman*
Pages	363–366	239–271 and 283–289	321–415

Further reading

Cook, S (1996) *Customer Care – Implanting Quality in Today's Service-Driven Organisations*, Kogan Page, London

Gross, S and Pfain, B (1993) 'Innovative reward and recognition strategies in TQM', *Conference Board Report, No. 1051*, pp 19–20

Johnson, N (1994) *The Secrets of Telephone Selling*, Kogan Page, London

Lancaster, G and Simintiras, A (1991) 'Job related expectations of salespeople – a review of behavioural determinates', *Management Decision*, Vol. 29, No. 2, pp 48–57

Peel, M (1993) *Customer Service*, Kogan Page, London

Simmons, S (1996) *Flexible Working*, Kogan Page, London

Case Study 15

Restructuring and Rewarding the Sales Force

Introduction

Designing a suitable financial plan for compensating salespeople is an important, difficult and highly perplexing task.

Little has changed since Smyth[1] introduced this Harvard Business Review article where he stressed there was no simple formula by which the optimum incentive opportunity can be determined. Management had to:

> ... exercise judgement in arriving at the answer, taking into account the company objectives, the characteristics of the selling job and the sales support provided to the field sales force.

Motivating and rewarding the sales force has always been a controversial issue, exceeded only, in recent years, by debate over the rewards appropriate for directors of privatised industries. Traditionally, the sales force have been regarded as a stand-alone group with their own remuneration scales, including a heavily weighted element of bonus or commission. Their uniqueness has been based on their requirement to play a number of roles which Langley[2] saw as 'Representative, Researcher, Initiator, Administrator, Communicator and Negotiator'.

To carry out these different roles successfully, they need a longer list of skills than most, including technical expertise, product knowledge, social skills/empathy, self-reliance and confidence, influencing abilities and flexibility.

In most organisations, they also have a separate career path and rarely change to other disciplines. This separateness has led to considerable authority over personnel matters remaining with the sales management team with few human resource practitioners having the experience or confidence to challenge their expertise. There has been no need to engage in empowering exercises in these confines – their power was never diluted.

Often the personnel department is forced, because it is less powerful in corporate terms, to accept and administer schemes which sit ill with remuneration policy for the rest of the staff and have to be kept separate from them.

This case study deals with a major organisation in the financial sector facing up to some of the implications of the market freedoms and competition introduced by Margaret Thatcher in the 1980s in this sector. It particularly relates to the culture and reward system which is appropriate when an organisation changes its marketing and sales culture. It examines some of the dilemmas which face the innovator in a traditional environment and the narrow range between success and failure in a high risk strategy.

Background to the case

Money Bank PLC has a large and long-established retail banking network. The arrival of competition from building societies in the mid-1980s produced many changes towards a more customer-friendly and proactive banking environment. One of those changes was the increased freedom to market additional products. In the late 1980s an explosion of new pensions and life assurance products were launched in the market place, taking advantage of pension legislation and the long 1980s stock market boom. Money Bank joined in this rush, deciding to link to a major insurance company.

For the first three years, the main selling activity took place in the banking halls, firstly through a special counter and then through dedicated areas with comfortable chairs and coffee on tap. Extensive product training took place for branch and regional employees interested in this developing area and many became extremely knowledgeable of the intricacies of the various pensions and life assurance deals. The results, however, were disappointing and the share of the market captured by Money Bank was below forecast.

In 1990, a new Director, Martin Reynolds, was appointed with specific responsibilities to expand the pensions and life assurance unit. Unusually, he did not come from banking but was head-hunted from a large mutual life assurance company where he had spent the last five years as a junior director successfully using modern sales techniques to increase its market share from six per cent to eight per cent. His own career path there was blocked and he enthusiastically grasped the opportunity to transfer this success into a traditional banking unit.

At the same time, the Human Resources Director, James Watson, who had been in post for six years following a successful 20-year mainstream banking career, was busy expanding his own department's role. One of his recruits was Jane Moore, who also came from outside banking. She had spent her early career with an FMCG and then moved to McTavish Glenn, a major consulting firm that had been originally accountancy-based but had now moved into the equally lucrative general and organisational consultancy realm. This included payment systems and Jane had specialised in this area for two years in a wide variety of organisations, public and private.

Jane's role, as James saw it, was to work alongside Martin to help re-vamp the sales operation and install a successful reward strategy. One of the lessons that Jane had learnt at McTavish was the need to try to carry the sales force along with any major re-structuring. After some initial meetings and time to gain understanding of the business, Jane proposed that some or all of the existing force be surveyed prior to any changes being decided. With some reservations, Martin agreed although he wanted this to be carried out within six weeks.

The survey

This was the first time that such widespread consultation had taken place prior to the implementation of changes to their terms and conditions. Consequently, few staff believed that they could influence the new package, most believing that the key decisions had already been taken.

100 staff were selected at random, representing good, average and poor performing groups, to take part in discussions at seven regional centres. Over a three-hour period, Jane carefully listened to the sales force's views on their existing package including the base salary, the grading and bonus systems and the benefits.

The remainder of the sales force, about 450 staff, were sent an open letter which sought their comments on all aspects of their package. There was a very disappointing response here with only 18 staff taking the opportunity to respond. Jane was also invited to attend meetings with the regional managers whose views showed a remarkable degree of convergence with the sales force. It was clear that the sales force would be responsive to some changes but nothing too drastic.

The second part of Jane's strategy was to put forward the possible options for change.

Options for change

(The existing salary structure is set out in Table 3.5.) The life assurance advisor (LAA) was branch based while the pensions advisor (PA) was based at the regional centre and spent the majority of time in the field. No bonus system was in force, although the performance-related pay scheme, introduced three years before, influenced the speed of salary progression within the grade and gave occasional one-off bonus payments. Promotion from both positions was to senior personal finance planning manager (SPFP) who controlled the pensions operation but acted only as advisor and motivator to the life assurance staff who still reported to the branch manager.

The LAA and PA positions had been evaluated at assistant branch manager status under the Hay job evaluation process. As a result, a new recruit to these positions was immediately promoted to this grade and received a salary

Table 3.5 *Existing salary structure*

Job title	Salary	Increments
Life assurance advisor	£16–19,000	8
Pensions advisor	£17–20,000	8
Senior personal financial planning manager	£21–27,000	6

increase and a company car, in the case of the PA. If they were later identified as not being suitable for the sales role, it was difficult to return them to mainstream banking. It was also inequitable that an inexperienced seller was rewarded in the same way as an experienced colleague, particularly when they were able to generate little or no income for the bank. As the full sellers' package was given at the time of appointment, there was no recognition in salary terms when they completed their training and became accredited.

A further problem was that the only route to promotion was into a sales management role as an SPFP manager. As a result, good experienced sellers were taken out of the front line and their experience and income generation potential was lost. Moreover, good sellers did not necessarily become good managers. Finally, the rapid growth in the market had led to many promotion opportunities so the sales force had become dominated by new and inexperienced staff.

The organisation structure also needed revision. LAAs came chiefly from the branch network and their loyalty remained to the branch. Where that loyalty was strong, they did not always spend all their time on selling activities, helping out the branch in other ways during times of crisis. This often clashed with the sales objectives and was a source of confusion in responsibilities and reduced selling performance.

The solutions

Jane saw that action was required in a number of areas. Firstly, the structure had to be revised to fit the changing requirements; secondly, the basic rates needed re-jigging and thirdly, the motivational issues needed addressing.

Structure and basic rates

It was apparent that a successful sales operation required a separate control unit. This could be either completely controlled from the regional unit with the sales force based there or retaining the LAAs in the branch and training them in the more complex pensions area. The branch-based operation had the advantage of the passing trade where customers were able to talk about their requirements often without an appointment. On the other hand, customers could still continue to collect the literature in the branch and appointments could easily be made there for a later date. Experience had shown, in any case, that the 'on spec' appointments rarely produced a sale without a follow-up discussion as customers did not have the necessary information with them concerning existing pensions and life assurance. On balance, a regional unit with dedicated sales staff and a clear reporting structure seemed the best option.

This would also make it easier to set up a separate salary and promotion ladder outside of the traditional main branch banking grading structure. Jane's proposal is set out in Table 3.6.

Table 3.6 *Proposed basic rate structure*

Job title	Salary	Increments
Trainee financial advisor	£13–14,000	2
Financial advisor	£15–17,000	4
Senior financial advisor	£18–20,000	4
Field force manager	£22–28,000	6

Internal staff could now be recruited to the trainee financial advisor position on a salary close to their existing rate which meant that they could move back into the branch network if they proved unsuccessful. The re-entry would be to another branch and the spell in sales could be looked at as a period of experience which was useful in the career path leading to branch manager. A trainee would be promoted to financial advisor within one to two years, depending on performance.

The top 25 per cent of financial advisors could look forward to promotion to senior financial advisor (SFA) where a few differential benefits would apply (better private health insurance, for example). Jane saw this as an opportunity later on to make progress on a flexible benefits package where SFAs would have a larger cash sum on which to choose their benefits.

Motivation

The structure proposed should go some way towards meeting career aspirations and Jane would make separate proposals on the development requirements which would be intensive, comprehensive and expensive. Her proposals, accepted in the main, added up to ten per cent of the total sales budget.

In considering the motivational elements, Jane was aware of the American literature where expectancy theory (Vroom[3]) was very influential on sales force remuneration. Studies by Weinrauch and Piland[4] had reinforced the need to have a clear and highly valued financial incentive procedure to ensure the required goals were reached.

The existing structure had no place for bonus or commission. The traditional stance of the bank had eschewed such practices in the branch network. Having a separate structure would allow a fresh start here.

Jane could see two options. The first (Option 1) would be to move slowly into this field with opportunities to develop later. The second (Option 2) would reflect the 'big bang' approach where there would be a direct jump into a highly motivational setting.

Option 1

A threshold level of sales would be set which would, in general, cover the advisor's costs. Once the threshold was exceeded a bonus of £70 would be paid for every £1000 of commission generated for the bank. This would be paid out quarterly. A higher threshold would be set for the senior advisors, but they would get £90 per £1000 commission.

Trainees, after initial training, would be eligible for £30 per £1000 commission with a lower threshold. Field force managers would receive 12.5 per cent of the bonuses paid to their staff. There would be a limit of £3500 maximum bonus for the advisors and £6000 for the senior advisors in a financial year. The 'on target bonus' would be 60 per cent of these figures.

A fifth bonus could also be earned. This would be based on quality criteria, including customer service standards, administration and regulatory compliance. It would be in five grades and the payment would range from zero per cent of the sales bonus to 40 per cent in ten per cent jumps.

Although the bonus would be paid quarterly, it would be accumulative over the year so the sales force could not 'fiddle' the bonus by forcing all their sales into one or two quarters to achieve high bonus rates.

The payment of the fifth bonus would ensure that the quality areas would not be ignored and field sales managers would be able to reward responsible, reliable advisors whose bonus earnings were not excessive. The cautious element of this proposal was reflected in the cap on earnings.

Option 2

This option was the same as Option 1 but had two substantial differences.

The thresholds were set at a figure approximately 150 per cent of the sales costs but the bonus was set at £50 (trainee), £100 (advisor) and £130 (senior advisor) per £1000 commission earned. There would be no bonus limits.

Both these changes rewarded the high performer in a much more substantial way and could be considered to encourage ambitious salespeople to join the bank and to strive for very high sales levels. At the same time, it penalised the poor to below average performer who would receive little or no bonus.

The discussions

Jane talked these proposals over with James, in the first instance. Although he recognised the need for a higher motivational element, he took some persuasion to include Option 2 in the formal proposal to be discussed with Martin. He did not see the Bank's culture changing so quickly and saw problems with the regulatory environment where the greater emphasis on targeting high sales levels would be frowned upon.

Martin, on the other hand, did not see the proposals as radical enough. He accepted readily the organisation structure but considered the split between basic salary and bonus to be too heavily weighted in favour of the basic salary. He wanted to see a basic salary which was reduced by at least 20 per cent and a much higher bonus potential. Ultimately, he believed there was a place for some senior sales advisors to be paid simply by bonus as existed in certain parts of the industry already, although he did recognise that this was probably a step too far at this point in time.

One further proposal he made was for an accelerator to be applied to Option 2. Rather than paying all bonuses for advisors at the rate of, say £100 for each £1000 of commission earned, he wanted a series of stepped payments per quarter, as set out in Table 3.7.

Table 3.7 *Martin's proposal on stepped payments*

First £5000 commission	£50 bonus per £1000 commission
next £5000 commission	£100 bonus per £1000 commission
next £5000 commission	£120 bonus per £1000 commission
above that level	£150 bonus per £1000 commission

This would encourage good performers to strive for even higher sales rather than rest on their laurels. He was totally opposed to any limit on bonuses and regarded the fifth bonus as arguably of little value. The three options, as they now became, are summarised at Figures 3.16 and 3.17.

Sales £	Advisor Option 1 £	Senior Ad Option 1 £	Advisor Option 2 £	Senior Ad Option 2 £	Advisor Option 3 £
16000	0	0	0	0	0
20000	280	0	0	0	0
25000	630	450	100	0	50
30000	980	900	600	0	350
40000	1690	1800	1600	1300	1700
60000	3080	3600	3600	3900	4700
66000	3500	4140	4200	4680	5600
80000	3500	5400	5600	6500	7700
87000	3500	6000	6300	7410	8750
10000	3500	6000	7600	8900	10700

Figure 3.16 *Sales bonus options*

The decisions

Jane watched the arguments between Martin and James with increasing anxiety. She saw it as a clash of the traditional banking culture meeting the raw market-driven sales culture and wondered if it was possible for a meeting of minds. The debate went to board level. James knew that the retail banking management would be unhappy with losing all authority over life assurance sales and the survey had shown that the existing sales force were not ready for profound change. He therefore used all his authority to successfully gain the Board's approval of Option 1 for a two-year trial period.

The trial

Organisation and recruitment

The initial changes went very smoothly. Branch management had become

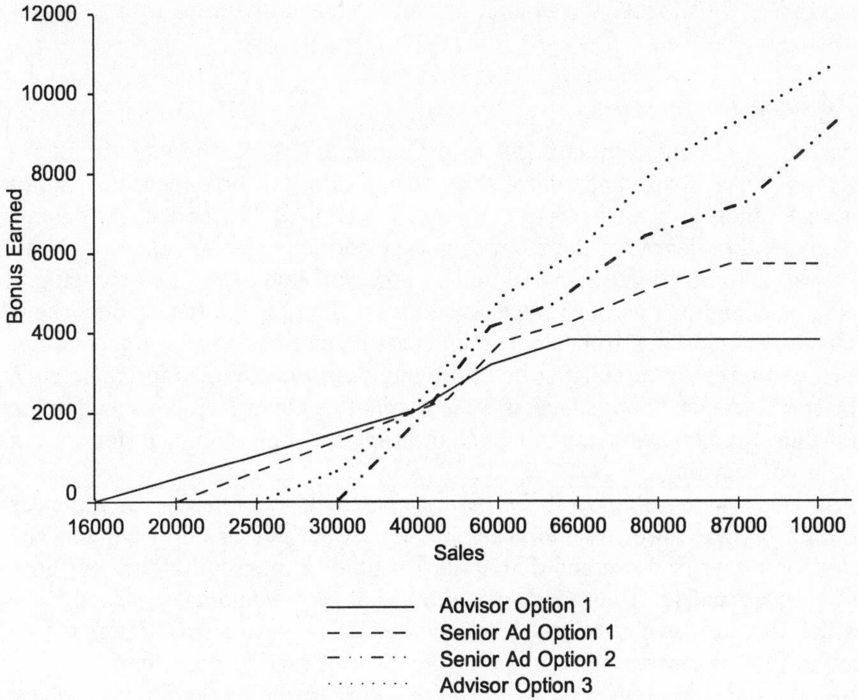

Figure 3.17 *Sales bonus options (graph)*

resigned to the loss of the life assurance sales operation following Martin's appointment and branch staff showed no resentment of the separate and potentially more lucrative reward structure for the advisors. They recognised the need for long and sometimes unsocial hours and the peripatetic nature of the work justified the company car. They knew that there was fairly open access to that section if they were ambitious. Most branch staff were happy to play their part in ensuring that interested customers were put in touch with the advisors with speed and efficiency.

The separate job family was an important means of achieving the flexibility to respond to particular markets if required, without a knock-on effect to other staff groups. The existing sales force gave a guarded welcome to the changes, which involved some temporary basic pay safeguarding where the advisor's basic pay was higher than under the new scheme. Applications for the senior advisors positions were over-subscribed several times.

The structure allowed recruitment from outside the Bank into the trainee position and for those applicants with sufficient sales experience to go directly to sales advisor. A short burst of management recruitment resulted in a few senior advisors and field sales managers being appointed. During the first 18 months, a small number of trainee advisors did not make the grade, despite the newly-introduced assessment centres Jane had recommended, but over 80 per cent of those from the branch network achieved re-entry without major problems.

The bonus

It was in the bonus payments where problems emerged. The majority of the existing sales team and all of the new recruits approached the bonus arrangements with enthusiasm, especially when, at the series of regional meetings, they learnt of their 'on target' performance.

It was an unfortunate sense of timing, however, that led to the new scheme being launched just as the ravages of the recession hit the financial markets. Individuals held back from further financial commitments and organisations were uninterested in starting or improving pension schemes for their staff. The result was that bonus targets were not met and levels of bonus paid in the first four quarters were much less than predicted, being only 70 per cent of 'on target' earnings.

All sides were unhappy at the result. The Bank was unhappy as the sales productivity was lower than forecast so the cost of sales was over budget. The sales force felt let down and demoralised as the promises of higher earnings did not materialise. A number worked out that they would have earned more on the old performance-related pay scheme. There were a small number who earned the maximum bonus, despite the difficult market conditions.

As the quarterly bonus payments were below target, so the fifth bonus was also disappointing. The conscientious advisor who followed the procedures and paperwork and provided a good service to customers, without producing excessive sales, received very small fifth bonuses despite getting the 40 per cent ratings. What was more, field sales managers tried to help their advisors' earnings by giving consistently high ratings. This led to the method of grading being seen as arbitrary by the sales force and excessively generous by the Bank.

The outcome

For James and Jane the trial had been a disappointment. James wanted to revert back to the old scheme but Jane saw this as a backward and unacceptable step. On the other hand, she was uncertain what to recommend. She lacked sufficient conviction to argue that the targets should be lowered in response to the recession, knowing that the bank would argue that this would mean that their profits, already depleted by the recession, would be depleted further.

She also knew that the bank would argue that selling was always recognised as a higher risk profession giving better than average earnings when times were good. The Bank would not be inclined to maintain their earnings when times were hard without a very good reason. The need was there, she recognised, to attract and retain high-performing staff and to remove the 'jobs for life' mentality.

Martin was quite sure what action to take and felt justified in his original proposal. A number of the sales force had, despite the market, reached their maximum. He believed that a good proportion of the others, realising that the bonus would be hard to achieve, had relaxed and accepted that their basic rate was at a reasonable level and this, together with some reduced bonus, would carry them over. They were not sufficiently motivated under this scheme. His original proposal, with lower basic and higher bonus would force them to work harder.

A meeting was fixed with the Board, which Jane had been invited to attend, where James and Martin would argue out their sides of the case. On the way, Jane heard on the car radio that LAUTRO had fined a major insurance company £400,000 for 'substantial compliance deficiencies' relating to their mis-selling of pensions during the late 1980s.

Student activities

1. Why is there such a wide range of views on the appropriate way to reward the sales team?
2. What was the value of the consultation process and how could it have been improved?
3. What features of Langley's definitions are suited to the sales force in this case study?
4. What would have been the likely consequences of adopting Option 2 at the time instead of Option 1?
5. Should any of the incentives reflect team goals and how would they be incorporated into the final reward package?
6. What should Jane recommend at the Board meeting?

Standard reading

	Armstrong and Murlis	*Armstrong*	*Milkovich and Newman*
Pages	247–261	369–382	598–601

References

1. Smyth, R (1968) 'Financial incentives for salesmen', *Harvard Business Review*, February
2. Langley, M (1987) *Rewarding the Sales Force*, IPM, London
3. Vroom (1994) *Work and Motivation*, Wiley, New York
4. Weinrauch, J and Piland, W (1979) *Applied Marketing Principles*, Prentice Hall, New Jersey

Further reading

Cannell, M and Wood, S (1992) *Incentive Pay – Impact and Evolution*, IPM and NEDC, London

Merrick, N (1995) 'Putting pushy salespeople out of commission' *People Management*, May 4
Morden, A (1991) *Elements of Marketing*, DP Publications, London

Case Study 16

A High Flying Sales Contest at Gate Products

Introduction

Direct selling activities are the butt of many a comedian's joke. The unwanted telephone call at home, the foot-in-the-door salesman and the endless junk mail would long ago have extinguished this very unusual and un-British practice if it was not for two factors.

Firstly, the public do not disapprove of the practices all the time. In fact, they can be welcomed if carried out at the right time, in the right way, under the correct form of control. Recently, at a loss for a new meal to cook, my wife opened the door at 5.00 pm to a purveyor of up-market frozen dishes. He was apologetic, friendly, pleasantly convincing but not pushy and had a nice line in ready-to-cook garnished cod. A deal was struck, £30 of cod finished up in the freezer and we were sitting down to a memorable family meal at 5.45 pm. There are other well-known examples of the direct selling operation, such as Avon cosmetics, where the selling part can be just one item of a satisfying social event.

Secondly, for a number of special businesses, it has proved successful over a long period of time. To put it simply, it works! The mark-up in shops for the majority of products is anything from 35 per cent to 50 per cent so there are considerable savings to be made by cutting out the middle man and going directly to the customer. Like a high performance car, however, this form of selling can be prone to accidents if the driver is not trained properly, does not take the right amount of care and is not motivated to get the best all round long-term results.

Only a few companies have trod this path and all have realised the importance of correct staff recruitment and selection, which usually involves psychometric testing for substantial long-term sales drive together with effective staff training and control systems. It has also been recognised that there is a need to continually excite and motivate the sales force. It is a high risk strategy for both the company and the individuals who choose to work in this way and earnings can vary enormously, reflecting this risk. It is not unknown for six-figure earnings to be reported but there is also a very high turnover of staff who either cannot make a living or a small minority who try to abuse the system.

This case study looks at the experience of one company which has operated in this environment for a long period of time and has reached a high level of sophistication in its operations.

Background

Gate Products* has a turnover of £85 million selling a range of products for the home and has been in business for 30 years. It is now a subsidiary of a FTSE 250 company. Covering the whole country, the sales force is divided into twelve divisions and 111 areas. Direct selling started from day one of the company and the selling force now runs to over 650. With the exception of the divisional managers, all the sales force are self-employed on commission only.

The remuneration pattern is as follows:

1. Divisional managers have a basic salary of between £30,000 and £50,000 and also receive a targeted bonus package based on all the sales in their division, called an 'on target bonus'. Together, this brings their annual earnings to anything between £50,000 and £100,000.
2. Area managers receive a commission for their own sales of around 15 per cent and also an override of the sales in their area bringing their annual earnings to between £30,000 and £90,000.
3. Sales representatives (mostly men but some women) receive commission and, in addition, service and loyalty bonuses. Their earnings can vary greatly from zero, if they sell nothing, to £70,000 for an exceptional salesperson in an exceptional year. The average hovers around the £25,000 mark.

Area managers and sales representatives provide their own transport, telephones, sick pay and pensions and these substantial costs have to be deducted from the remuneration to get the sums into context. The commission structure is very complex depending upon a number of factors such as the source of the sales lead, the product mix, special promotions and whether the product is sold on a cash or finance deal. Control measures are in place to guard the quality of sales and reduce commission where sales are inappropriate or where customers cancel. Promotion is almost entirely internal and this is recognised as a very important motivator. All divisional managers can truthfully say, as they interview the applicants in their substantial homes, that they achieved this exalted station by hard work and application and that any sales representative with grit and determination can do the same.

Sales contests

Beyond the sales commission, the company motivates the sales force through extended sales contests. MCB, a leading consultancy in communication and

---

* The company's identity has been changed for reasons of confidentiality

motivation, have been the originator of these contests for the past seven years. Bill Price, Managing Director, defines three major objectives in these activities:

- to communicate the sales targets and the level of success that can and has been achieved by teams and individuals;
- to reward successful members of the sales force in the form of cash bonuses, holidays and other benefits; and
- to recognise their contribution through publicity in the form of mentions and photographs in the contest newsletter and presentations of certificates and awards by senior management at sales functions. (Research has shown that these non-financial benefits are seen as very important to employees in any organisation but particularly to members of sales forces.)

The contests have to be centred round a theme and these have included the wild west, skiing, grand prix motor racing and great railways with prizes linked to those themes.

Bill was quite clear that the incentives must match the audience and the company culture to have a good chance of success. For example, the type of financial rewards for Gates would not be suitable for a clearing bank where MCB had recently run a contest. Here, the prizes were low key and the benefits to come out of the contest were chiefly those of communication of the performance standards required to lift the bank's promotional image, traffic flow and housekeeping.

The details

The summer contest for 1994 was called 'Island Magic' and the prizes were all linked to this theme. The performance measures were converted into a common currency which was 'yards round the island'. There was a standard conversion of the cash value of every sale into a number of yards plus extra yards for particular business gained, say, on finance or by cold calling. The more yards obtained, the greater the chance of winning prizes.

The incentives were arranged to motivate and reward on both a team and an individual basis and to be attractive to the top performer as well as an average performer. At the beginning, representatives and teams were divided into five leagues depending on their performance since the start of the year. The highest league had more prizes but there were still a number to be won by individuals and teams in the bottom leagues that made an improvement over the course of the contest. Half way through, there were promotions and demotions for those individuals and teams at the top and bottom of their league. This is illustrated at Table 3.8.

The prizes were as follows:

1. Each week, there were awards to the top six representatives and two area managers who got to choose, in order of performance, from a range of six island linked items, including expensive sun-glasses, a Sewills barometer and a pair of silver lobster cufflinks.

Table 3.8 *Island Magic Incentive*

Representatives' League

Representatives will compete in the Leagues each month by achieving movement around the Island in yards. The more yards you obtain the higher up the league table you will move. In the Representatives' League you will obtain yards from the following:

		Plus a boost bonus for:	
All Contest Business	÷ 5 = yds	3 in a Road	1,000 yards
All Self Generated Business	÷ 5 = yds	4 in a Road	1,400 yards
All Finance Business	÷10 = yds		
All New Business (Self Generated)	÷10 = yds	5 or more in a Road	2,000 yards

Area Managers' League

Area Managers will compete in their Leagues each month by achieving movement around the Island in yards. The more yards the Area achieves, the higher up the league table you will move. You will obtain yards from the following:

All your Area Representatives' Contest Business	÷ 5 = yds
All your Area Finance Business written by Representatives	÷10 = yds
PLUS	
Area Managers' Self Generated Business	÷ 5 = yds
Area Managers' New Business (Self Generated)	÷10 = yds
Area Managers' Finance Business	÷10 = yds

	No. in LEAGUE	AWARDS	PROMOTED	DEMOTED
'E' REPRESENTATIVES LEAGUE				
A	Top 50	9	X	7
B	Next 100	7	7	5
C	Next 100	5	5	3
D	Next 100	3	3	1
E	Balance	1	1	X
B + T REPRESENTATIVES				
A	Top 100	4	X	1
B	Balance	1	1	X
SPECIALISTS				
A	All	1	X	X
AREA MANAGERS				
A	Top 30	5	X	3
B	Next 40	3	3	1
C	Balance	1	1	X

2. The top 20 representatives each month, ie a total of 60 over the three months of the contest, were invited to a roulette lunch at a top London hotel where they competed to win £8000 in a treasure chest (chips provided free on the basis of the sales during the contest to date).
3. There were also league 'Magic Island' prizes of days out for two. They took place at three locations: Monkey Island, on the River Thames near Maidenhead, including a river trip and a dinner at Oakley Court; secondly, an action-packed watersports day in the Midlands, including marine jets and speedboats and finally, a weekend at a country club in the Isle of Man.
4. The end of contest prizes were luxury four-night holidays for two in a five-star hotel in Cyprus with a full programme of events. This would be won by the top three area teams and the winning representatives, a total of more than 30 couples. Other prizes included divisional contest prizes of a 'Magic Island' trip and, for the winner of the team knock-out competition, a presentation lunch with top sales management. In this contest, the bottom seven performing teams each week were dropped leaving a group of 20 or so teams left in the contest on the last week. The winner would be the best performing team on that last week.

The contest was complex to set up and, to an outsider, sometimes difficult to understand but it proved successful over the years in overcoming a number of potential problems.

(a) How to keep the enthusiasm going for an extended period. The regular sales newsletter and the regularity of the prizes mean that the momentum is kept up throughout the 13-week period. The league structure allows teams to make up lost ground in the last few weeks and win some of the prizes.
(b) How to avoid the situation where the same individuals win the contests every time. The same individual and team cannot win more than one prize so the opportunity is spread to a wide area.
(c) How to ensure that a wide number of staff earn some of the rewards. Due to the design of the prize structure, as many as 250 area managers and representatives will win some form of prize over the contest.
(d) How to make the rewards attractive. The prizes, especially the end of contest prizes, are expensive and research has shown that luxury holidays are seen as the most attractive prize both to teams and individuals. They become an 'event' which is remembered over a number of years and help to bond the team. The 'action days' are also seen as memorable where the competitive drive can be channelled into a 'fun' event.
(e) Whether to include partners in the prizes. This has proved difficult at times in the past where complications have arisen over the choice of partners and how they take part. The compromise is now working well where the partner is invited to some events, particularly the holidays, but there are still some left for the employees themselves. This is being kept under close review.

Desiderata	Cash, etc	Recognition awards	Merchandise	Travel, etc
Family influence: will the whole family be excited by the incentive offered?	No: the family considers cash just a small addition to regular income – if they ever get to hear about it.	No: usually the family hears about this award only after it is won and then only by the winner's family	Yes: most families select awards and encourage participants to earn them. (See Note 1)	Maybe: only if the participant and his family feel they have a good chance to qualify for an award.
Choice: will all participants be able to select the award they want most?	Yes: although cash will often disappear in routine household bills.	No: self-explanatory.	Yes. (See Note 2)	Group travel – No. Family holiday award – Yes.
Number of winners: can all participants win according to performance?	Yes: the amount can be in proportion to effort.	No: if they could, it would not be recognised.	Yes: in proportion to effort and results.	Group travel – No. Family holiday award – Yes.
Appeal to average: will the awards appeal greatly to the middle 80% of participants?	Maybe: some may feel they will be inadequately rewarded for goals assigned.	No: self-explanatory.	Yes: even a relatively inexpensive prize award can be a much desired luxury.	Group travel – No. Family holiday award – Perhaps.
Pride: will the award cause winners to enjoy maximum praise and acclaim?	Hardly: except for family, who would show friends a bank deposit entry?	Yes: definitely when the rules are equitable.	Yes: the participant is recognised as being an award winner.	Yes: another form of top recognition award.
Excitement: can the awards be widely and powerfully promoted?	No: there is nothing more ordinary than cash.	Yes: until participants realise who will or will not win.	Yes: participants look forward to earning awards they feel they cannot afford to buy.	Yes: nothing is more powerful.

Desiderata	Cash, etc	Recognition awards	Merchandise	Travel, etc
Lasting value: will the award be a long lasting reminder of success?	No: cash as an award disappears as soon as it is pocketed, deposited or spent.	Yes: obviously.	Yes: also has use and enjoyment values.	Yes: if everything goes well.
Cost: is the cost of the award good value for what you paid for it?	Maybe: but what happens when the campaign and award terminates? (See Note 3)	Yes: and it usually costs so little.	Yes.	Yes: group incentive travel also has features that individuals and money cannot buy.

Note 1 Families are inveterate browsers. If you show them as well as tell them what they can set their sights on, you will make your objectives live in their minds through their objectives.

Note 2 Analysis of many thousands of merchandise award orders shows that some 75 per cent of items are partner/home orientated, 15 per cent home/children orientated and the participant seldom gains more than 10 per cent.

Note 3 This is important and deserves an illustration of its own. Here is the 'time and motive study' of the typical motivation programme.

Figure 3.18 *Comparison and evaluation of various types of awards*

Student activities

1. In evaluating the motivational effect of the contest, how does the contest match up to the requirements of expectancy theory?
2. Take the part of a hard-working, middle-of-the-road self-employed sales representative. What would be your balanced view of the contest? What would you see as its major benefits? Would you see any drawbacks?
3. Imagine you are setting up a computer service bureau with a team of three sales representatives. Argue the case for and against contracting the team on a self-employed basis.
4. Why does the complexity of the sales contest not present any problems in practice?

Standard reading

	Armstrong and Murlis	*Armstrong*	*Milkovich and Newman*
Pages	324-329	369-382	598-601

Further reading

Fisher, J (1994) *Staff Incentives*, Kogan Page, London

Greenberg, J and Greenburg, H (1991) *Creating Sales Team Excellence*, Kogan Page, London

Jolson, M et al (1993) 'Transforming the salesforce with leadership', *Sloan Management Review*, Spring, Vol. 34, No. 3, pp. 95-106

Williams, M (1994) 'Something for everyone', *Personnel Today*, May 3

Appendix A

Contents – advice for practitioners

In the Daily Telegraph Business Enterprise book, *Motivating Through Incentives*, a guide to the value of contest rewards is given in the form of the chart reproduced below (Figure 3.18).

PART 4
PAYING TEAMS

Introduction

In the field of research into reward management, there has been a rising interest in the 1990s in the theory and practice of paying teams. This interest arises from three sources:

1. Organisations which have downsized and de-layered are paying more attention to the creation of empowered teams and stressing the key value of teamwork amongst employees. In some cases, this is rhetoric but there are sufficient numbers who have entered this sphere with serious intentions who see teamworking as a major source of improved quality, productivity and customer service (Hay[1]). They see pay as the clearest method of delivering a message to an employee to reinforce the value of teamwork. Researchers are keen to see whether this works out in practice.
2. As we have seen in previous case studies, individual incentive schemes have had a mixed press. They cut across the teamwork values by the divisive process of paying differentially and blur management's messages. As interest in individual schemes declines, the interest in team-based schemes grows.
3. There is some limited evidence that payment for teams is more acceptable to the workforces and schemes could therefore have a longer shelf life. It is asserted that there is a strong link between teamwork and employee involvement in the business which can strongly influence an organisation's overall long-term performance. Researchers are looking to investigate the power of this link and the outcomes arising.

However, it is almost impossible to discuss the payment for teams without investigating how teams function and what makes them succeed or fail – but there is no space to cover such a huge area in this publication. There are some key texts listed at the end of this section which attempt to fill this gap.

The spectrum of team pay

Team-based pay cases come in all shapes and sizes. One way of differentiating them is on a grid with the one axis representing how influential the team is in determining the payment and the second axis representing how quickly the payment is made. This grid is shown in Figure 4.1.

At one end of the stratum, is the direct selling sales team that wins awards in sales contests (details were given in Case Study 16). They have a high influence over the result and the payment is made very soon after the end of the contest.

At the other end of the spectrum, there are the final payments made under the profit-related pay (PRP) schemes, such as The Burton Group PRP Scheme in Case Study 19. As in most PRP schemes, the influence that the 'team' has on the payments is very small (they are not informed of the profit target as this is regarded as share sensitive). The company regard the outcome as a form of a 'thank you' to ensure that there is some equitable share of the profits. The payment is made some time after the end of the financial year. There are also some immediate payments on account which are, in reality, a small part of total pay.

Table 4.1 Team-based pay schemes

	Immediate payment	Profit-related pay schemes on-going	Vauxhall Motors employee recognition scheme	Direct selling commission only team
Time to wait for pay	**Medium-term payment**	Gainsharing scheme –Large Unit	Gainsharing scheme –Small Unit	Dartford team pay scheme
	Longer-term payment	Profit-related pay –end payment	John Lewis Partnership profit-sharing	Executive Pay Portsmouth Hospitals NHS Trust scheme
		Low Influence	**Medium Influence**	**High Influence**
		Influence of teams/employees on Reward		

Other case studies sit in different parts of the spectrum. In Dartford Council Team Pay, Case Study 17, the teams have considerable influence over their results as they help to set the objectives and carefully monitor the progress. Payment is made shortly after the year end.

For the John Lewis Partnership, Case Study 20, the profit-sharing element of pay is quite substantial having risen as high as 24 per cent in the late 1980s. Although the team is the whole work force, their degree of involvement as 'partners' places them in a higher position of influence than on a conventional profit-sharing scheme, although the timing of the payout is the same. There is considerable stress placed on communicating organisational performance through the weekly journal.

Gainsharing schemes, such as those at BP and Ingersoll Rand in Case Study 18, fall in the middle of the spectrum. Their degree of influence varies depending on the size of their unit, ranging from a medium influence in a small operating unit to a lower influence for a whole factory. Payment can also vary but most pay a certain amount on account either monthly or quarterly. Given the high profile in the US, it is surprising that they have been introduced so rarely in the UK.

For teams at Vauxhall Motors in Case Study 26, payment for their innovatory ideas is as quick as management can manage, to avoid the time delays associated with a conventional suggestion scheme. The team's influence on the results can vary between being very substantial for an accepted and successful scheme to much less so for one that fails the hurdle of acceptance.

Finally, executive pay, such as for the RTZ Board in Case Study 25 and examples of group management pay, such as the scheme in Portsmouth Hospitals NHS Trust, detailed in Armstrong[2] come in the category of being highly influential as to the value of the reward, but the wait can be extended. For some executive share options, the wait can be three years or more.

Common features of success

Brown[3] has set out three clear factors that correlate with team-based scheme successes:

- a clear strategy, with objectives to engage employees in a collective effort to achieve business goals;
- involving employees in the team reward system, including designing the measurement process and taking decisions over the pay distribution; and
- defining the team correctly, so that team membership is directly relevant to the task in hand. Small teams where targets can be clear and immediate, such as in sales, service or credit control; larger teams for indirect activities where the performance cycle is longer and more difficult to measure.

Research findings

There have been a set of recent research findings in the US reporting the success of team-based schemes (Cooke[4], Kruse[5], McAdams and Hawk[6]). These have concentrated on gainsharing and profit-sharing schemes and the success measures were principally financial. There were also some strong indications that employees had become more involved and that absenteeism and turnover had reduced.

Team-based pay appears to be growing at a rapid rate in the UK (Armstrong[7]) but from a very limited base, so research findings are thin on the ground. Given the extent of interest in the subject, they will probably not be long coming.

References

1. Hay/CBI (1995) *Trends in Pay and Benefits Systems*, London
2. Armstrong, M (1996) *The IPD Guide to Team Pay*, IPD, London
3. Brown, D (1995) 'Team-based reward systems', *Team Performance Management*, Vol. 1, No. 1, pp 23-31
4. Cooke, W (1994) 'Employee participation programmes, group-based incentives and company performance', *Industrial and Labor Relations Review*, 47:4, pp 594–610
5. Kruse, D (1993) *Profit Sharing: Does it Make a Difference?*, Kalamazoo, Missouri
6. McAdams, J and Hawk, E (1994) *Organisational Performance and Rewards*, American Compensation Association, Phoenix
7. Armstrong, *op. cit.*

Further reading

Gross, S (1995) *Compensation for Teams*, American Management Association, New York

Case Study 17

Team Pay at Dartford Borough Council

Introduction

Dartford Borough Council is one of the smaller district (second-tier) councils employing around 300 staff. This is considerably reduced from the total in the early 1980s due to the process of Compulsory Competitive Tendering (CCT) which leaves the Council with a high proportion of skilled enabling staff, mostly managerial, supervisory, technical and contract management.

By the late 1980s, Dartford was encountering the same recruitment and retention difficulties faced by most local authorities, particularly those close to large centres of employment. Situated in North Kent, just outside London, the market for professional staff – legal, planning, accountancy, for example – had become so competitive that the national pay and grading system (NJC) simply did not offer sufficient remuneration.

An immediate solution was a performance management and performance pay system and this was introduced in 1989 on an individual basis at the same time as new contracts of employment. As part of the new package, the gradings of officer posts were re-evaluated using the Hay scheme and additional benefits were introduced. Staff could earn up to 15 per cent performance pay through the achievement of individual targets set at the beginning of the financial year.

A review of its first year of operation in November 1990 showed that the scheme was working in a far from satisfactory way. It was clear that there was an inconsistent approach by senior managers when identifying targets and appraising staff which reflected their different styles of management. The scheme also appeared to be unpopular with staff as a divergence of payments between colleagues became apparent. Although the operation of a formal appraisal system brought organisational improvements, these were difficult to quantify in precise terms and were obscured by the need to create divisive bonus payments.

In February 1990, Richard Doré joined the Council as Head of Personnel and Administrative Services. His experience had included a scheme for teamworking and team bonuses and he believed that this type of operation would carry more credibility in the culture of Dartford.

Rewarding team working

Commencing in 1991, the Council adopted a scheme based on the measured performance of teams of staff against agreed team targets. This reflected the basic 'team' approach of most work areas in the Council and was intended to motivate all team members. It was considered to be easier to measure real improvements in productivity and service performance in groups than by individual measures.

The individual appraisal scheme would continue to operate as a vehicle to review the personal development of staff and would also operate to appraise the incremental progression of staff through the grading scale. It was recognised that staff would continue to be awarded increments through the normal service entitlements but this could be withheld if individual performance levels were unsatisfactory.

1. Size of teams – there were no pre-determined recommended size of teams. In general, they remained in their functional slots so that, for example, the post room team was five strong and the highways management team included 15 staff. It was important that there was a distinct identity between members.

   It was possible for staff to be members of more than one team. This occurred in a number of situations:

   - for managers who would be part of a management team as well as their own department team;
   - for staff who would be part of a matrix or cross-functional team working on a particular large project which, in itself, justified team status under the scheme; and
   - when staff took on a new job through transfer or promotion during the course of the year.

   In these situations, an employee would be credited with part of the team bonus for each team in which they were a member. An example would be a manager who may be credited 20 per cent for the management team, 60 per cent for the department team and 20 per cent for a project team.
2. Cascade of targets – the targets for the chief executive, management team and directorate management teams are established by the council members (elected councillors). The targets are divided into three main areas:

   - service targets, which are a combination of performance indicators set out by the government under the Citizens' Charter and those recommended by the Audit Commission together with other service targets agreed by the council members;
   - project targets, which can include major areas of capital expenditure (building work or computerisation), work associated with major planning/construction work in the area (Channel Tunnel Link, Bluewater shopping centre) and projects to achieve accreditation such as ISO 9000/Investors in People; and

- management targets, which can include quality, financial targets and improving time-scales for performance.

These targets will feature in various degrees in most of the teams' overall targets as cascaded down through the individual departments.

3. Target definition – it was established at a very early stage that targets should not duplicate items in individual's job descriptions. The premise was that an employee should not be paid twice for doing the same job. The targets should have a measurable output and must be time-based. They should also involve the whole team in as even a way as possible so that team members have the opportunity to contribute and the sharing of the rewards are seen to be as fair as possible.

   The rewards should be related to achievements and not to routine activities. However, it was recognised that this would be a grey area and could vary between those staff who carried out a higher proportion of routine administrative day-to-day work (reception, switchboard) and those whose work consisted of a collection of specific projects (planning and development projects staff). Richard Doré's role here was crucial to keep a watching brief on the targets at the start of the year to ensure that they kept, by and large, within the original guidelines and that they were reviewed at six-monthly intervals by managers.
4. Number of targets – the normal number of targets for each team was between four and seven but they ranged between three and ten depending on the nature of the team's work and the importance of the target.
5. Bonus calculation – at the end of the year, the achievement of each team in meeting their targets was to be assessed by two measures. Firstly, how many of the targets had been reached in percentage terms. Secondly, how had the team performed in quality terms in its motivation to reach its targets as measured on a scale of one to six (see Figure 4.1) and the impact that the achievement of targets made on the division, directorate or the Council as a whole. If it was judged that the team had acted in a less than satisfactory way, ie performance levels five and six, then no bonus at all was payable.

A theoretical bonus of 15 per cent maximum could be achieved. This could be awarded if the team achieved all of its targets on a performance rating of one (exceptional high performance). This payment was based on the minimum salary point of the individual's grade at April lst in the previous financial year. The Team Bonus Matrix (see Figure 4.2) shows the bonus payable under other levels of achievement. For example, achieving 75 per cent of targets at a performance level of two would produce a bonus of seven per cent.

There is one final adjustment made to these bonuses. At the end of each year, the provisional results are reviewed by the senior management team to iron out anomalies and inconsistencies. The face value achievement, in financial terms, is then matched to the budgetary provision for that year. If the budget does not cover the full cost of the percentage payments, there has

TEAM TARGET PERFORMANCE LEVELS

6	Basic requirements not met. Unacceptably poor performance in quality and/or quantity. Improvement is required.
5	Less than satisfactory performance. Achievement is below what can reasonably be expected. Members of team require help to improve their performance.
4	Satisfactory performance. All that could reasonably be expected has been achieved at a satisfactory quality but further improvement may be possible.
3	Good level of performance. Expectations exceeded and a good all round quality of performance.
2	High performance. Expectations well exceeded in both quantity and quality and unexpected and significant changes have been handled to a good standard of performance.
1	Exceptionally high performance. Targets achieved to an outstanding performance level in both quantity and quality including unexpected and significant changes.

Figure 4.1 *Team target performance levels*

NORMALISED TEAM BONUS MATRIX

% Team Targets Completed	TEAM PERFORMANCE LEVEL					
	1	2	3	4	5	6
61 – 70	5	3	2	1	///////	///////
71 – 80	9	7	4	2	///////	///////
81 – 90	11	9	6	3	///////	///////
91 – 99	13	11	8	5	///////	///////
100	15	13	10	7	///////	///////

Figure 4.2 *Normalised team bonus matrix*

to be some scaling down across the board. This will depend on the overall performance of the Council and its funding situation. In 1994-5, for example, the payments were scaled down by 22 per cent so that the average payments overall to members of staff were five per cent.

The following are two examples of the above calculations:

Example 1

Employee is paid £15,000 on a scale with a upper limit of £16,000. He is in one team whose performance is rated at level two and they achieve 95 per cent of their targets. This gives a theoretical bonus of 11 per cent. This is scaled down by the personnel committee by 20 per cent, giving a final bonus of 8.8 per cent. The amount payable is 8.8 per cent of £16,000 = £1400.

Example 2

Employee is paid £10,000 on the top of his scale. He is in two teams, the first at 75 per cent and the second at 25 per cent (which represents the division of his time). The first team achieve 80 per cent of their targets at a performance level of three. This gives a bonus of four per cent. The second team achieves 92 per cent of their targets also at a performance level of three to give a bonus of eight per cent.

He gets 75% of 4% (team l) = 3%
He gets 25% of 8% (team 2) = 2%

Total bonus = 5%

This is then scaled down by 20 per cent to give a final bonus of four per cent. The bonus paid is four per cent of £10,000 = £400.

Scheme evaluation

The scheme has been in operation for five years and indications remain strong that it is seen as successful and reasonably fair by the staff. In 1994, a survey was carried out with the staff consultative group and their overall view was that the scheme should be retained. It was much preferred to individual performance pay. Trade unions are represented in the group but there are no formal negotiations over the scheme.

A second source of evaluation was a report by Price Waterhouse, the Council's external auditors, who carried out a review of the impact of the scheme in 1995. They reported that it was robust and that it had achieved genuine and cost-effective improvements in performance. The bonuses had been earned and represented value for money.

Richard considers that the scheme has a number of strengths.

1. The process of consultative target-setting enables the teams to stop and question what they are doing and the contribution of their work to the team's overall achievements. For example, the number of formal reports has been reduced by team members saying to their recipients, 'How valuable is this report? What do you do with it, apart from filing it? Can you get this information more easily elsewhere?'. This type of questioning could only have taken place through the process of review and reflection.
2. The cascading of the Chief Executive and management team's targets ensure that the overall Council goals are clearly spelt out to all the staff. Despite the small size of the Council, it is easy to forget essential communication processes and team target-setting ensures that team members know and understand the Council goals. They can go further by questioning these goals and contribute towards new goals for future years, particularly in areas such as the preservation and development of essential services where they are consumers as well as providers.
3. The team targets also help to link in with the steady cultural change that is affecting all councils. The government initiatives through the Citizen's Charter to improve the quality of service to the public was received with caution but the overall drive was understood and supported. The use of performance indicators was seen as a sensible move in this direction and are essential planks in the relevant team targets. Simple areas such as targets for the time and manner of answering telephone calls became immediate team targets for the administrative front-line staff and were further supported by customer care training courses and surveys. A more complex area is the drive by the Council to achieve Investors in People and ISO 9000 accreditation. These could only be achieved through a team effort in all departments involved in the process and they easily became key team targets. Staff have responded with interest, concern and

application to the task in hand. This was followed by considerable satisfaction by staff at all levels when these targets were successful. Rather than just being a matter for congratulation for the figurehead Head of Service, it became a much wider matter of reward for all the teams involved.

4. Another example of the scheme supporting change was when the Council changed political control in 1994, since when there has been a strong move to consult more closely with the public. The setting up and operation of a number of Neighbourhood Forums became team targets and were successfully completed within the time-scale.
5. There is some evidence that peer pressure is growing within teams to ensure that all team members perform to the required standard. It is possible that a target may not be fully achieved by the lack of enthusiasm of one of the team members and the team can suffer financially. For this reason, teams have become much more focused in their work and are more careful to communicate their progress to each other and identify possible causes of target failure so these can be eliminated at an early stage.

Despite the overall success, Richard is conscious that more work needs to be done. There are still some possible areas of weakness.

(a) The scheme can possibly work against teams dealing with more routine matters. For example, it is difficult to devise targets for the post room that are not entirely related to their fundamental job, namely to deal with the incoming and outgoing post accurately within the defined time-scale and to provide a messenger and courier service. Targets are less likely to have a major impact on the organisation so the ultimate percentage bonus for teams like these can work out to be less than may equitably be argued. As they tend to be on lower pay scales, in any case, their ultimate bonus is also rather low.

(b) The other side of the coin is that staff who deal with significant matters, such as the planning and development implications of the Bluewater shopping site (the latest and probably the country's largest out-of-town shopping development which is being built within the borough) have a substantial impact on the overall work of the Council and there can be a tendency for their targets to be crucial and the rewards greater. The evidence is not necessarily conclusive on this point but Richard has felt a need to keep this point in mind when reviewing the targets and bonuses.

(c) There are inherent difficulties in all performance management schemes and this is no exception. Staff expect to get at least level three, if not level two and these assessments occasionally cause tensions. The main problem is not with respect to wholly measurable targets (although these are difficult enough) but dealing with changed circumstances during the course of a year where targets may become easier or more difficult due to external circumstances. There is no easy solution here except to say to staff that decisions made regarding these changes can go either way – the credit for achievements has to be judged as a whole.

(d) Team sizes have been an issue, although less so now. The revenues division team started at 40 strong but this was found to be too large as the good level of performance of some sections was not recognised. The division has now been divided into four teams and this appears to be working better.

(e) Absence has not been an easy issue to settle. At present, for the individual, an absence of more than six weeks reduces their team pay; it has been clear that, for the team, absence has made targets more difficult to reach. Team pressures do seem to be having some effect on absence and the overall absence rate is currently two and a half per cent which compares very favourably with other local authorities.

Conclusion

As a pioneering council on team pay, Dartford are proud of their success so far but are conscious that all incentive and reward schemes need to be watched closely to ensure they are not manipulated or go stale. It is important that the original objectives of the scheme are being met and that steps are being taken regularly to ensure that this happens.

At the end of the current performance year (March 1997) it is intended to review the operation of the scheme and recommend any necessary changes to the personnel committee. It is unlikely, however, that these will change the thrust of the scheme overall.

Student activities

1. Evaluate the benefits of paying for team performance against individual performance in a local authority setting. Would your answer be any different if the setting was a financial services company?
2. How would you deal with the situation where the apparent performance and team rewards for one team were substantially higher than all the other teams?
3. Analyse the system for measuring team success. Would you recommend any further measures? Would a third party assessment be appropriate in any circumstances?
4. Read the IRRS article on 'Team rewards for the benefits commission'. Compare and contrast the methods of operation and the apparent success.

Standard reading

	Armstrong and Murlis	*Armstrong*	*Milkovich and Newman*
Pages	283-284	299-313	333-334

Further reading

Armstrong, M (1996) 'How group efforts can pay dividends', *People Management*, Jan. 25, pp 22-27
IRRS (1996) 'Team rewards, Part 1', *Pay and Benefits Bulletin 396*, March, pp 2-6
IRRS (1996) 'Team rewards, Part 2', *Pay and Benefits Bulletin 400*, May, pp 3-8
IRRS (1995) 'Team performance bonuses at the Benefits Agency', *Pay and Benefits Bulletin*, January, pp 6-9
Smith, A (1992) 'Team prize', *Personnel Today*, Nov. 10th

Appendix A

Team pay – advice for practitioners

In Michael Armstrong's *IPD Guide on Team Pay* (1996) he concludes that good teamwork may be enhanced by the reward system but there are other ways of developing it as well. Here are six of his recommendations:

- devise and implement commitment and communication strategies which develop mutuality and identification;
- keep emphasising that constructive teamwork is a key value in the organisation and ensure that the top management team practises what it preaches;
- create teams which are largely self-managed or self-directed, whose members jointly set their own specific short-term objectives within the framework of broader corporate and functional objectives and define the measures they will use to monitor their own performance;
- use team training to improve team processes including objective setting, planning and monitoring performance as well as interpersonal skills;
- set overlapping or interlocking objectives for people who have to work together. These will take the form of targets to be achieved or projects to be completed by joint action; and
- assess people's performance not only on the results they achieve but also on the degree to which they are effective team players.

Case Study 18

Gainsharing at BP and Ingersoll-Rand

Background

Gainsharing is a most attractive and equitable concept and one that has been operated successfully in North America since the 1930s. For no obvious accountable reason, it has scarcely surfaced in the UK, despite the similar economic and social environment. Schemes are operated chiefly in an industrial setting but US experience is that they are being extended into service and non-profit making organisations.

The essential feature is that the benefits of increased organisational performance, including productivity, cost reductions and improved quality are passed on to employees who are instrumental in accomplishing these improvements. The cash payments arising from these gains are usually made on a equal basis to the group of employees involved in the form of a percentage of base pay although they are occasionally shared equally, irrespective of base pay.

Types of schemes

Scanlon plan

This is now seen as the pace-setter, started up in the 1930s to save companies from imminent collapse in the Depression. Joseph Scanlon was a one-time prize boxer who turned to accountancy and eventually went to work in a steel mill and became the local union president. When the steel mill faced closure, Scanlon, helped by his accounting training, could see that productivity was desperately low and managed to persuade the company on a joint plan for company salvation. Working with the unions, the aim was to lower labour costs without lowering wages and to help teams of employees to identify how they could work to improve the company's performance.

This proved successful and was adopted at a number of other threatened industrial concerns, with full co-operation from the unions. Table 4.2 shows a typical example of how a scheme works.

One of the immediate advantages arising from the introduction of these schemes is the improvement in employee involvement and the identification of the employees with the success of the company. This point was picked up in an early survey of operating schemes which found that operatives and supervisors rated most highly the way the scheme improved morale and commitment (Goodman et al[1]). More recently, gainsharing has been recognised not just as a way of reducing the cost base but to support the company philosophy of involvement and empowerment, particularly as an aid to organisational change and development.

An innovation associated with these schemes was the setting up of productivity committees where managers and employees came together regularly to discuss current performance and ideas to make improvements – a foretaste of quality circles.

Table 4.2 *Example of a Scanlon Plan*

Historical data over past 3 years		
Sales Value of Production (SVOP)	=	£20,000,000
Total Wages Cost	=	£5,000,000
Wages as a percentage of SVOP	=	25%
Gainsharing pool starts to operate when the wage percentage drops below 25%		
Operating period January 1996		
SVOP	=	£2,000,000
Target wage bill (25%)	=	£500,000
Total Wages Cost – actual	=	£420,000
Gainsharing pool	=	£80,000
Divided 50% to employees	=	£40,000
Say, 1000 employees	=	£40 per employee for the month

Rucker and other plans

The main criticism of the Scanlon Plan was that it was too simple a measure for labour costs. Subsequent developments have utilised 'value-added' measures (Rucker Plan), the ratio of output using standard labour hours to input using actual labour hours (called Improshare) and a gainsharing variant, called 'winsharing' which widens the goals beyond labour costs to other performance measures such as customer value and quality improvement as described by Schuster and Zingheim[2].

The BP exploration plan

BP is the best known UK example of a sustained gainsharing plan. It operates in a number of varying ways in separate parts of the organisation and has recently been extended to the retail division. This exploration plan arose from two sources. Firstly, an overhaul of the company's centralised reward structure and the greater emphasis on each of the 'assets' (exploration units) earning its keep with the full co-operation of its employees. Secondly, there had been successful pilot gainsharing schemes in two of the large oil production units in Alaska in 1992 and this lead to a momentum to spread it to other parts of the organisation.

Following a UK pilot later that year, a full-blown scheme was launched in 1993 covering 2500 employees working on 17 assets in the North Sea. The scheme was divided into two parts:

- for the asset-based staff (those whose time was allocated to one asset) the shared rewards were linked to the performance of that particular asset. Originally this covered about 1100 staff but the development of the scheme allowed an increasing number of employees to be attached to an asset so that, by 1995, this figure had risen to 1800; and
- for the remaining staff supporting more than one asset, the 'umbrella scheme' was devised where rewards were linked to the performance of all the assets. This mostly applied to the central support staff.

Gainsharing targets were established relating to oil production, costs (especially labour costs), plus safety and environmental issues which were tailored to the particular asset. A valiant attempt was made in the difficult task of creating a 'level playing field' to make sure some assets did not earn bonus more easily than others. The other unique measure was the price of North Sea oil which had a fundamental effect on profitability. This was a common measure which applied to all of the assets.

Payments would be triggered when the targets were exceeded. There was a 20 per cent cap in the first year, reduced to 15 per cent in subsequent years. Regular meetings were held at each of the BP assets locations between management and employee representatives.

Results

The results in the first two years of operation were very positive. For 1993, staff received payments ranging from three per cent to 13 per cent with an average of seven per cent. For 1994, there was an advantageous North Sea oil price which helped 1800 employees earn gainshare bonuses varying between one per cent and 20 per cent with an average of around eight per cent. The actual figures were regarded as too sensitive for publication outside the organisation.

Just as important, the feedback from staff indicated that there was a growing understanding of the business and cost environment which made employees consider the wider implications of their work, particularly where mistakes could be costly. When applied on a local basis, there was also more pride in the performance of their asset and a small degree of competition to be a high-performing unit. Line management of the assets have taken well to spreading the concept of ownership to the staff by regular briefings and discussion groups. It has been voted a success all round.

The Ingersoll-Rand scheme

The first introduction to gainsharing plans in Ingersoll-Rand in the USA was in 1985 at the Painted Post company, a manufacturing subsidiary with 400 employees. The main products are gas and air compressors with the accompanying service and repair facilities. There were three elements in the plan:

- increasing productivity, measured as the labour cost percentage of sales;
- savings on waste, measured by the reduction in spoilage and scrap; and
- savings on supply costs.

The base year was 1984 when the labour cost as a proportion of sales value of production was 16 per cent, the waste was three per cent and the supply costs were four per cent. An example of the way the scheme was implemented is set out in Table 4.3.

The gainsharing bonus is paid on a quarterly basis as a percentage of salary. No bonus is paid when an employee is absent for any reason, including sickness.

The reserve is established in order to safeguard the company against any years with lower than normal performance which may arise from difficult market conditions or plain bad luck.

Table 4.3 *Painted Post gainsharing example for a full year*

Sales value of production	$40,000,000	
Labour cost saving		
Target saving (16%)	$6,400,000	
Actual labour costs	$6,200,000	
Gainsharing labour bonus	$200,000	$200,000
Waste saving		
Target waste (3%)	$1,200,000	
Actual waste	$1,050,000	
Gainsharing waste bonus	$150,000	$150,000
Operating supplies saving		
Target supplies cost (4%)	$1,600,000	
Actual supplies cost	$1,500,000	
Gainsharing supplies bonus	$100,000	$100,000
Total gainsharing bonus		$450,000
Reserve set aside for difficult times		$100,000
Available for distribution		$350,000
Employee share = 65%		$227,500
Participating Payroll		$4,000,000
Employee bonus ($227,500 as a percentage of $4million)		5.68%
Reserve balance to carry forward		$100,000

Employee Involvement Teams (EITs)

The company recognised at an early stage that the success of the plan would largely be determined by the extent to which all employees got involved in the company objectives of making saving and improvements. EITs were set up in each department and on each shift with the objectives to be:

- employees to use their creative powers to make suggestions to improve productivity and quality;
- to set up an effective two-way communication medium;
- a useful vehicle to initiate and support the change process; and
- to assist in the educational process: for employees to understand costing processes; for engineers to discuss the realities of their engineering ideas; for management to explore the improvement process and understand motivational and operational difficulties.

EITs were given authority to implement ideas when they cost $200 or less and did not impact on another department. Ideas costing more than $200 or having an impact outside the department would go to the EIT Steering Committee for evaluation.

The EIT Steering Committee had the following functions:

- oversee the operation of the EIT teams;
- encourage the teams to take on significant projects;
- review ideas rejected by supervisors and managers;
- co-ordinate a review of ideas that cut across more than one department;
- provide regular communication on EIT activities; and
- act as a mechanism to provide greater trust, confidence and teamwork.

The Bonus Committee

The Bonus Committee is made up of four union and four company representatives. It meets once a quarter to review the calculation of the bonus and the outcomes and ensure these are communicated to the workforce effectively. This includes explaining if the figures have deteriorated and what may have been the causes.

Student activities

1. Compare the operation of the two schemes. Does the nature of the business affect the way the scheme works?
2. Imagine that the cost of supplies increase in the Ingersoll-Rand scheme but it is not possible to increase the price of the finished goods. The gainsharing bonus therefore drops. Draft a communication to the employees explaining this.
3. A major fire occurs on one of the BP North Sea platforms causing it to be closed down for four weeks. This badly affects the output over that particular bonus period. An investigation shows that the fire resulted from freak weather conditions. Should the gainsharing bonus be affected?

4. Draw up a detailed agenda for an EIT meeting at Ingersoll-Rand and a meeting at one of the BP asset locations. How would you measure the success of these meetings?

Standard reading

	Armstrong and Murlis	*Armstrong*	*Milkovich and Newman*
Pages	330-339	314-318	334-353

References

1. Goodman, P, Wakely, J and Ruh, R (1972) 'What employees think of the Scanlon Plan', *Personnel*, Spring, pp 22–9
2. Schuster, J and Zingheim, P (1992) *The New Pay*, Lexington Books, New York.

Further reading

Cooper, C, Dyck, B and Frohlich, N (1992) 'Improving the effectiveness of gainsharing: the role of fairness and participation', *Administrative Science Quarterly*, Vol. 37, pp 471-90

IRS Pay and Benefits Bulletin (1996) *Gainsharing at BP Exploration*, February

Welbourne, T and Mejia, L (1995) 'Gainsharing: a critical review and a future research agenda', *Journal of Management*, Vol. 21, No. 3, pp 559-609

Case Study 19

Profit-related Pay at the Burton Group

Introduction

Tax relief for profit-related pay (PRP) was introduced in 1987 and, after a slow start, has now spread widely throughout the private sector. The original tax relief was one third of the PRP to a maximum of £3000 but this was increased in 1991 to 100 per cent of £4000 or 20 per cent of total pay, whichever is the lower. The huge expansion in take-up under the scheme can be seen from that date. From less than 1500 schemes covering 400,000 employees in 1991, the latest figures for the fiscal year 1995-6 is 10,519 schemes covering over 2.6 million employees and this is still increasing at a fast rate.

So fast, in fact, that profit-related pay has become a victim of its own success. The cost to the taxpayer, which is likely to be in excess of £1 billion in 1996-7, has prompted the government to reduce the tax benefits from 1998 and to phase them out altogether by the year 2000. Not many new schemes are likely to start after 1998, therefore, and it will put some organisations who already have PRP schemes in a quandary. They will find it difficult to eliminate the scheme, telling their employees that it was only introduced for tax purposes. On the other hand, they will be under pressure to make up the loss of tax relief suffered by employees, pressure that few employers in times of good profits will be unlikely to resist too much.

The maximum tax relief is worth £960 to the standard tax payer and £1600 to the higher-rate payer. Most of the early schemes were replacements for existing cash profit-sharing schemes, such as those operating at Gallagher or the John Lewis Partnership but recent introductions have tended to feature salary conversions and this case study is one in point.

Background

The Burton Group PLC is the largest fashion retailer in the UK with leading stores such as Debenhams and fashion multiples including Dorothy Perkins, Principles, Top Shop and Burton Menswear trading from over 1600 sites in the UK.

The group went through very difficult times during the recession in the early 1990s, where a combination of over-exposure to property and too many brands operating in isolation from too many unmodernised shops in the wrong locations, had lead to poor trading conditions. 'Entrenched in a markdown mentality' as John Hoerner, Chief Executive explained in the 1995 *Annual Report and Accounts*. The consequence was massive losses in 1991 and a new set of top management appointed in 1992.

By 1995, the situation had been reversed through the repositioning of brands, a reduction of debt, a programme of shop modernisation and disposals and a general improvement in the retail consumer outlook. The profits for that year increased to £98 million, an increase of 140 per cent from the previous year and the share price, once less than 30p, had risen to over 140p bringing the company back into the FTSE 100 group.

Introducing profit-related pay

An Inland Revenue Approved Profit Sharing scheme had been in place since 1979 but the elimination of profit during the recession had meant that no issue of shares to employees under the scheme had been made since 1989. Given this history, the company had to be confident that any new scheme linked to profitability would have a good chance of success and also have credibility with its employees. A major emphasis of the new management team had been on the importance of improved performance and of employees being focused on effective selling in all the divisions, so a means of rewarding employees through a scheme linked to overall profit would be in line with the company reward strategy.

In itself, PRP was not seen as a major motivational element but one of a collection of policies and benefits that helped to identify the employee with the performance of the organisation.

Arthur Andersen, the international consultancy, was chosen to put together the Burton Group's scheme. Their experience in this area was extensive with successful implementations at companies such as Mercury Communication.

In August 1995, the company wrote to all employees to introduce the Burton Group PRP scheme which would be effective from the following month. Under Inland Revenue rules, 80 per cent of eligible employees needed to join for the scheme to go ahead.

The details

How it works

Employees in the scheme have their basic pay and any overtime split into two parts. 80 per cent will be taxable as previously while 20 per cent becomes non-taxable PRP. The non-taxable PRP element is related to the profits of the group and a profit pool is set up each year from which the PRP payments are made. The size of the pool cannot be known until the company publishes its results for the full year but employees do not have to wait until this time to receive their PRP. The company is sufficiently confident concerning the profit targets that 90 per cent of the PRP is paid out on a monthly (or weekly) basis. The balance of the PRP pool is paid out at the end of the year assuming that profit targets are met. Examples of pre-PRP and post-PRP earnings are shown on Tables 4.4 and 4.5.

Table 4.4 *Pre-PRP earnings*

WHAT ARE THE BENEFITS?

The benefit to you is an increase in take-home pay throughout the year and – after the year-end – a final payment worth around 2% of take-home pay. So, PRP will have increased your total take-home pay by between 3% and 7%, depending on your salary and your personal tax allowances.

Here is an example for somebody earning £10,000 a year.

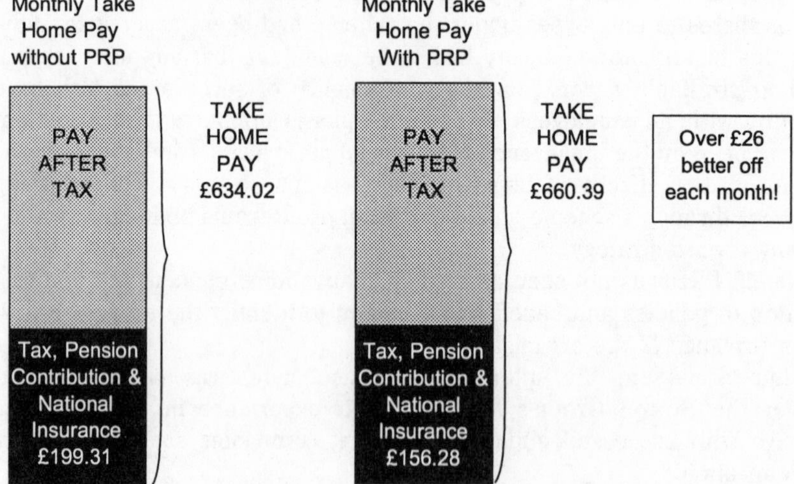

So, in this example, your monthly take-home pay increases by over 4% plus the final payment of £200 (less National Insurance and pension contribution). This gives you a total increase in net pay of 6.3%.

Effect on pay review

Most organisations introducing the scheme ask employees to take a small cut in their basic pay because the effect of the non-taxable PRP element is sufficient to give them an overall increase in their take-home pay. The Burton Group chose a different approach. Employees were not asked to take a decrease but were told that the pay review due to take place in March 1996 would only apply selectively, targeting the higher level performers rather than the normal performance-related review covering all employees. This was because the introduction of PRP had the effect of giving employees a pay increase of between three and seven per cent.

Table 4.5 *Post-PRP earnings*

Here are some other examples of how much PRP can be worth:

Current Basic Salary £	Monthly Take-Home Pay (ie before PRP) £	Monthly Take-Home Pay *With* PRP £	+	Planned Final PRP payment after year end £	Total Increase as a % of Current Take-Home pay
6,000	417.33	428.15		120	4.6%
7,000	474.50	487.12		140	4.7%
10,000	634.02	660.39		200	6.3%
12,000	740.35	771.99		240	6.5%
15,000	899.85	939.40		300	6.7%
20,000	1165.69	1218.42		400	6.9%
25,000	1446.28	1496.28		400	5.8%

These examples assume that:

- You have a single person's tax allowance
- You pay National Insurance at the contracted out rate
- As a member of the Burton Group Pension Fund, you contribute 4% of basic salary.

The tax rates are correct from 5 April 1995.

The profit targets

It is obligatory under the Inland Revenue rules to have profit targets from which the PRP is derived but there is no obligation to disclose these targets to employees. The information is, of course, market sensitive so no disclosure was made.

Who can join?

Prior to 1995, organisations could exclude employees working less than 20 hours a week but the Finance Act in that year eliminated that option. They did so because such a large proportion of part-timers are female that the exclusion could be regarded as discriminatory as identified by the 1994 House of Lords decision in *Equal Opportunities Commission* v. *Secretary of State for Employment*, (1994 1 All ER 910).

The Burton Group faced something of a dilemma here. A very high proportion of the Group's employees were part-timers and the majority of these paid little or no tax. For them, the PRP scheme would have no advantage so they would choose not to join. Without an 80 per cent agreement, the scheme could not go ahead.

To overcome this problem and also to provide a safety net in case of

Table 4.6 *Benefits*

Not only will you benefit when the bonus of 2% of annual basic pay plus overtime is paid, you also see an IMMEDIATE INCREASE IN YOUR TAKE-HOME PAY because you don't pay tax on the 20% of your pay which is paid as PRP. So,

Current Weekly Pay	Weekly Increase In Take-Home Pay Single*	Married*	Year End Bonus	Total Annual Increase Single*	Married*
£	£	£	£	£	£
80	0.88	–	77	124	78
100	3.67	–	97	280	97
130	4.78	4.78	126	364	364
150	5.51	5.51	145	420	420

* All calculations use 1996/97 tax and National Insurance rates and the single and married persons allowance.

unexpected poor company performance, Burtons decided to pay a year end bonus of two per cent of annual pay to all staff working 16 hours or less a week. For example, an employee on £50 a week would receive a year end bonus of £53. In this way, they would receive a benefit by joining the scheme although this would be financed entirely by the company. An example of the calculations is shown on Table 4.6.

The only employees excluded were those who joined after the start of the company's financial year. They could join the scheme in the following year. Those on contracts of six months or less are excluded.

Communication of the scheme

Apart from the issue of a booklet explaining the scheme to all employees, a series of presentations were made at all main stores, distribution centres and head offices and to all personnel staff. A freephone 'hot line' was set up to answer any employee questions which was run by Arthur Andersen.

Outcome on employees joining

The information pack made it clear that employees needed to do nothing to be in the scheme. If they did not want to join, they had to write to the PRP co-ordinator. In the event, 99 per cent of employees opted to join the scheme. The reasons given by the very small minority of employees who decided not to join (about 400 employees) were:

- those who had decided to leave within the next few months; and
- those who were in receipt of state benefits who would lose benefit if they received any additional pay at that point in time.

Results expected

At the time of writing, the scheme has yet to complete one full year's operation so no watertight predictions can be made. However, the improved interim results and the strong current trading position indicate that the profit targets will be reached, if not exceeded.

On the basis of these expectations, the Burton Group will have shared the benefits of PRP by making the March 1996 pay review selective and employees will have benefitted by an increase in take home pay of between three and seven per cent. Subsequent March pay reviews would not be affected by the introduction of PRP.

Student activity

1. Taking the Burton Group scheme as a typical example, how successful do you consider that schemes have been in meeting the government aims behind PRP?
2. PRP is sometimes called a group incentive scheme, sometimes an employee benefit. Set out the arguments on either side and justify your own view.
3. Why have the government regulations insisted on an 80 per cent employee take up for the scheme to qualify for tax relief?
4. Set out the main similarities and differences between PRP and profit-sharing schemes. Can they run alongside each other?

Standard reading

	Armstrong and Murlis	*Armstrong*	*Milkovich and Newman*
Pages	347-352	314-318	341-342 and 354-359

Further reading

Ernst & Young (1995) *Profit-Related Pay*, London, Summer

IDS (1996) *Profit-Related Pay*, Study No. 603, London, June

Inland Revenue Tax Relief for Profit-Related Pay: Setting up a scheme (pamphlet) (1995)

IFF (1994) *Profit-Related Pay: An Employer Survey*, (an IFF Research Report for the Inland Revenue)

IRRR (1994) *Profit-Related Pay in the 1990s*, Report No. 568, pp 2-11

IRRR (1995) *Spectacular Growth in PRP Continues*, Report No. 581, pp 4-8

McLean, H (1994) *Fair Shares: the Future of Employee Financial Participation in the UK*, Institute of Employment Rights, London

Suter, E (1994) 'Equal rights for part-timers, *Personnel Management Plus*, April, p 16

Case Study 20

Profit Sharing at the John Lewis Partnership

Partnership is justice. Better than justice, it is kindness. Partnership is a matter of facts, not words (John Spedan Lewis).

Background

The John Lewis Partnership is one of the largest retailers in Britain with 23 department stores and 112 Waitrose supermarkets. The combined turnover for the year ending January 1996 was £2.8 billion with a trading profit of £173 million. The unique nature of the company is that it is genuinely a partnership and that the profits of the partnership belong to the employees (partners) who currently number 34,000.

The system of sharing profits with employees began in 1906 when Spedan Lewis, the son of the original John Lewis, started experimenting with sharing power with his staff, using a staff council, a committee for communication and a house journal. He had realised at that time that the Lewis family were drawing more from the successful business than the whole employee payroll put together. He became concerned to devise a more equitable system, particularly as he was conscious that he was born to the business (he had been given a quarter share on his 21st birthday) and had not built it up from scratch. He took the process further in 1914 when his father, who had bought the controlling interest in Peter Jones Ltd in 1906, gave the store to Spedan telling him he could do what he wanted with it as long as he did not leave the John Lewis store until 5.00 pm! Peter Jones was then making a loss and Spedan told the staff that if they worked with him to make it profitable, they would have a financial share in the success.

By 1920, the business had become profitable and the first distribution of 'partnership profit' was made of seven weeks' pay to all employees. In 1928, on the death of his father, Spedan became sole owner and a year later he established a trust for the benefit of employees, selling his dividend rights (worth around £1 million) and allowing the partnership to purchase them with an interest-free loan which was spread over 25 years. By 1950, he had established a written constitution for the business and transferred completely his rights of ownership to trustees.

Spedan Lewis retired in 1955 at the age of 70 and there have only been three Chairmen since: Sir Bernard Miller from 1955 to 1972, Peter Lewis, nephew of the founder, from 1972 to 1993 and Stuart Hampson from 1993 to present.

Shared ownership

Before describing the operation of the profit-sharing scheme, it is important to understand how the Partnership operates.There are a number of interesting philosophies which underpin the ownership structure of the organisation. Firstly, the theory that partners, who may neither aspire to be managers nor possess the ability to be one, are seen as individuals with a valid contribution to make. They have a right to question anything they do not understand and to receive frank answers. Secondly, the theory that a partnership should allow the members the satisfaction of sharing in the advantages of ownership:

- knowledge through effective and thorough communication;
- power through the democratic exercise of voting; and
- finance through the operation of the profit-sharing scheme.

There are three effective authorities of the Partnership:

The chairman

He is normally appointed by his predecessor and appoints the holders of the senior positions in management. He is in a strong position to influence policy but if he does not use his power and influence in a proper, acceptable and successful way, he can be removed from office by the Trustees. This has not happened so far.

The central council

There are 130 members in the Council. Up to 20 per cent can be appointed by the Chairman, usually from the ranks of senior management. The others are appointed yearly by secret ballot throughout the partnership. Any partner is able to stand and is entitled to reasonable help in electioneering.

The Council elects three Trustees of the constitution through whom the Council can remove the Chairman. They also elect five directors to the Central Board. The Council has to be consulted if at least three of these directors consider that a proposal or issue discussed at the Board is of such importance that consultation is necessary. This could be issues such as store closures or environmental issues. Any subject can be discussed by the Council and recommendations are made to the Chairman, who has to take these matters to the Central Board and justify any rejections or amendments.

The Council has control over one per cent of the company's payroll (equal to over £3 million in 1996) and this money can be used at their discretion to finance expenditure on welfare matters, such as leisure facilities, financial help for partners, providing retirement homes or charitable causes.

There are also Branch Councils at each store, usually with a Central Council member who carries issues from the branch to the Council.

The central board

This consists of the Chairman, his deputy, five directors appointed by him and five elected by the Central Council. The Board make executive decisions, including the amount of the Partnership bonus.

Supporting the administration of the whole scheme are the Registrars who work alongside the heads of stores and branches. They are responsible for seeing that management, other partners and the representative institutions operate within the Partnership's constitution and they usually edit the local magazine (*The Chronicle*).

Profit-sharing scheme

The profit-sharing bonus is paid to partners each year in the form of a percentage of their base salary. Figure 4.3 shows the level that has been paid since 1975.

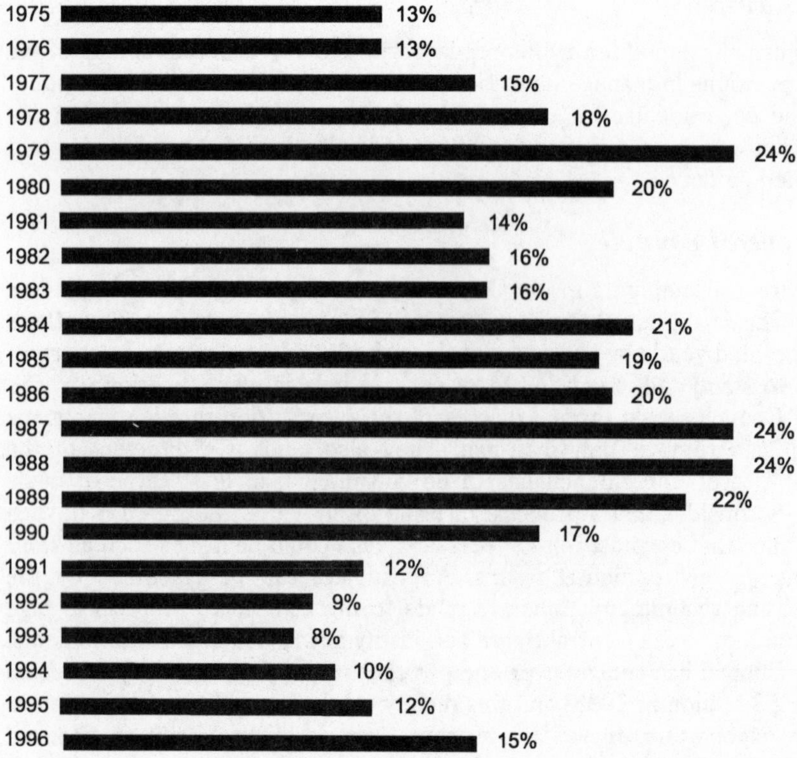

Figure 4.3 *Partnership bonus levels*

The three factors which influence the level of profit to be shared amongst partners are:

- the amount of profit made by the organisation;
- the amount of that profit that needs to be retained in the business to finance expansion and investment; and
- the cost of each one per cent of bonus, which is dependent upon the payroll costs reflecting, in turn, the number of partners and their rate of pay.

For the year ending January 31st 1996, the profit earned in total was £150 million, up by 28 per cent on 1995 and was a record figure exceeding the previous record of £131 million made back in 1989. After tax and interest payments, the Board decided to retain £64 million for expansion and investment and distribute the remaining £57 million to partners, giving them a bonus of 15 per cent of their salary, compared to 12 per cent the previous year. The cost of a one per cent bonus had risen by six per cent due to the rise in the number of partners and the annual pay increase.

A substantial part of this bonus is paid in the form of the government approved tax-exempt profit-related pay (PRP) scheme. In 1996, this percentage was 80 per cent, up on previous years.

As Figure 4.3 shows, there has been considerable variation in the bonus payments, particularly in recent years. 1993 was a poor year with a bonus of only eight per cent and the bonus for 1996 is still well short of the halcyon years of the 1980s when bonuses were in the 20 to 25 per cent range. There have been other bad years, including the 1930s when bonuses slipped below ten per cent and a period after the second world war when bonuses disappeared altogether.

Supporting the participative culture

Profit-sharing is one outcome of the ethos of the organisation. From an early date, there has been an exceptional emphasis on communication, employee welfare and corporate responsibility.

Communication

The Partnership call their communication programme 'Sharing Knowledge' and regard it as perhaps more important than sharing power and profit and a central prerequisite of a real partnership between management and employees.

As well as 32 local journals produced by the stores, the central editorial department publishes *The Gazette*, now in its 75th volume. Much of the journal contains the normal contents of a house magazine – news, social events, leisure, new products, appointments, obituaries – but there are two areas which make it uniquely different:

1. It has full details of the previous week's trading showing week-on-week

percentage comparison with the previous two years in each of the stores including a league table of performance in certain selected areas. This is detailed information which is not provided to shareholders (or investors) in the conventional PLC.

2. It has the most open form of letters section you will find in any house publication. It is company policy for a comprehensive system of correspondence columns to be encouraged. Anybody can write and they can be open or anonymous. Although all anonymous letters have to be vetted by the Chairman before publication, he has to certify that the publication of a letter would be harmful to the business for it to be stopped and this happens very infrequently. On each letter, a comment must be made by the appropriate manager. For example, in the edition of May 11th 1996, an anonymous partner called 'Sore' complained about their disappointment on buying an expensive pair of shoes in the Oxford Street store. The service from the assistant was poor, the ordered shoes took a month to arrive and they were a poor fit. The reply from the managing director of John Lewis apologised and explained the difficulties arising from refurbishment, offering a re-fit, etc. This is not unusual for a private correspondence between a customer and management but quite unusual for a house magazine with a circulation of 34,000. It clearly demonstrates the commitment to open and honest communication, warts and all!

Each store has an informal committee for communication, made up of non-managerial staff with a chairman from head office which meets four times a year so there can be two-way discussions dealing with store issues. The issues raised and the answers are published in the local house magazine.

Employee welfare

The company has invested heavily in health and welfare facilities for employees. There are two country clubs, two countryside hotels and a flurry of music, arts and sporting societies. Sick pay is substantial, there is a 70-strong occupational health service and there is a generous pension scheme. An elected committee deals with a hardship fund for partners with health or legal problems.

Corporate responsibility

The emphasis that the company has placed in this area is demonstrated in a number of ways:

(a) Environmental issues – a seven-page brochure is issued to employees dealing with the progressive approach to a variety of green subjects ranging from tropical hardwoods, through to detergents, energy conservation, CFCs and packaging.

(b) World issues – the stance on child labour and animal testing is quite marked and well publicised.

(c) Support for the arts – partners can obtain a 50 per cent subsidy on up to 12 theatre, opera, classical concerts or film trips a year to a maximum cost of £360 and visits to museums and art galleries are also subsidised. The company also sponsors a number of concerts and exhibitions directly.
(d) Directors' pay – if the company was a PLC, it would rate among the top 150 in the UK. Taking this into account, the pay of full-time directors verges on the modest (1995-6 figures). The base pay is comparable to other companies its size, with the Chairman earning close to £300,000 and six directors earning between £140,000 and £210,000 per annum. However, there is only the profit-sharing arrangement to add on (15 per cent for all partners) and there is no other bonus payment, nor are there any potentially lucrative share option schemes available elsewhere. There is no remuneration committee and decisions on pay are taken by the Chairman and the Board who have to answer, ultimately, to the partners.

Conclusion

The policies of this most unusual company fit into a coherent and well-structured whole and the reward system matches the major element of mutuality, namely that the partners share some of the risk and gain some of the benefits. This principle goes much further in practice than with conventional profit-sharing schemes. In the late 1930s, profits evaporated and none were paid out to the partners. By the late 1980s, a profit share of 25 per cent emerged but this was cut in half five years later. In other words, there was a real reduction of earnings of over 12 per cent. Together with the other principles of full and effective participation and communication, the reward systems add a final piece to this fascinating integrated jigsaw.

Student activities

1. What are the main reasons that the risk-sharing elements of the profit-sharing scheme have not been adopted by more than a handful of other organisations?
2. Draft a memorandum to staff explaining the payment of the eight per cent profit-share bonus in 1993.
3. What types of disciplines (pay and otherwise) does the partnership approach impose on the employees which would not be the case in other organisations?

Standard reading

	Armstrong and Murlis	*Armstrong*	*Milkovich and Newman*
Pages	347-352	314-318	341-342 and 354-359

Further reading

Adams, C (1994) 'Profit-sharing and employee involvement: are they compatible?', *University of Melbourne, Department of Economics*, July, Research Paper

Anfuso, D (1995) 'PepsiCo shares power and wealth with workers', *Personnel Journal*, June, Vol. 74, No. 6, pp 42-49

Fowler, A (1994) 'How to link pay to company profits', *Personnel Management Plus*, May, Vol. 5, No. 5, pp 24-25

Hampson, S (1995) '80 years of partnership', *Involvement*, No. 627, pp 16-17

PART 5
BENEFITS

Introduction

In 1993, the US Chamber of Commerce reported that the cost of employee benefits as a percentage of payroll had risen from 25 per cent in 1959 to 41 per cent in 1993 and averaged nearly $15,000 per employee. General Motors pays out more in benefits than it does for the steel for all its motor cars! Although medical insurance costs play a far higher part in employee benefits in the US, the equivalent UK costs cannot be far behind, given the perfidious and unstoppable drift towards company cars.

Benefits, therefore, are horrendously expensive and have to earn their keep. They have to be part of a cost-effective recruitment and retention strategy, not introduced and varied piecemeal in response to anecdotal market evidence.

Making benefits pay

This section covers four case studies where serious attempts are made to use benefits as an integrated part of total remuneration and corporate strategy. There is one example of the introduction of flexible benefits (Case Study 21 – Mercury Communication) where the opportunity for employees to take responsibility over the benefits they want reflects the company ethos of empowerment and flexibility in the workplace. If individuals can design their own benefits package, then they can transfer that skill into designing solutions for their own work-related problems. The additional advantages in terms of cost curtailment is also discussed.

Another area of an integrated solution is in Case Study 22 where Hascot Western Langley have put together an attractive collection of family-friendly benefits which match the requirements of a high proportion of the workforce. This has been carefully targeted and costed so that the payback is easily identified. They have avoided the broadbrush benefit of flexitime, so popular in the 1980s, because the benefits for the employer are too difficult to define and the temptations of working the system too high for the employees. (John

Garnett, long-time Chief Executive of the Industrial Society, would not touch the system for this reason.)

Case Study 23 looks at the practical difficulties of merging the two fundamentally different types of pension schemes, defined benefit (final salary) schemes and money purchase schemes. Despite the extensive 'contribution holidays' enjoyed by most large companies with defined benefit schemes in recent years, there are very few new schemes of this type being started because of the future funding uncertainties. In fact, a number of well-known organisations, such as both Lloyds and Barclays Bank, are beginning to phase them out, recruiting new staff onto the safer and more predictable money purchase schemes.

Finally, Case Study 24 examines how a share option scheme can help to encourage employee involvement and commitment to the organisation if it is launched properly. It is interesting to note that the cost of tax relief in 1995-6 for share option schemes was £330 million.

Future benefits

Much of the current discussion centres around the complex tax advantages of various benefits and the piecemeal government approach to encouragement (£40 million to set up creches) and discouragement (reducing benefits and tightening up loopholes on company cars and free petrol). Company policy does change in line with tax advantages on offer although that is generally the worst reason to change course.

Although dealt with under the section on team pay, the present position on profit-related pay is the most odd. The cost to the exchequer for tax relief in 1995-6 was over £800 million through the relaxing of concessions in the early 1990s and the rapid expansion in scheme introductions that followed. In comparison, the cost for 1991-2 was only £40 million. Yet most analysts remain sceptical that the British versions of profit-related pay, most of which are tied to the most tax-advantageous method, have the desired effect of increasing employee involvement and commitment. Certainly there is major doubt that it is good value for the general tax payer. From many employees' viewpoint, it could be argued that it is a useful source of extra pay, but little more.

Further reading

Beam, B and McFadden, J (1992) *Employee Benefits*, Dearborn Financial Publishing, Chicago

Caulfield, S (1990) 'Benefits in a changing workforce', *Compensation and Benefits Review*, July/August, pp 71-75.

CBI/Towers Perrin (1994) *The Benefits Package of the Future*, London

Dreher, G et al (1988) 'Benefit coverage and employee cost: critical factors in explaining compensation satisfaction', *Personnel Psychology*, Vol. 41, pp 237-54

Rosenbloom, J and Hallman, G (1991) *Employee Benefit Planning*, Prentice Hall, New Jersey

Woodley, C (1990) 'The cafeteria route to compensation', *Personnel Management*, May

Case Study 21

Flexible Benefits at Mercury Communications

Introduction

As with many HRM-related schemes, the origin and development of flexible benefits packages (sometimes known as 'cafeteria benefits' or 'flexible remuneration schemes') took place in the USA in the 1980s. Between 1980 and 1988, the number of such schemes rose from eight to 800 (Hewitt Associates[1]). The tax regime, both in the USA and in Australia, has been kinder in this area than in the UK. Studies in the States have shown that increase in job satisfaction and organisational commitment are associated with the move to such a package (Barber, et al[2], Heshizer[3]).

The development has been hastened by a number of factors. Firstly, organisations are increasingly moving away from rigid, collectively determined pay and benefits agreements towards individual contracts which allow for far greater flexibility on the part of both employer and employee. Secondly, the convergence of employment practices in trans-national companies will encourage the spread of such new concepts (Hay Group[4]). Thirdly, the computer technology capable of handling the complex decision process involved has developed and is within a reasonable cost (Johnson[5]). Fourthly, there are a number of consultancies which are actively researching and developing the idea. Fifthly, although the UK tax regime has not been particularly helpful to the concept, the 1986 Social Security Act, which enabled employees to opt out of company pension schemes and take out personal pensions instead, inaugurated the process of instilling in the minds of employees the fact that decisions on benefits were not solely in the hands of the employer. Sixthly, the nature of the employment scene has been changing substantially since the early 1980s with a far higher proportion of women in the workplace. The pattern of benefits they are looking for does not necessarily mirror the traditional male oriented package on offer. Finally, a number of corporate newcomers in swiftly growing industries (notably the financial and communications sectors) wanted to stress their innovative role, particularly where they wished to recruit and retain skilled employees. It reflected their policy of differential competitive positioning in the market place. This case study is one in point.

Background

Mercury Communications was established in 1982 and is 80 per cent owned by Cable and Wireless and 20 per cent by Bell Canada. With the opening up of the telecommunication industry in the UK and around the world, the company expanded rapidly to reach a workforce in excess of 10,000 by 1994. The majority of the employees are engineers but the customer-facing activities including operator services, sales and customer support, form a significant group There are over 100 locations within the UK.

The customer has typically seen Mercury as an alternative to BT, providing a land-based telephone service to business and residential sites via a digital network. However, the nature of telecommunications has changed rapidly in the past ten years with the integration of mobile communication, computer and television hardware with information and entertainment networks. Mercury has increasingly seen itself as a high-technology organisation in a competitive environment.

As the company grew rapidly, it adopted the working practices of a fully flexible organisation with functional reporting lines operating in conjunction with programme groups and virtual teams, together with flexible and location-independent working. The HRM practices reflected this growing flexibility with an avoidance of rigid job grading schemes and status-based rewards. Leading edge practices such as 360 degree appraisal, individual development plans and innovative performance pay schemes sat alongside a very competitive employment package.

The starting point

The standard benefits pack to all staff on permanent contracts in 1992 was as follows:

- 25 days annual leave;
- free private medical insurance;
- employee assistance programmes;
- save-as-you-earn share scheme;
- final salary pension scheme;
- staff discounts;
- sick pay and maternity provisions above statutory levels;
- death in service cover; and
- company loans.

This package cost over £50 million per annum (£5000 per employee) in order to attract and retain the calibre of employee necessary to support the strategic goals of the business.

It was known that employees place a different individual value on each benefit depending on their age and personal circumstances. The Mercury workforce reflected a considerable social range and it began to be realised that the benefits programme was the one key component of the employment programme which did not include provision for the individual. For example, the appraisal, career development, training and remuneration policies all focused on the individual employee as a key factor but the benefits programme tended to assume that everyone was the same.

Furthermore, employees had little or no idea of the huge cost of the benefits and therefore little real appreciation of their value.

The movement towards introducing flexible benefits was supported by the following perceived advantages:

- employees could choose benefits that satisfied their unique needs;
- flexible benefits would help meet the changing needs of a changing workforce;
- flexible plans would make introduction of new benefits less costly. The new benefit would merely add to the wide variety of elements from which an employee could choose;
- the total cost would be contained at the maximum set by the organisation;
- the package would be more attractive to applicants;
- Mercury would be seen as an innovative employer in the market place where the cultural ethos was reflected in employee pay and benefits; and
- employees would become comfortable with their benefit choice and be less likely to leave for a more hostile and anonymous benefit environment.

Getting going

An internal feasibility study was started in 1992 looking at the actual cost of benefits provisions, the take-up of the current benefits, opportunities for flexing and which employees would be covered together with tax, pricing and control systems issues. A study of newly-introduced UK flex schemes was carried out with four companies agreeing to participate in the research. Senior executives were interviewed with positive results. All of them felt that flex was entirely appropriate for the Mercury culture and, most important of all, they were unanimous in the view that Mercury should introduce flexible benefits for all employees.

As a result of these studies, the consultants William Mercer were asked to do a full feasibility study and this was presented to the Mercury Board and approved in May 1993.

Due to the fact that the Mercury scheme would be the biggest of its kind in the UK, it was decided to introduce the idea to a pilot group of employees in advance of the main launch. This was done in order to test the systems, administration and communications aspects and give the opportunity for feedback before the main launch. The scheme was called FLEX and piloted to 400 employees in April 1994, principally in the research and development area. It was a voluntary arrangement, and 34 per cent took up the offer by varying their benefit provision. The most popular benefit to change was annual leave (15 per cent) followed by dental insurance (13 per cent) and pension (ten per cent). Overall, the general feedback was very positive.

A project team of 18, made up of the employee benefits manager, Russ

Watling, and staff from human resources, pensions, payroll and other involved departments, developed the scheme over the next nine months.

The full launch

In January 1995, the full-scale launch took place. Substantial time and money was spent on the communication process which consisted of on-site presentations, newsletter articles and individual consultations. A firm of independent financial consultants assisted with pension counselling, which was available on a helpline and through surgeries at the 50 Mercury locations. The most substantial cost was in the production of a FLEXPACK, a 16-page A4-sized booklet. They were sent to each employee's home because so many of the flex choices were family-type decisions. The pack included an eight-page benefit statement which detailed all the core benefits that the employee was receiving at that time. A calculation was shown of the available choices and their costs on an actuarial basis. It was made clear that the choice made by the employee was incorporated into their contract of employment.

Seven flexible benefits were offered on the menu:

- pensions;
- life cover;
- health care;
- dental insurance;
- annual leave;
- childcare vouchers; and
- cars.

Each employee was given a standard entitlement for health care, pensions, annual leave and life cover. Under the FLEX scheme they could increase or decrease this benefit by transferring money-equivalent 'credits' between each benefit, or by taking any surplus as extra cash with their salary or by spending some of their basic salary on extending benefits. Employees entitled to a company car could use this benefit in the same way.

Those employees who wanted to opt for dental insurance, childcare vouchers or a lease car could purchase these benefits from their basic salary (or from their transferred 'credits'). Once all these decisions were taken, they had to remain in place for 12 months.

Detail of benefits

Pension

Employees in the pension scheme accrue retirement pension at the rate of 60ths for each year of service under the Cable and Wireless scheme. In other words, 30 years of service will provide an employee at normal retirement with 30/60th pension (or one half of final salary). For this benefit the employee contributes five per cent of pensionable salary.

FLEX offers four new options where employees are able to trade up in order to accrue pension at a faster rate and either plan for early retirement or improve their existing pension potential. These options are to pay extra contributions to buy pension at the rate of 55ths, 50ths, 45ths, or 40ths. In the case of an employee who contributes at 50ths for 30 years, the pension at normal retirement age would be 30/50th (or 60 per cent of final salary). Employees pay these extra contributions out of their FLEX credits or directly from their base salary. An employee can also decide not to take any company benefits at all.

Life cover

Life cover is four times pensionable salary for employees in the pension scheme but there is no cover for those outside the scheme. Under FLEX, employees can trade down to three times salary or twice salary and transfer that credit or take it as cash. Employees outside the scheme can buy life cover at twice, three times or four times salary.

Health care

Private medical cover had been provided for some years on the basis of employees' family status, ie single employees received single cover, married employees received married cover, etc. This meant that there was duplication of cover for some employees with working spouses already receiving medical cover in their own employment. Under FLEX, employees could trade down to single cover and use the credits elsewhere. Employees could also upgrade their cover to purchase, say, BUPA medical screening or higher maximum treatment limits out of their salary or using credits saved elsewhere.

Dental insurance

Employees could choose to upgrade their standard plan to cover NHS service for themselves to one that covers private treatment for themselves and their immediate family.

Annual leave

The standard leave entitlement is 25 days. Employees could choose to vary this by purchasing up to an additional five days (ie up to 30 days' leave) or receiving credit for up to five days (ie down to 20 days). Each day is priced at 1/260th of the individual's annual salary. Any change in this area must be approved by the employee's line manager.

Childcare vouchers

These were launched at the same time as FLEX and could be used to pay a nursery, childminder, nanny, creche, friend or relative. They are purchased in £1 units out of salary or from credits. Mercury had investigated starting up creches but found them to be too expensive. They have estimated that employees make a six per cent saving by purchasing vouchers and a free childcare help and advice line has also been provided.

Cars

Employees provided with company cars could trade up or down or receive a cash benefit instead. It is also possible for employees without company cars to join a lease purchase scheme from external suppliers using cash or credits from the FLEX scheme.

Administering the scheme

34 per cent of employees made a decision to FLEX their benefits. When their choices were made (they had a four-week deadline) then the in-house computer system went to work to integrate those choices with the Peterborough Software Uni2000 Personnel and Payroll system using a graphical use interface.

Once the decisions have been made, they remain in force for a year with only the occasional necessary change brought about through a lifestyle change (marriage, divorce, etc). After the high administrative costs of the first year, the administrative costs are now much reduced with a busy spell in the last two months of the year and little work in between.

Scheme evaluation

The annual company-wide attitude survey in April 1995 found 75 per cent of employees happy with the flexible benefit concept although 47 per cent were worried about overcommitting themselves under the scheme.

Student activities

1. If the concept of flexible benefits is so attractive, why is it that few employers have taken it up in the UK?
2. Identify the key features detailed in this study of the process of introducing flexible benefits.
3. Read *Reward Management* by Armstrong and Murlis, page 416. Do you agree with their prognosis?
4. Is their any link between flexible benefits and expectancy theory?

Standard reading

	Armstrong and Murlis	*Armstrong*	*Milkovich and Newman*
Pages	367-385 and 401-417	325-339	416-482

References

1. Hewitt Associates (1988) *Fundamentals of Flexible Compensation*, Wiley, New York
2. Barber, A *et al* (1990) *The Impact of Flexible Benefit Plans on Employee Benefit Satisfaction*, paper presented at the 50th annual meeting of the Academy of Management, San Francisco
3. Heshizer, B (1994) 'The impact of flexible benefit plans on job satisfaction, organisational commitment and turnover intentions', *Benefits Quarterly*, Vol. 4, pp 84-90
4. Hay Group (1992) *Compensation and Benefit Strategies for 1993 and Beyond*, Hay Management Consultants, Philadelphia
5. Johnson, R (1996) *Flexible Benefits, A How To Guide*, International Foundation of Employee Benefit Plans, Brookfield, Wisconsin

Further reading

Coopers and Lybrand (1993) *Flexible Benefits*, CCH Editions, Bicester

IDS (1995) *Flexible Benefits*, Study No. 589

Watling, R (1996) *Flexible Benefits – A Practical Guide*, Technical Communications Publishing, Brill, Buckinghamshire

Case Study 22

Family-friendly Benefits at Hascot Western Langley

Introduction

It is reported that more than one million employees take a day a month off sick to care for children and elderly relatives (IES[1]). Others find they cannot continue to work with a less than sympathetic employer and resign leaving the employer to incur all the costs of recruiting and training a new member of staff. As each new recruit can cost £4000 to £5000, this is a substantial expense. Given that it has become the policy of all political parties to support and improve the position of women in the workplace, it is not surprising that new concepts have arisen to avoid these largely unnecessary costs.

Employers with a more progressive outlook have adopted an integrated approach with a mixture of clear equal opportunities policies and practices, job re-design and family friendly benefits. Hascot Western Langley are one such company that has found that this approach pays off both in terms of costs and in terms of better employee relations.

Background

Hascot Western Langley (HWL) are a textile company with a wide range of fashion goods. Previously two separate companies, one in the UK and the other in Canada, a merger took place in 1993. Production of the high fashion garments is sourced from a variety of countries, including India and the Far East, but 25 per cent is still manufactured in Canada and the UK.

In Romford, Essex, HWL employ around 700 staff, 500 of whom are female. Fashion companies have always had a good share of female staff but in the last 30 years this has permeated throughout the business to reach the boardroom. By the early 1990s, the chairman and personnel director of the HWL were both women.

Both directors had realised that the company had invested considerable time and money into the training of women at all levels and were acutely conscious of the degree of specialised skills which young executives possessed. The fashion trade in the UK is not a large industry and skills in design and manufacture are in short supply, invariably subject to poaching as well as natural wastage. By the late 1980s, the turnover rate had become unacceptably and damagingly high and it was clear that both sources of loss had to be tackled in a distinct way. The other cultural aspect of the industry is the discipline of fashion deadlines where employees often have to 'go the extra mile' to complete the clothes collection in time for the fashion shows. It was felt that the company should make some effort to repay this degree of dedication by going an extra mile themselves.

Analysing the problem

The staff turnover, 90 per cent of which was women, was analysed through statistics and exit interview evidence. There were a number of employees who were clearly poached by other fashion companies through the offer of higher salaries and perks, but this was a minority. A much higher proportion left through pregnancy and did not return or left some months after returning, having found the conflict between the demands of jobs and young children too much. A smaller proportion left to look after a sick relative, usually an aged parent.

In the case of women returnees, little or no effort had been made at that time to ease their passage back to work beyond the statutory minimum. The situation had been viewed through the eyes of line managers who would prefer them to come back full-time with the minimum of delay or, in some cases, not come back at all. Special arrangements had been made in a few particular cases but these were local agreements which had begun to cause murmurings when requests to replicate them elsewhere were refused.

It was clear that a company initiative was needed to tackle the problem and the improvement in benefits was seen to be a most important step.

A new approach to benefits

Childcare

The most difficult problem faced by employees wanting to return was the need to provide satisfactory child care provision. Few had immediate recourse to an easy solution of full-time, willing grandparents or friendly, available neighbours. There were two possible solutions here – providing a company creche or providing childcare vouchers.

At first sight, the company creche on the premises appeared to be the best solution. The advantages were that the mother would not have to make an extra journey and would be able to drop in during the day, the quality of the childcare could be guaranteed and the size could be matched to the expected requirement. However, there were snags to consider.

1. Finding a suitable location on the premises would be costly in terms of converting to the required health and safety standards and it would need to be distant from circulatory areas due to the noise levels.
2. There would be the natural temptation for mothers to drop in too often to the creche during the day which would not be too pleasing to line management.

3. Other less sympathetic employees could resent the presence of children on the premises – some, apparently, came to work to get away from them.
4. There are few creche management companies in the vicinity so it was likely that the company would have to manage it itself. Was the company prepared to do this or should it stay simply in the fashion business (the 'stick to the knitting' argument). In the disaster scenario, when the creche staff happen to be all ill at the same time, this would stop all their mothers working.
5. If the creche always had vacancies, this would add to the costs. If the creche was always full and had a waiting list, this would also create problems such as when an employee wanted to return to work – would they have to wait? Could some vital members of staff jump the queue?
6. The operating costs per child per month was something in the order of £300 and a decision would have to be made as to the level of subsidy. To make it free would present a very high cost. However, the lower the subsidy, the more the employee would have to contribute and putting up the cost to employees each year could be seen in a negative light. After all, none of us really appreciate the subsidised canteen and we all complain when the prices go up!
7. The mother may not get on with the creche staff (and vice versa) leading to difficult internal wrangles and a genuine dilemma for the mother. Should she withdraw the child and lose the benefit, or soldier on with an unsatisfactory arrangement which could affect her work?

For all these reasons, the company decided instead to give a childcare allowance. The same arguments seem to have convinced many employers because there are still only an estimated 500 or so employers with creche facilities catering for only two per cent of the UK employees' children, despite £10 million worth of tax incentives. There were other advantages for the allowance:

(a) It gave freedom to the parent to spend it as they wished and to choose the best care for their children.
(b) There was a psychological advantage that employees would be pleased when the value of the subsidy was raised. If necessary, it could be pegged without causing discord. No money would have to be collected from an employee.
(c) There would be no time and effort spent in finding premises, running the creche or deciding on waiting lists.

There was, however, a somewhat unexpected cost. Childcare benefits would have to be offered to both male and female employees or it would clearly be a discriminatory act. Although only one parent can give birth, so maternity benefits can be limited to the mother, both parents have children so there is no possibility of imposing restrictions by sex. However, it is unlikely (not impossible, but unlikely) that male employees will bring their children into work for the creche so they would not take up that benefit. On the other hand, they will all gratefully receive a childcare allowance or voucher. In effect, the cost could almost double.

In 1996, HWL paid a monthly allowance of £66 for the first child and £44 for the second and subsequent children up to five years old. It is not paid to employees on temporary contracts. If they had provided a company creche, it would have been a tax-free benefit for the employee and tax-deductible for the employer. However, the provision of a voucher is seen by the Inland Revenue as a taxable benefit, though not a charge on National Insurance. There is therefore a saving to both parties compared to a salary payment.

Summer play scheme

Recognising that the long summer holiday can be a nightmare for employees with children at school, the company finances a free four-week play scheme at a local leisure centre for five to 11 year olds. It has 24 places and it is booked on a first come, first served basis. Needless to say, it has proved very popular.

Working hours flexibility

The company offers three choices of hours to make up the 35-hour week:

- from 8.30 am to 4.30 pm;
- from 9.00 am to 5.00 pm; and
- from 9.30 am to 5.30 pm.

These times are not contractual but employees are asked by their line manager to choose one and to keep to it so that the department has good coverage at the start and end of the day.

There are benefits for all parties in this arrangement unlike a flexitime system where experience has shown that it generally operates in favour of the employee and there are fewer companies now moving in that direction.

Maternity and paternity policy

HWL has recently extended maternity rights to 52 weeks of maternity leave, of which 20 weeks are on full pay. It gives a few extra weeks for employees to make up their minds on the thorny question of whether to return to work or not. When employees do return, they can work three days a week for the first eight weeks.

Paternity leave of five days on full pay is a right that employees can take up any time in the first year of their child being born.

Other policies

Free breast cancer screening is provided on a regular basis. Compassionate leave on full pay can be granted for up to five days for deaths and serious family illnesses. There is a pre-retirement scheme which allows a phased reduction of hours over the last six months at work. Opportunities for homeworking on either a part-time or full-time basis are carefully discussed with employees who wish to move in this direction, initially on a trial basis from both sides and with extensive evaluation.

Comparison with other organisations

The balance of the benefits and the clear messages which are sent to employees in terms of equal opportunity issues have ensured that HWL are in the top echelon of family-friendly benefit providers There are only two areas where other organisations have moved further down the line, namely career breaks and job share.

Career-break schemes were first introduced in the financial sector, notably Lloyds and Barclays banks. Employees have the right to return to work any time within a five-year period from the birth of their child, although the actual date of return has to be mutually agreed to fit a current vacancy. During the period of the break, it is agreed that the employee comes into work for a few weeks each year to keep up their skills and keep abreast of new developments. There is no continuous employment and each period of temporary employment is a new contract. This arrangement has the benefit for both the employee and the employer in that the employee does not feel pressured into returning to work while the baby is only a few months old and the stress that can bring into the workplace. The costs to the employer are fairly minimal and the only minor disadvantage could be that more employees may have longer breaks than under the statutory scheme so there may be a higher initial cost in training.

Job share is a more controversial issue. Despite a few high profile sharing job shares in the public sector (personnel director in a London borough, for example) most employers find it difficult to come to terms with job shares in all but the most routine positions. Difficulties with continuity and relations with the public are the usual stated reasons, all of which can be rebutted by anecdotal but limited experience. Business reasons for refusing to allow a returnee to job share have been generally accepted by tribunals in the few cases which have been brought and it remains a grey area.

Conclusion

Altogether, the cost to the company of these family-friendly benefits is around £130,000 per annum or around two per cent of payroll costs. This is equivalent to the recruitment and training costs of around 35 employees. It is difficult to estimate whether the policy has reduced staff turnover as the economic outlook has improved so much in the last three years and this has had an impact on the absenteeism and turnover rates. There are also not many companies with which to compare, although HWL's rate is slightly less than the industry average.

The main benefit is seen as the perception by employees that the organisation has made a real effort to help those who have young families and are trying to juggle work and family life. This has emerged from a number of employee attitude surveys taken recently. There was strong support for the concept that employees will respond to the additional effort made by the company 'going the extra mile' themselves in terms of working at home, having working breaks and being very focused on deadlines.

There is no doubt that the company considers these benefits to be in the interests of all parties and they are gradually being extended elsewhere. Advice and encouragement comes from the Equal Opportunities Commission and from an organisation called Parents at Work, who organise an annual competition for employers. The nine 1996 finalists ranged from the giant Abbey National Building Society down to the Royal Liverpool Philharmonic Society who have less than 100 employees. All have taken innovatory initiatives including on-line childcare information (Price Waterhouse), a 'Childcare Charter' (Heysham Power Station) and a 'Working Parents Support Group' (British Airways). The area of support here is getting bigger each year.

Student activities

1. Write a letter to the Chancellor of the Exchequer setting out the case for child care allowances to be free of tax and National Insurance for employees.
2. Compare the importance of the introduction of family friendly policies with other equal opportunity initiatives in the workplace.
3. Why has job sharing been so slow to develop in the workplace compared with other temporal flexibility measures, such as flexible hours, flexitime and part-time working?
4. Examine the demographic, political, economic and social forces that are encouraging an increasing proportion of women with young children back to the workforce.

Standard reading

	Armstrong and Murlis	*Armstrong*	*Milkovich and Newman*
Pages	376-377	325-339	471-472

References

1. Bevan, S. (1997) *Who Cares? Building a Business Case for Carer-Friendly Employment Practices*, Institute of Employment Studies, Brighton

Further reading

Crofts, P (1995) 'Report prompts call for national childcare policy', *People Management*, June 29

Employers for Childcare (1995) *Good Childcare, Good Business*, September

Evans, J (1995) 'Firms broaden family policies', *People Management*, March 9

Finch, S (1993) *Childcare for Personnel Managers*, Working for Childcare, London
IDS (1995) *Childcare*, Study No. 574, March
IDS (1989) *Job Sharing*, Study No. 440, August

Further information

Employers for Childcare, Cowley House, Little College Street, London, SW1P 3XS. Tel: 0171 976 7374

National Childminding Association, 8 Masons Hill, Bromley, Kent, BR2 9EY. Tel: 0181 464 6164.

Parents at Work, 77 Holloway Road, London N7 8JZ. Tel: 0171 700 5771.
(Working For Childcare is at the same address – tel. 0171 700 0281.)

Case Study 23

The Pensions Paradox

By Pam Stevens, Lecturer in HRM, Dearne Valley Business School

Introduction

The following case study involves two companies in the computer services and software industry who are both experiencing high labour turnover and considerable market pressures. They are not direct competitors as they provide computer software to differing market segments: one specialising in software for the retail and distribution sector while the other specialises in software for the public sector such as the National Health Service and local government. They have, however, recognised the potential benefits of merging their two companies to capitalise on each other's strengths and bring together their considerable computer expertise.

Merger talks have been going on for several weeks now and one of the 'sticking' points has been the respective occupational pension schemes. The following case study outlines the background to each of the companies and explains why the merger talks may be running into difficulties over this issue.

Retails Services Ltd (RSL)

RSL employs 93 people primarily at its headquarters in Leeds where it has been based since 1988. Its founder and current Managing Director, Joe Broadbent realised the potential for computer software to the retail industry, particularly following the boom in catalogue shops on the high street and more recently, home shopping channels on television. The company's computer software is designed to provide total retail business support, including product and price management, branch merchandising, purchasing, warehousing, EPOS (electronic point of sale) communication and management information.

Turnover has practically doubled every year since 1988 so that the current turnover is close to £8 million, although this is expected to stabilise over the next few years. The company introduced a money purchase pension scheme in 1989 when it realised that one of the key questions asked by both prospective and existing employees was about the benefits provided by the company. It was tricky enough at the time to attract people with the highly specialist computer skills necessary for the company's growth and the benefits package seemed to be critical in wooing people away from more established national computer companies.

Joe was also keen to contain costs and told his accountant to, 'Get me a pension package which will give us good value for money and won't cost the earth'. The accountant introduced the scheme in 1989 with the company paying three per cent and employees paying a minimum of three per cent and a maximum of 15 per cent within Inland Revenue rules. It was placed with a well known life assurance company. 30 employees joined at the time (about 60 per cent) Since then, many employees have left the company and others have joined.

Suidar Ltd

Suidar's history goes back further than RSL as it began as the computer department of a large manufacturing organisation and branched out as an independent company in 1978. It currently employs 112 staff and is based in Milton Keynes. The last 18 months have been worrying times for Suidar and their board of directors are very keen to progress the merger talks with RSL. It is jointly owned by three of the founders including the Managing Director, Alan Kent who is now 58.

Suidar's markets have practically collapsed with the continuing downward spending of its major customers in the public sector. Neither the new National Health Trusts nor county councils are spending much money and even if the company submits tenders for work, the orders take anything up to two years to come in. There was a brief flurry of activity when it seemed that the move to local-pay bargaining in the Health Trusts would generate some orders for Suidar's computerised job evaluation scheme but then it all just fizzled out. The company are desperate to expand their market and customer base.

It was the marketing manager, Sharon Rogers, who first realised the opportunities that a merger with RSL would bring. She had come up with the idea after buying a clock radio from the home shopping channel on TV. She was very impressed by the way her order was handled and processed: the radio was delivered the following day accompanied by a membership card with introductory offers. She realised that there had to be an efficient information system providing this high quality service and her enquiries led to RSL.

The problem was trying to find a way to interest their Managing Director in a deal with Suidar. She came up with the idea of geographical synergy where both organisations could gain substantial benefits. The merger talks had been progressing well with each company's respective lawyers ready to draw up the final merger agreements. At this point, Richard Hale, Suidar's Personnel Manager, showed to his directors the many differences in the two companies' pay and benefits structure. Differences in bonuses, holidays and hours of work could be sorted over time but the pension schemes were quite different and merging them would have considerable financial implications.

Table 5.1 *Pension scheme comparison*

	Suidar	RSL
Type of scheme	Defined benefits (60th's)	Money purchase
Employer contribution	13%	3%
Employee contribution	5%	3%-15%
Permanent health insurance	Yes	No
Death in service	3 x salary	1 x salary
Trustees	2 Directors	1 Director
Dependant's benefits	50% pension	none
Minimum age of joining	20	23
Service required before joining	None	1 year
Part-timers eligible	Yes	Yes
Index-linked on retirement	Yes	No

Table 5.1 sets out these differences which are at either end of the spectrum in pension terms.

The Suidar scheme is managed by an insurance company whose manager is a close friend and golfing partner of Alan Kent. Pensionable pay is defined as basic earnings plus overtime plus bonuses.

A recent review to check the performance of Suidar's pension fund investments has shown that the assets of the scheme represent 142 per cent of the benefits which have been accrued to members after allowing for expected future increases in earnings. The actuaries have indicated to the pension trustees that the scheme is at the point of being over-funded due to the high funding rates of both the employees and the employer and high performance of the investments, particularly equities. This, together with the fact that the average age of the employees is only 37 and that none of the current members of the scheme are due to retire for another eight years, means that the company has a substantial surplus in the scheme.

The merger looms

Reports of this surplus have leaked out to Suidar employees and this, coupled with the current merger rumours, is fuelling concerns amongst them that the value of their pension scheme is being used to make their company more attractive in the merger talks. Indeed, some are worried that the excess monies will be used to shore up the company's finances and there will be no money left in the pension fund when they retire.

As far as the directors of the two companies are concerned, the sticking point in the merger talks is not so much about clarifying the position of Suidar's surplus (see details of 1995 Pensions Act in Appendix 1) but rather the issue of which scheme to adopt and how to go about it.

From Joe Broadbent's viewpoint, he was appalled at the funding rate of 13 per cent and would prefer to stay with RSL's simple and cheap pension scheme. Given the age and the nature of staff turnover in the computer industry, he did not consider that a good pension scheme means very much to employees anyway as long as a basic scheme is on offer. His own scheme, needless to say, is a separate one.

For Alan Kent, however, the pension is important for his staff because so much of their work is for the public sector and staff are very aware of this one major benefit of working in the public sector. Take away Suidar's attractive pension scheme and a number of employees would be persuaded to leave Suidar for the numerous local authority and health service jobs on offer.

Employees of both organisations have started to get worried and reports of conversations overheard in the canteens and car parks are coming back to the respective boards.

At Suidar:

> Look, I haven't been working for this company since 1980 just to see the value of my pension disappear in a puff of smoke.

> It's all right for some – they won't lose out. I bet they have already worked out ways to milk the scheme for their own ends!

At RSL:

> I don't intend to work for this company for four years, let alone 40. What use is an expensive pension scheme for me?

> I've paid into this scheme for six years and when the companies are merged, it will be left as a small remnant of a pension eaten up by expenses.

As the uncertainty continued, employees eligible after one year's service held back from joining either scheme. Richard Hale was constantly approached by employees asking what was happening and he managed to persuade his board to arrange a meeting for staff to ask questions. In preparation, he worked out in his own mind the advantages and disadvantages of both types of scheme and summarised this for issue to the staff at the meeting. He had to be careful to make it neutral as he could not be sure which way the two companies would jump if they could finally agree terms.

Defined benefit scheme (sometimes called final salary scheme)

Advantages

For the employee, the benefits are predictable and give more security. In this case, benefits tend to be more generous and comprehensive. An employee could calculate what his or her pension will work out at with a given number of years of service, an estimate of the final salary and an assumption of, say, five per cent roll-up of their annual salary. For the employer, although the costs may be unpredictable, the existence of the scheme is a good selling point in recruitment terms.

Money purchase scheme (sometimes called defined contribution scheme)

Advantages

For the employer, the costs are predictable in that the contributions are defined. For the employee, the final benefits are unpredictable, depending on the way that the pension fund has performed during its life and the value of the annuity that can be purchased on the day of retirement. (This, itself, will depend on current interest rates and the performance of the investment market, principally the stock market). However, performance of money purchase schemes have, on occasions, out-performed defined benefit schemes.

Richard entered the meeting with a degree of apprehension. Answering questions from employees who were all in different career, financial and personal situations and making sure that none of the answers could be misconstrued as advice (which he was not authorised or licensed to give) would not be an easy business!

Student activities

1. Consider the two alternative pension schemes for two employees at Suidar.
   (a) Harry, aged 53 with 12 years' service, earning £35,000, married with two children at university and one other small pension scheme.
   (b) Jane, aged 28 with five years' service, earning £22,000 married with one child and no other scheme.
2. Carry out the same analysis for these employees if they worked for RSL with service of six years each.
3. From the viewpoint of both the managing directors, what would be an acceptable compromise on the pension issue, given that they both consider the merger to be vital to their interests? Is there a possibility of a hybrid scheme?
4. What does the future hold for occupational pension schemes? Will companies continue to offer them in 20 years' time?
5. What are the ethical implications of the 'whistle-blowing' sections of the 1995 Pensions Act?

Standard reading

	Armstrong and Murlis	*Armstrong*	*Milkovich and Newman*
Pages	386-400	340-352	459-464

Further reading

Hunt, P (1996) 'UK pensions in the 21st century – how will the next generation pay for its retirement?', *Winning entry in AXA Equity and Law essay competition*, available from the Success Foundation, Ludlow Avenue, Luton, Beds.

Industrial Relations Law Bulletin 532 (1995) *Pensions Act 1995*, November

IPD (1996) *Guide on Trusteeship and the Pensions Act 1995*, London

Oldfield, M (1994) *Understanding Occupational Pensions*, Tolley, Croydon

Reardon, A (1993) *Pensions Handbook*, Longman, London

Self, R (1993) 'Changing roles for company pensions', *People Management*, 5 October, pp 24-29

Appendix A – Pension Act 1995

Selected features

Most of the provisions of The Pension Act 1995 come into effect from April 6th, 1997 and their main purpose is to tighten up the administration of occupational pension schemes and improve their security.

Trustees

The Act provides that the members of a pension scheme may nominate and select trustees whose responsibilities will include supervising pension fund investments for the best interests of present and future beneficiaries. In schemes of less than 100 members, a minimum of one trustee may be nominated. Where there are more than 100 members, this rises to a minimum of two employee trustees. They will normally serve for a minimum of three and a maximum of six years and can only be removed from office by the employer with the agreement of the other trustees.

The member trustees will have the following rights:

- the right to paid time off work for performance of their trustee functions and for relevant training;
- the right not to suffer any detriment by reason of acting as a trustee; and
- the right not to be dismissed for performing the duties or functions of a trustee which would automatically be deemed to be unfair.

Regulatory body

A new body, the Occupational Pensions Regulatory Authority (OPRA) has been set up with the power to fine individuals and/or corporate bodies and to impose severe sanctions on trustees, employers and professional advisers who do not carry out their responsibilities in a proper manner.

Whistle-blowing

Pension scheme actuaries and auditors have a statutory responsibility to bring into the open evidence of material non-compliance with the Act. Employees and trustees are protected from being sued for breach of confidence if they report material non-compliance.

Case Study 24

SAYE – A Tool for Employee Involvement?

By Pam Stevens, Lecturer in HRM, Dearne Valley Business School

Introduction

One of the first acts of the Thatcher administration was to introduce Save-As-You-Earn (SAYE) share option schemes through the 1980 Finance Act. It was seen as a way that the employee could identify with and gain benefit from the success of the organisation over a long-term basis. It has become more tax efficient over the years and increasingly popular. Over 1000 schemes have been approved and it is estimated that options have been exercised by over three million employees since the start. It is not clear how many have retained the shares or have taken their profit and run. Nor has any research been done to see at what level it may motivate the shareholder.

Background

Gold Sports Shoes (GSS) specialises in manufacturing trainers, aerobic and running shoes, and football boots and is owned by Gold and Co PLC. Its Leicester factory employs 600 employees, down from a high of 1000 in 1990 caused by a series of redundancies. The latest round of redundancies led to a series of highly disruptive union ballots, although the workforce eventually voted against taking industrial action.

The cutbacks arose from the increasing competition from the Far East where the labour costs are far lower. GSS has held onto its market share of 11 per cent by a large increase in productivity through automation and by the parent company's 'buy British for quality' campaign.

Payment for operatives is still largely on a piece-work basis although this is starting to be eliminated by the arrival of automated equipment. There is a large research and development section due to the highly technical nature of the product. Trade union membership is around the 75 per cent mark and increasing after each redundancy exercise.

Company initiatives

Recent initiatives have included a number of quality drives which have not been altogether successful and niggling quality problems have continued to plague the customer services department. For example, eyelets on shoes have not been correctly punched or the sole of the shoe has the habit of becoming unglued. A more serious issue involved a claim by a British Olympic athlete that a trainer made specially for her led to an injury with her achilles tendon.

The company responded by inviting the athlete to become a 'consultant' to the company and they have agreed to sponsor her for the 'millennium' Olympics in Sydney. The sponsorship deal is seen as very important as it has become one of the spearheads of a revitalised marketing exercise called 'Going for Gold'. This has been combined with a company-wide strategy to boost market share and profitability over the next five years. It has been accompanied by a new company logo depicting an imitation of an Olympic gold medal and a new company mission statement:

> Gold Sports Shoes is committed to the Olympic spirit of helping British athletes to excel through the provision of sports shoes of the highest possible quality.

In addition, all products of the company are now stamped with a 'Go for Gold' slogan which is being supported by a national advertising campaign featuring the sponsored athlete performing on the track. The final part of the campaign was a linked employee initiative called 'The Gold Standard' where departments and employees agreed a set of quality, productivity, customer service and other targets, both individual and team-wise. Assessments were made from time to time and a set of cash and non-cash rewards were given to successful individuals and teams; nothing too large, £100 per employee, but it meant a successful way of reinforcing of the importance of the standards. This got underway towards the middle of 1992.

SAYE Share Option Scheme – 1990

The parent company, Gold & Co PLC, launched their first SAYE scheme in 1990. The intention was to allow employees to share in the growing success of the organisation and to acquire a stake in the business in which they worked. An employee entered into a contract to save for five years with a building society (SAYE) for an amount up to £100 a month. At the end of that five-year period, the employee had the option to purchase shares in the organisation at the option price announced in 1990. This price was 160p which was the share price current at that time, less a ten per cent discount.

As the shares had been at only 120p in 1988, it seemed to be a scheme which could not fail and a large take-up was expected. The parent company had left each of its subsidiaries to introduce the scheme in its own way. In most subsidiaries, a limited amount of marketing led to a take-up of about 20 per cent of employees, not a long way off the norm for a first scheme and the parent company was satisfied with the outcome.

In GSS, however, the take up was much less, at only eight per cent. This was chiefly because the announcement of the introduction of the scheme coincided with the announcement of the first tranche of redundancies and the company therefore made SAYE a very low-key affair. An announcement was printed in the company newsletter, giving brief details and asking employees who were interested to contact the Company Secretary, Karen Richmond for an application form. A few notices were pinned around the factories. Of the eight per cent who entered the scheme, most were employees in management or administrative positions who had directly contacted Karen to get all the required information.

Over the next twelve months, the company went through an extremely successful period with new launches and favourable fashion publicity. The share price climbed and reached a high of 481p in the latter part of 1992. A number of employees were surprised and a little angry that they had not been encouraged to enter the scheme, particularly when they learnt that management and administrative employees would seem to reap the benefit of an easy, tax-free gain.

SAYE Share Option Scheme – 1993

The second scheme was launched in the middle of 1993. It had been planned since the start of the year when the share price was 440p, but, by the time of the actual launch, the share price had slid to 180p and it had further to fall towards the end of the year to a low of 85p (see Table 5.2). The slide had chiefly been caused by the loss of some overseas markets and a product scandal in two other subsidiaries. The company had to issue a profit warning by the middle of the year.

The share option price was fixed at 162p again including the usual ten per cent discount. Not surprisingly, the take-up around the company was very low, only five per cent despite much wider publicity and a more careful communication programme. The chief executive of Gold & Co PLC made a video which was shown in the canteen at lunchtime and a brochure was issued

Table 5.2 *Share performance 1990–1996*

Year Ending 31 Dec	Share Price at Year End	Earnings (loss) per share	Dividend per share
1990	200p	1.25	0.5p
1991	212p	1.66	1.0
1992	481p	5.88	1.5
1993	85p	(5.94)	0.5
1994	160p	3.25	1.5
1995	245p	4.0	1.75
1996 (May)	280p	5.5	na

in the pay packets to all employees. Karen was sure that on this occasion nobody was left in the dark and she would not be attacked for keeping the scheme quiet.

SAYE Share Option Scheme 1996

The third SAYE scheme was to be launched towards the end of 1996. By this time, there had been a recovery of the share price to 280p. Karen sat down with John Davidson, the Human Resources Manager to decide on the strategy for the third launch.

They started by reviewing what had gone wrong with the first two launches and set them out as follows:

1. The timing of the 1990 scheme was unfortunate. The strategy behind the scheme was to encourage employees to share in the success and to motivate them to work harder so the company would prosper. This was unlikely to succeed when, at this point in time, jobs were disappearing so the signal was a very mixed one. As the scheme was new, employees did not want to give a long-term financial commitment.
2. The second major mistake was the casual and off-hand way in which the scheme was announced, it did not bounce with confidence.
3. The scheme appeared to be one that was restricted to management areas.
4. The launch of the 1993 scheme seemed to start very well with expenditure on a video by the managing director. As it turned out, this was probably a bad mistake – he hardly ever visited GSS, never went down to the shop floor and was a poor public speaker. The video had not been produced to a high enough standard.
5. The brochure was reasonable but it was clear that brochures rarely made people sit up and commit themselves.

When reviewing the scheme itself, it was certainly a success for those that joined the 1990 scheme. When they exercised their option in 1995, they paid 160p for their shares which were worth 245p immediately and had subsequently risen as high as 300p. Employees who had saved £50 a month for the five-year period (£3000 over the period plus a bonus of an additional 12 contributions making a total of £3600) would now be sitting on a paper profit of well over £2500.

For those who joined the second share option scheme, it looked even better in the sense that the share price had already increased by almost 90 per cent, despite the initial drop. With luck, it would continue upwards for another two years to give handsome profits for those willing to take the risk.

This was one of the key words – risk. SAYE schemes in industries with a volatile share price (such as computers and other high technological companies or any industry with an element of fashion) are asking employees who invest to share the risks. Investments may not be a sure-fire winner as in blue chip industries but they should still have a good chance of rewarding the risk-taker over the long-term period. The other point to remember is that employees are under no obligation to actually exercise their option if, say, the share price has collapsed. If they do exercise their option (and the vast majority do) they carry the same risks as any stock market investor except that they tend to have their eggs in one basket.

The second key word was long-term. It is not a 'fast buck', but a steady, long-term investment for those employees who would not want access to the money over the five years. That would usually not apply to the low-earning factory operative or those who lived from hand to mouth.

Taking these points into account, they sat down to work out the best way ahead.

Student activities

1. Set out what you see as the best package to launch the 1996 scheme and justify your decisions.
2. Is there any way that the scheme can be integrated with the Gold Standard campaign? Is there any connection?
3. Write a question and answer booklet for staff which would pre-empt the likely questions.
4. One of the applications for the scheme is from an employee who you know has very limited resources and is not known for taking sensible financial decisions. They want to save £80 a month. As head of personnel, do you see any ethical reason for intervening here?

Standard reading

	Armstrong and Murlis	*Armstrong*	*Milkovich and Newman*
Pages	309-323	318	–

Further reading

IDS (1995) *Profit Sharing and Share Options*, Study No. 583, August

IRS (1995) 'A share in the firm', *Employment Review*, No. 589, August, pp 12-16,

Jackson, C and Nicholl, V (1995) 'UK share option schemes and deferred share arrangements – either or both?', *Benefits and Compensation International*, April, pp 16-21

Kent, S (1996) 'ESOP Fables', *Personnel Today*, January 30th, pp 23-26

Klein, K (1987) 'Employee stock ownership and employee attitudes: a test of three models', *Journal of Applied Psychology*, Vol. 72, No. 2, pp 319-322

Rosen, C and Young, K (1991) *Understanding employee ownership*, ILR Press, Ithica, New York

PART 6
MISCELLANEOUS CASES

Introduction

There is no straightforward link for the five cases in this final group so the subjects are dealt with individually. That is not to say they are isolated or unique, they all have links with the other sections and a significant place in the general reward framework.

Boardroom pay

Boardroom pay is perhaps the most controversial of all pay subjects and one which is constantly dissected in all sectors of the press. Should top executives be paid so much? Was it right for Michael Eisner, Chief Executive of the Disney Corporation, to be awarded stock options valued at $300 million on top of his $750,000 salary in 1993? (O'Byrne[1]). Should George Simpson be able to earn up to £10 million over his first five years as Managing Director of GEC? (Cave[2]). Should Sam Chisholm, CEO of BSkyB , have received over £3.5 million in pay and benefits between 1995 and 1996?

The subject has been rarely out of the headlines. When it was disclosed, in 1916, that Lord Northcliffe, the founder of the *Daily Mail* and later owner of *The Times*, was receiving an annual income of over £1 million from his newspapers, (probably worth around £25 million or more today) there was considerable press coverage in his rival papers. Questions were asked in Parliament as to why, in the middle of a war, with its additional privations for the average citizens, one person should seem to be paid so excessively.

Views vary in different quarters. It is not just the left that rail against the mysteries of top pay. A large institutional investor sold shares in Matthew Clark, the UK cider maker, in protest at the payment of £431,000, including tax liability, to a director for moving house 105 miles (Lewis and Wood[3]).

Cultural differences appear in this arena when the average ratio of chief executive's pay to lowest operator's is examined. In America it is 35:1, but it is only 15:1 in Japan and goes down to 3:1 in Norway (Kalleberg and Lincoln[4]; Littlechild[5]).

Justification for high payments to directors can take the following forms:

- the market for top executives is world-wide so British companies have to pay comparative rates or they will lose the best people to the Americans, the Japanese or the Swiss;
- a high proportion of pay is in the form of performance bonuses which are only paid if the company does well. It is not unknown for directors to take pay cuts when their companies suffer (P&O in 1996, or Proctor and Gamble in 1994). This is a win-win situation, where shareholders are pleased as earnings per share rise and the organisation can afford to meet the bill for the bonuses;
- the pay of Board members is a very small part of total employee costs, but the decisions directors take can be absolutely crucial to the organisation; and
- giving very high packages to board members is an incentive to young executives to stay with the organisation. Too often in the 1960s and 1970s, talented young executives left to become rich by starting (and eventually selling) their own business, impoverishing the ranks of the large UK companies that can truly create a country's wealth.

Public disquiet has been directed of late to pay in privatised industries, where the level of risk and competition is much lower than in conventional private sector operations, yet pay levels have climbed steeply since privatisation. Executive pay therefore became included in the remit of the Cadbury Committee on Corporate Governance and, following slow progress here, to the Greenbury Committee on director's remuneration.

Case Study 25 deals with the Board remuneration at RTZ PLC, a company that has met all the requirements of the Greenbury Committee and whose scheme links with team-based pay as the measurements of performance are collective. It describes the issues which have led to recent changes and the reporting openness which is associated with the scheme.

City pay

Staying in the City, Case Study 29 provides an example of the alien world of market traders whose esoteric skills produce huge rewards for most and the occasional spell in a Singapore reformatory for the small minority. This is truly a global 24-hour market place with a high level of risk, entered at one's peril. Few studies have been made of reward strategies here. The links are very close to individual performance pay as the traders work alongside the two market-driving forces, greed and fear.

Other cases

Case Study 26, which looks at Vauxhall's employee recognition scheme, has links with most other sections. *Individuals* and *teams* can be rewarded for the efforts they have made in putting up a proposal. There are a number of cash and non-cash *benefits* on offer and the scheme has become embedded into the ethos and *structure* of the pay system. It was not established primarily as a vehicle for pay, rather as one of employee involvement and productivity improvement, but it is pay which *reinforces* the behavioural changes, giving an incentive for employees to look at positive advances in methods of operation and then rewarding them subsequently for ensuring that the new idea actually gets implemented properly and is made to work.

The case on equal pay, Case Study 27, looks at the intricacies of what, on the surface, looked like a comparatively straightforward case but was transformed into a complex, time-consuming and legalistic action. Tribunals were never supposed to work in this way and the procedures are due for an overall review, particularly in respect of the role of the independent expert and their report.

Statistics throw an interesting light on equal pay claims. In 1995, there were 1766 such claims, of which 637 were for work of equal value arising from employees in 31 companies. In only 11 cases did the tribunal case go far enough for independent experts to be appointed. The complexity of the proceedings means that the applicant needs to have legal support from either the unions or the Equal Opportunities Commission (EOC) to be able to proceed. Employers equally dislike the proceedings and will either try to settle the case quietly or fight it fiercely if the loss could prove expensive or cause havoc to their pay structure.

Case Study 28, by contrast, looks at the introduction of a performance management system in Malaysia, which was used to underpin changes in a reward system. It provides an insight into the approach made in a utility company in the East to the concept of measuring performance and the need to gently alter the established culture to ensure new approaches are successfully put into place.

References

1. O'Byrne, S (1994) 'What pay for performance looks like: the case of Michael Eisner', *Journal of Applied Corporate Finance*, October, pp 135-6
2. Cave, A (1996) 'Anger over GEC's £10 million package for Simpson', *Daily Telegraph*, 28 August
3. Lewis, W and Wood, L (1996) 'Institution sells cider shares over director's allowance', *Financial Times*, 13 August
4. Kalleberg, A and Lincoln, J (1992) 'The structure of earnings inequality in the United States and Japan', *American Journal of Sociology*, Vol. 94, supplement S121-S153
5. Littlechild, D (1996) 'Pay equity holds firm in Norway', *People Management*, June 13, 1996

Further reading

Brewster, C and Tyson, S (eds) (1991) *International Comparisons in Human Resource Management*, Pitman Publishing, London

Conyon, M (1995) 'Directors' pay in the privatised utilities', *British Journal of Industrial Relations*, Vol. 33, pp. 159-72

Gregg, P *et al* (1993) 'The Disappearing Relationship between Directors' Pay and Corporate Performance', *British Journal of Industrial Relations*, Vol. 31, pp. 1-10

Hastings, S (1989) *Identifying Discrimination in Job Evaluation Schemes*, Trade Union Research Unit Note No.108, Oxford

Incomes Data Services (1994) *Equal Pay – Employment Law Handbook*, Series 2, No. 3

Rubery, J (1992) *The Economics of Equal Value*, Equal Opportunities Commission, London

Wilkinson, B and Leggatt, C (1985) 'Human and Industrial Relations in Singapore: the Management of Compliance', *Euro-Asian Business Review*, Vol. 3, pp. 9-15

Williams, A and Crabb, S (1995) 'Quelling the storm over top salaries', *People Management*, 9 March, pp. 22-5

Case Study 25

Executive Pay at RTZ PLC

Introduction

RTZ PLC is the largest mining company in the world with active interests in North and South America, Europe and a dozen or more countries in Asia, Australasia and Africa. In 1995, the process of dual listing took place with CRA Ltd, another large mining company based in Australia and the combined group turnover exceeded £5 billion in that year. There are a total of 51,000 employees, including 14,000 in Australasia, 9000 in Africa and 8000 in North America. The company has been among the top 20 companies by value listed on the Stock Exchange for over 25 years and is currently valued at over £10 billion.

During the 1970s and 80s, the company diversified laterally, notably into cement, and downstream, into a wide range of manufacturing activities associated with metals, timber and the home improvement market. This policy was reversed in the late 1980s and the 1990s with the disposal of the entire cement and manufacturing interests and the purchase of BP's mining interests.

Existing executive remuneration

Up to the early 1990s, the company had a conventional executive pay scheme comprised of base salaries, annual bonuses and share options. As with many companies of its size, it aimed to pay around the upper quartile in terms of base salary and total remuneration. Directors had three-year rolling contracts of employment.

1. Annual bonuses – the Nomination and Compensation Committee (NCC), comprised of non-executive directors, determined the annual cash bonus which consisted of two elements. The first related to improvements in RTZ's earnings per share; the second related to the individual's personal performance. The combined value had a maximum of 40 per cent of the base salary.
2. Share options – directors were issued with options to a value of four times salary and these were 'topped-up' when exercised or when there was a significant salary increase.

Prompting the change

There were a number of sources for a reconsideration of executive pay which began in 1993 and continued during 1994:

- the major shareholdings in all FTSE companies are held by pension funds and life assurance companies. Both the National Association of Pension Funds (NAPF) and the Life Offices Association (LOA) have begun to take a much closer interest in good corporate governance and have indicated their preference for longer-term executive reward based on performance;
- the company wanted to link rewards for directors and senior executives more closely with rewards to shareholders. In particular, they wanted to eliminate as much as possible the judgmental elements, especially in the annual bonus;
- the movement to accentuating corporate, rather than individual awards was considered important to reinforce the concept that the Board acted collectively in decision taking;
- increasingly, share options were found to be somewhat capricious in reward terms. The gains were often related to the timing of the grant rather than individual or corporate achievement. The policy of 'topping-up' encouraged early exercise of options and these all too easily became 'bed and breakfast' operations with share options exercised and then sold immediately. Long-term shareholdings were not specifically encouraged; and
- although of somewhat minor significance, the granting of options in this way diluted the existing shareholdings.

The revised scheme

The objectives of the new proposals were governed by four principles:

- rewards were to be linked to shareholders' wealth appreciation and to superior performance against peer competitors;
- subjectivity was to be eliminated by bench marking against published factual statistics independently calculated;
- executive share ownership was to be developed by mandating that the larger proportion of bonus earned was paid in shares (purchased in the market and therefore not diluted) to be retained for extensive periods; and
- the schemes should take into account the long-term and cyclical nature of the mining industry.

When the new scheme was introduced, the executive directors' cash bonus scheme was terminated and it was decided that no further options would be awarded under the 1985 Executive Share Options scheme. Another substantial change was that directors' contracts of employment were reduced to two years without compensation.

Two new plans were introduced, the Mining Plan and the FTSE Plan.

The Mining Plan

This scheme compares RTZ's total shareholder return with 15 international comparator mining companies over a four-year performance period. The comparator companies are mostly North American and South African companies, such as Anglo-American, Alcan and BHP. The Total Shareholder Return (TSR) for each company is evaluated on the basis of the cash flows assuming the purchase of the share at the beginning of the period, the sale of the share at the end of the period and receipt of dividends during the period. Currency movements are neutralised in this calculation.

For main board directors, bonuses arising from the plan are expressed as a percentage of each director's salary, depending on the performance against the comparator group as follows:

Upper quartile	60%
Second quartile	40%
Third quartile	20%
Lower quartile	0%

Around 180 other employees take part in the scheme and, for them, the target percentages are lower.

For directors and senior executives, half of the after tax value of the bonus is given in cash and the other half is invested in RTZ shares which have to be retained for a further three years. During this period, recipients get dividends but may not sell or transfer the shares. For other executives, the payment is made in cash.

Example of the operation of the Mining Plan

Performance of TSR by RTZ

Share value at January 1st, Year 1	800p
Share value at December 31st, Year 4	1100p
Increase in value	300p
Dividends during period	200p
TSR	500p

This represents a gross return of 62.5 per cent over four years, equivalent to around 13 per cent per annum.

Comparator companies

Company 1	25%	Company 6	14%	Company 11	9%
Company 2	20%	Company 7	12%	Company 12	6%
Company 3	19%	Company 8	12%	Company 13	4%
Company 4	17%	Company 9	11%	Company 14	1%
Company 5	16%	Company 10	10%	Company 15	–2%

With a TSR of 13 per cent, RTZ would come sixth in this group; this would place it in the second quartile, entitling a bonus of 40 per cent.

Let the director's basic salary be £150,000. The bonus would then be £60,000 (40 per cent) of which a half (£30,000) would be cash and the remaining half would be in the form of shares. The payments would be pro rata-ed for executives and professional grades.

This is a simplified example which does not take into account the timing of the dividend or complications such as script issues.

The FTSE Plan

This Plan replaced the share option scheme. At the beginning of each performance period, a notional 'bench mark' number of RTZ ordinary shares is ascribed to each director. This number equates to the largest number of shares which can be bought using a specified percentage of the director's basic salary as at the previous December 31st. The percentage of salary is fixed by the NCC and they have currently set the level at 100 per cent for main board directors with appropriately lower levels for other senior staff.

The amount they actually get ascribed to them depends on the performance of RTZ shares compared to the top 48 companies in the FTSE index over a four-year period (using similar comparisons to those used in the Mining Plan). The allocation is then:

Performance of RTZ shares	%-age vested
In top quartile	All 100%
In second quartile	66.7%
In third quartile	33.3%
In bottom quartile	zero%

Example of operation of FTSE Plan

A director is paid £150,000 pa at the beginning of a period and the share price is 750p. The director would be notionally ascribed 20,000 shares (100 per cent). At the end of the period, RTZ's share performance is ranked in the 19th place. Thus, 66.66 per cent of the notional shares would be vested, ie 13,333. These shares have to be kept for a further two years.

In both the Mining Plan and the FTSE Plan, the shares are bought in the market place by the Employee Share Ownership Trust (ESOT) on behalf of the participants which prevents dilution. During the fixed retention period, the executives receive dividends but may neither sell or transfer the shares, for example, into a PEP.

Scheme evaluation

It is too early to say how successful the scheme is as it is based on long-term performance. The shareholders' meeting passed the proposals with none of the local difficulties faced by boards such as Barclays Bank where there was a substantial minority shareholders vote from institutions against the new executive remuneration scheme.

The scheme meets all the requirements of the Greenbury Committee, particularly those related to long-term remuneration and the recommendation that directors should be encouraged to hold their shares for a period after vesting and that their contracts should not exceed two years.

Results announced for the year ending December 1996 showed a second quartile performance in both plans.

Student activity

1. Compare the executive remuneration detailed in the latest annual reports for four large PLCs chosen at random. The comparison should include:
   - the level of total board salaries and their constituent parts (basic, bonus, benefits, share options and pensions);
   - how the bonus arrangements are set out, including the performance measures used and the maximum that can be earned;
   - the level of pension contributions by the company;
   - the length of service agreements and whether any director has received compensation for loss of office over the past year; and
   - how the directors' remuneration scheme matches the recommendations of the Greenbury Committee.
2. Examine the latest copy of the RTZ annual accounts. Consider the performance of the organisation and the payments to directors under the two bonus schemes and comment on the outcomes to date.
3. Consider if there is any way these performance measures and payments can be transferred to the public sector.

Standard reading

	Armstrong and Murlis	*Armstrong*	*Milkovich and Newman*
Pages	418-426	353-363	584-593

Further reading

Arthur Andersen (1996) ***Boardroom Pay in UK Quoted Companies***, London

Conoley, M (1995) 'Executive share options: a new dilemma for HR', ***People Management***, August 10

Hewitt Associates (1995) 'Corporate governance and executive remuneration, ***Executive Compensation***, Vol.1, March

Institute of Directors (1992) ***The Remuneration of Executive Directors***, The Director Publications Ltd, London

IRS (1995) 'Greenbury: a brake on boardroom pay?', ***Pay and Benefits***, August

Williams, A (1994) ***The Truth About Executive Pay***, Kogan Page, London

Wright, V (1993) 'Directors' remuneration', ***Human Resource Management and Strategy***, Croner Publications, London

Case Study 26

Paying for Innovation – The Vauxhall Experience

Introduction

In recent years, suggestion schemes have had a bad press in some quarters. They have had an undervalued and old-fashioned feel about them, often reflected in the image of the 'suggestions box' with paint peeling off, that sits in the corner of the works canteen in the 1950s Ealing comedies.

They originated as a genuine attempt to harness the enthusiasm and experience of the workforce to produce new ideas in the workplace and to reward those ideas that proved successful. As ideas increased in number, it became necessary to formalise the scheme of rewards. What had originated as a quick 'thank you' to a bright young production recruit by the works manager on his own initiative in the 1950s, became part of personnel systems in the 1960s to ensure parity, fairness and consistency across the shop floor.

For some of the schemes, the formalisation produced dysfunctional results. In the least successful schemes, decisions could no longer be taken instantly – they had to be first considered by a suggestions committee when it next met, then costed, evaluated and finally agreed by a director some months later. Even then, payments could only be made if the budget allowed. This was another instance of the many cases of dis-empowerment of supervisors and managers, along with recruitment, selection, quality and safety. The dead hand of central control usually meant a listless or even lifeless scheme, where the occasional attempt at resuscitation failed after a brief spell of activity. In any case, the scheme was isolated, playing no part in the general thrust of company policy, and was treated as such by management.

Unions co-operated in this viewpoint, regarding all ideas on improvements to be the role of management and not something that employees should bother themselves about, particularly as only the odd individual would benefit – that is, unless the suggestion was about improving the terms and conditions of employees, which was their job – for which they did not expect payment!

General Motors suggestion scheme

Not all schemes proved unsuccessful. By the late 1980s, the General Motors' (GM) (Vauxhall's parent company) scheme had been running for 35 or more years in their plants throughout the world producing some substantial results.

It was a scheme designed at GM headquarters to operate in the same way at each of the subsidiaries throughout the world. It had a 48-page scheme manual detailing all possible eventualities and establishing a clear pattern on such matters as which employees were eligible to make suggestions and which types of ideas could be rewarded. For example, ideas did not count in areas such as product styling for appearance only, or corporate or divisional policy on such matters as labour contracts.

Vauxhall had run this scheme diligently but, by the mid-1980s, it had begun to run out of steam and only had a limited impact. In its later years, the sums paid out rarely exceeded a few thousand pounds in a workforce which averaged more than 11,000.

Lean manufacturing

What changed this situation was the dramatic organisational developments arising out of the major threat to car manufacturing in the West. The success of Japanese car companies in the late 1970s and early 1980s prompted all American companies to totally review their way of working from first principles. So-called Fordism, the system of tight centralised control, where production innovations originated from and were tested by design and engineering departments and were costed to the last cent before being implemented through precise instructions to production operatives, was challenged by a succession of senior executives who went to Japan and discovered that involvement and participation could work, if it was associated with the right culture.

For example, in comparing the US and Japanese suggestion schemes, statistics in 1988 showed that the average Japanese worker produced over 100 times as many suggestions as the American employee and an adoption rate at 82 per cent was four times as great. The consequent savings were therefore very much higher.

A series of business initiatives called Lean Manufacturing and World Class Systems came on stream in the period 1984 to 1991 throughout GM which went a long way to meet successfully the competition from the Far East. Just-in-time materials supply, teamworking and empowerment were important pieces of the jigsaw. The Employee Recognition Scheme was one of the later introductions but has proved an extremely important factor in reinforcing the new style of business operations and the beliefs and values that underpin this process.

Set out in the Vauxhall magazine *Quality Network* in 1992, the importance of the need for the organisation to constantly change and innovate was emphasised:

- seek success through bold action and risk-taking, not security through the *status quo*;
- encourage personal initiative and new ideas;
- strive for continuous improvement in everything we do;
- eliminate every form of waste; and

- take pride in our organisation and be a contemporary company.

Vauxhall employee recognition scheme

To overcome some of the drawbacks of the old style suggestion scheme, important new objectives were set out for the new scheme:

- recognition and reinforcement of behaviour rather than focusing on cost savings;
- high rates of participation with a target of one idea per employee per annum of which 75 per cent would be implemented;
- large numbers of small improvements to the employees' own work areas;
- quick recognition and implementation, 70 per cent complete in one month;
- total involvement and commitment to the improvement process;
- provide frequent and regular opportunities for communication and positive recognition through the immediate supervisor whose role was to be enhanced;
- encourage people to work together to identify and solve problems and to communicate ideas; and
- guarantee that no compulsory redundancies would result from ideas put forward.

Pilot scheme

The new scheme was piloted in the paint shop at both Luton and Ellesmere Port and in the Luton head office in March 1991. One of the advantages of the paint shop was that the engineering staff were available on that site to evaluate the ideas beyond the supervisor's level so that the response time was very short. It was an immediate success at Luton. 52 per cent of employees participated in the six months' pilot compared to only ten per cent who participated in the existing suggestion scheme over the previous 12 months. On an annualised basis, six times as much savings were made. The success of the pilot led to the scheme being operational throughout Vauxhall Motors for its 10,000 employees by the end of 1992.

Operational aspects

The success of the scheme depended upon the careful specification of roles.

The supervisor

Encouraging and developing ideas became a key part of a supervisor's job. They encouraged employees to come up with ideas, helped them to complete the Improvement Idea Form (see Figure 6.1), focused participation on priority areas under their control, carried out the initial evaluation, discussed the ideas with the engineering or planning departments where this was

0058287

EMPLOYEE RECOGNITION SCHEME

Employee Recognition Scheme: Improvement Idea Form

(PLEASE PRINT FIRMLY) DO YOU AGREE TO PUBLICITY? YES/NO

NAME .... **FOLIO No.** .... **DIVISION No.** ....

(Please use the space provided on the reverse of this sheet for entering the names of other group members)

PART Nos.	EQUIPMENT No.	MODEL
	OPERATION No.	LOCATION eg column

Referred To

NAME	DATE

ALL RELEVANT INFORMATION MUST BE ENTERED IN THESE BOXES

YOU ARE REQUESTED TO USE SKETCHES, DRAWINGS AND ALL RELEVANT PART NUMBERS TO EXPLAIN YOUR IDEA

1 Briefly describe the **PRESENT METHOD**

2 What is **YOUR IDEA FOR IMPROVEMENT?**

3 My idea affects: ( ) Labour ( ) Quality ( ) Material ( ) Energy ( ) Other

4 **INITIAL (prior to any referral) AND FINAL EVALUATION REPLY BY SUPERVISOR** (*attach all supporting documentation.*)

Signature ______________________ **Date submitted** ____________
(Lead Author)

Received by (Signature) ____________ Print Name ____________ **Folio** ________ **Div No.** ________
(Supervisor)

This idea is submitted under the terms and conditions of the Vauxhall Employee Recognition Scheme as set out on the reverse of the Acknowledgement copy. I understand and agree that General Motors Corporation and its associated and subsidiary companies and assignees shall have the right to make full use of this idea. I understand and agree that the signatures above acknowledge receipt of this form and not acceptance of the idea for implementation.

Figure 6.1 *Improvement Idea Form*

necessary and assisted the idea to trial and final implementation. It was emphasised that, where possible, the employee making the idea would play a major part in its implementation. This, after all, would ensure that it was approached with enthusiasm, care and persistence. They also completed the Final Evaluation Reply on each ideas form.

More importantly, they had the authority to make an immediate award of up to £20 if the idea was one that they were capable of implementing in their area and considered that it would work and was of value. They could also give a spot prize of £5 if the idea was one of serious intent but could not be immediately implemented. Should the idea cover areas outside of their control or have more substantial benefits, then the idea would be handed over to the co-ordinator.

The co-ordinator

Responsible for departments or production units, the co-ordinator took the idea and ensured that it was evaluated speedily by the appropriate person or group. For example, an idea on materials delivery would need to be evaluated by the purchasing and logistics department. The results were fed back quickly to the idea generator and his supervisor and the co-ordinator had the authority to make awards up to £99. The co-ordinator was trained to look for hidden benefits as well as considering hidden costs.

The unit manager

As well as setting targets for the number and quality of ideas in his unit, the manager evaluates and implements the larger value ideas in his area and can make awards up to £5000.

The director

In rare cases, the director deals with wide-ranging ideas and can make awards up to the maximum figure of £12,000.

It was recognised that the scheme would fail if substantial management support was not available. This would come in the following forms:

- commitment by top management;
- training for supervision in their new role;
- education on how to find new ideas, how to solve problems, how to write good proposals and how to ensure they are implemented properly; and
- appoint recognition officers whose role is to promote the scheme at each plant, facilitate inter-plant referrals and participate in company-wide scheme developments.

Nuts and bolts

Inevitably, there continue to be some detailed rules. These are necessary to create parameters by which ideas and employees are eligible and how the sums of money awarded are calculated.

Eligibility

Employees up to the level of junior management can submit ideas as long as:

- it is not part of their job's responsibilities to suggest the improvement; and
- the idea represents a contribution beyond the performance normally expected of such employees.

All ideas are considered but there are some constraints. The following ideas are normally excluded which relate to:

- routine maintenance or repairs;
- minor errors in drawings or instructions;
- matters of GM policy;
- matters covered by contracts with others;
- advertising, PR matters and product appearance; and
- employee discounts, employee relations and social club matters.

All other ideas, including health and safety ideas, are encouraged although there are special rules for ideas emerging from normally constituted committees, such as the health and safety committee and the newly created Continuous Improvement Process Groups.

Calculation of award

Awards are based on 20 per cent of the total net savings during the 12-month period following implementation of the idea. There are detailed processes to establish the net savings, including calculating labour, material, energy and capital costs and even for better use of floor area and saving on conveyor down time.

Some ideas come forward which cannot be implemented. In these cases, a £5 'interest' payment is made which, in effect, says 'thank you – but sorry'. Where the benefits cannot be quantified financially, perhaps because they lead to improvements in the environment, quality or health and safety, then there is a degree of flexibility over the amount paid. The maximum for ideas that result in improvements, but not necessarily in savings, is £6000. An example here would be a patentable idea in the field of environment improvement or safety with enormous benefits which could be used throughout the organisation.

All awards up to £5000 are made free of tax (under an Inland Revenue extra-statutory concession A57 made in 1986) and all awards over £20 involve a presentation of an award certificate by the supervisor. Special recognition is given to employees who participate frequently or whose ideas are ineligible – they can receive merchandise and invitations to events or organised outings.

Successful ideas

During 1995, nearly 6000 ideas had been submitted and this had risen to over 7000 by mid-1996 on an annualised basis. Roughly 40 per cent of the ideas were accepted with a payout exceeding £500,000 per annum, an average of £71 per idea. The target of one idea per employee per year had been more than exceeded in many areas with the average payment in the course of a year climbing towards £55 per employee.

A selection of successful ideas include:

- connecting a bank of lights to the lighting control system to prevent them burning 24 hours a day. The cost was £46 to carry out the improvement, the saving was estimated at £1700 and the electrician who made the suggestion received £347;
- re-designing the label on dealer returns so the packaging can be reused. The cost was £50, the saving £4000 and the payment to the operative was £950;
- using timber off-cuts to make pallet posts. Costs of implementation was £70, the saving £1440 and the payment to the maintenance man £288;
- a drip tray was fitted to the trolleys carrying underbodies to prevent oil dripping onto the floor. £400 was awarded for this idea; and
- reducing the prepaint cycle on all paint machines thus leaving the dump line closed, minimising the excess paint being deposited to the coagulation plant. This saved raw materials and helped the environment. The cost was minimal, the saving £10,900 and the payment to the painter was £2185.

Increasingly, ideas are being put forward by groups of employees, sometimes whole teams. For example:

- ten employees shared nearly £7000 for their idea which prolonged the use of gloves and allowed many to be re-cycled;
- the trim shop maintenance team modified the software for the transfer of vehicles between conveyors which reduced the number of conveyor stops on final assembly. This cost very little, saved the company £15,000 and the team received £3000;
- a group of 40 plant team operators helped revise the layout and operation of general assembly. This saved over £15,000 in labour and materials producing a shared benefit of £3500 between the 40 employees; and
- 25 assembly operatives put forward a proposal to control their own quality more closely, thus reducing the need for an inspector. After a successful trial, a group payment of £5000 was made arising from the company saving of over £25,000.

Generating interest in the scheme

Campaigns

It was realised from the start that the scheme would need regeneration from time to time. To stimulate and maintain employees' interest, a series of campaigns was begun in 1994 which focused the ideas on particular areas and gave additional rewards.

The 1994 campaign was centred on health and safety ideas and each employee submitting an idea was awarded a free quality pen in addition to the normal cash awards. They also had their names entered in a prize draw at the end of the campaign where the prizes were 100 items of luggage. Over 700 ideas came forward in two months, double the normal number at that time.

In 1995, the emphasis switched to quality. This was broadly interpreted both in terms of production output and in quality of service to both internal and external customers. Here, the target was 1000 ideas accepted for implementation at which time the campaign would stop. Each idea would give the originator a wrist watch plus the opportunity for employees whose ideas were implemented to win a £500 holiday voucher and 100 Forest Green jackets. This campaign generated over 2000 ideas.

Euro '96 gave the company the opportunity to encourage football fans. All implemented ideas and their savings over the period January to May were recorded separately and the top ten per cent of originators and their supervisors at each location were put in separate draws. The prizes were 50 pairs of tickets for the Euro '96 matches with a top prize of tickets for the final as part of a luxury weekend in London.

The theme for the second half of 1996 was environmental ideas which tied in with the award to Vauxhall of BS7750 and emphasised the growing importance of environmental issues for the motor industry. Here the prizes would be an energy efficient light bulb for the first 400 ideas plus a number of family trips.

Training

From its implementation, training has played a key part at all levels. All supervisors and their teams have had short sessions on the mechanics of idea generation and an appreciation of the Japanese 'Kaizen' principle. Working together, they were coached in preparing a mock proposal and costing the benefits. Volunteers were invited to take part in Continuous Improvement Process teams who would meet to brainstorm ideas in their areas using techniques utilised in successful quality circle operations.

Co-ordinators received training so they had a thorough understanding of their role, not just in the mechanics and bureaucracy of the scheme but the dynamics of encouraging and supporting idea generation and implementation. For managers, the training was built into the complete programme of 'Lean Production' to harness ideas on improving productivity, quality and cost saving from all sources in their area.

Benefits to Vauxhalls

The success of the employee recognition scheme can be measured in three ways. Firstly, by the costs that have been saved. In the four years of operations, this has been estimated at around £6 million, of which around £1.5 million has been paid out in awards to employees. This figure for savings may be much higher as the recorded saving is only over the first 12 months of implementation and many ideas have a continuing benefit.

Secondly, by the number of employees participating and the total of ideas. In rough terms, around two-thirds of employees have put in one or more ideas since the scheme's inception and the average per annum is now approaching one idea per employee. This far exceeds the participation rate under the suggestion scheme and is in line with the original targets. It has, however, still some way to go before reaching the Japanese level of 30 or more ideas per employee per year.

Thirdly, in the reinforcement of the new culture and working systems of the organisation. For Vauxhall to survive as a viable manufacturing unit, the Lean Manufacturing Concept had to succeed. Higher productivity and better quality had to be achieved with a much reduced labour force and this would only work if there was a substantial degree of employee co-operation and support. The Employee Recognition Scheme was one of the major mechanisms that persuaded employees to take that extra step. The support was through:

1. Empowerment – the scheme was perceived as a de-centralising process by pushing responsibility for decisions on implementing improvements down the line to supervisors and, ultimately, the actual working teams. Employees gradually realised that they could change the way they worked, they could help to remove obstacles to smooth working and they could get seriously involved in the decisions that affected their normal day-to-day working. By being given responsibility for implementation, employees put far more effort into making new ideas work. 20 years of by-passing management and supervision and reducing the importance of their roles have been reversed.
2. Team-working – the growing encouragement for ideas to be generated by teams meant that the teams themselves became a far closer welded structure. In many cases, it is the integrated set of ideas on plant layout, assembly line operations or office procedures that make the major savings rather than isolated, incremental ideas. When ideas emerge carefully considered and costed by the team and approved by all the employees then implementation becomes a much easier process for all concerned producing a win-win conclusion in most cases.

The role of rewards

It is difficult to fully estimate how important are the extrinsic awards in the success of the scheme. In Japan, where awards are much lower, the culture places much higher value on public recognition by the company through a ceremony or publicity in the company magazine. Face may be lost if an employee does not produce sufficient worthwhile ideas.

In the West, tangible rewards are more generally appreciated although it is not always the amount of money that is the key. Research into sales force motivation shows that it is the combination of excitement, anticipation of the unknown (the big sale, the big idea), the sense of control and involvement and the thrill of success and recognition that are the major motivators. The scale of the actual payment comes some way down the list although it must not be derisory or demeaning. That is why the common market rate of paying around twenty per cent of the cost savings in the first year has been accepted as reasonable by employees across many organisations against the advice of some trade unions who have felt this to be insufficient. The addition of prize draws with a few sizeable prizes has latched on to the highly successful 'National Lottery' mentality.

The main perceived danger of the scheme is that employees will no longer produce ideas without some reward. There is the slippery slope of having to regularly launch new campaigns, think up attractive and universally acceptable new prizes and to try to prevent employees working the system by holding back on their ideas until the next contest. The ultimate minefield is that the fundamental purpose of the scheme, to harness genuine employee knowledge, competence and innovatory skills, may be lost in the steadily increasing hype necessary to raise the number of ideas and prove the continuing success of the scheme.

Student activities

1. Draft a questionnaire to employees to test the value of the rewards under the scheme.
2. Look at the Vauxhall Improvement Idea form. Devise three ideas for simplifying or improving this form.
3. Write a paper arguing the case for and against an Employee Recognition Scheme from the viewpoint of a shop steward.
4. Consider the ideas put forward by teams on page 272. What impact does this development have on job design for supervisors and engineers and are there any training implications?

Further reading

Arken, A (1996) 'Incentives to work safely', *People Management*, September, pp 48-52

Ekvall, G (1995) 'Participation and creativity – new forms of suggestion schemes in Sweden', *Creativity and Innovation Management*, Vol. 4, No. 3, pp 152-159

IDS (1995) *Suggestion Schemes*, Study No. 573, March

Lloyd, G (1996) 'Fastening an environment of employee contribution to increase commitment and motivation', *Empowerment in Organisations*, Vol. 4, No. 1, pp 25-28

Lummis, R (1993) 'Rover puts suggestions to competitive advantage', *Involvement and Participation*, No. 617, May, pp 12-14

Marx, A (1995) 'Management commitment for successful suggestion schemes', *Work Study*, Vol. 44, No. 3, pp 16-18

Pickard, J (1993) 'Handling proper suggestions on the shop floor, *Personnel Management Plus*, Vol. 4, No. 4, pp 14-15

Appendix A

For the practitioner

Gordon McPhail has run the Vauxhall scheme for five years and gives a few key pointers to success:

- keep it as simple as possible;
- give power to team members to investigate, test and implement ideas and to demand time and resources to get fast answers to their ideas;
- train management and shop floor thoroughly in the ideas generating and testing process;
- estimate rewards rather than have complex time-consuming calculations and remember to use points accumulation rather than cash when appropriate; and
- give strong encouragement to groups/team-based ideas storming, ideas events and try to get everybody involved with direct management support and commitment.

Case Study 27

An Equal Pay Claim at LCS

Background

LCS Ltd, is a computer services organisation owned by Peter Ludvig and Charles Brown and their families. Founded in 1976 as a niche player providing computer programmes for law firms in London, it expanded both geographically and product-wise so that, by 1995, it employed 600 staff in the UK with a turnover of £25 million and a healthy profit growth rising to £5 million in 1994. Its head office is in West London and it has eight regional centres.

Originally called Ludvig Computer Services, it now provides a complete IT package to small and medium-sized organisations. This involves integrated solutions, hardware and software to meet the clients' needs. 30 per cent of its business is still in the legal area but there is a growing proportion of the business directed to other areas, such as the motor trade and garden centres. A recent initiative in medical services IT for hospital trusts is proving very successful. Peter, the major shareholder, is chairman and chief executive; Charles is in charge of operations with specific responsibility for the regional centres.

Interjit Bhasra joined LCS in 1989 as Personnel and Training Officer. She had been recruited by Dave Allen who was the organisation's first Head of Personnel, appointed in 1987. It was Interjit's second position, having moved from a junior personnel role at the local hospital where she had gained three useful years of generalist experience after gaining an upper second class degree in Business Studies at Aston University. Her starting salary at LCS was £14,000 and this had risen to £19,500 by 1993 which she felt was a reasonable level at the age of 27. Due to the travelling involved, she had the use of a small company car together with free private mileage. By 1991, she had successfully completed her studies for IPD graduate membership. In 1992, she commenced a two-year MA course in Human Resource Management at Middlesex University.

Human resources department structure

At the interview, Dave made it clear that the team was a small one (just the two of them supported by a secretary) so it was important that they worked together in a very flexible way to carry out whatever projects arose – expected or unexpected. The department's responsibilities covered all areas of human resources in the organisation.

In general, due to geographical constraints, the day-to-day personnel work of the regional centres was carried out by the regional managers and Dave had developed the role of consultant to these managers. To assist in recruitment, he had just completed the trials of a standard set of psychological tests for managerial, technical and sales staff and convinced the directors that they should be used in all recruitment of these staff. The regional managers were, on the whole, happy to do so although some remained sceptical.

Dave had a very outgoing and well-rounded personality and had made a successful impact in most HR matters. The relationship with the co-owners, particularly the chairman, had developed well and he had played an important and successful role in a recent re-organisation.

Interjit's job

In terms of the specific areas, it was agreed that Interjit's responsibilities fell into three main categories: training, career development and general personnel duties while Dave would look after pay and rewards, performance management, management recruitment and employee relations.

Training

Taking up about 50 per cent of her time, Interjit carried out the following main activities.

Course development
On an annual basis she carried out a training needs analysis from which arose the requirement for a number of internal courses. These had included subjects such as customer care, desk-top publishing, effective recruitment interviewing, induction, time management and objective setting. She ran, on average, ten such courses a year. The staff that attended were primarily secretarial and administrative but she had developed and run a number of short modules which had been added onto internal conferences for supervisory and managerial staff. This idea had arisen from a brainstorming meeting with Dave, who had successfully sold it to the management team. Interjit had carried out most of the development work and the delivery was shared with Dave.

Course organisation
The training needs analysis also produced a requirement for external courses which she would research, book and evaluate for all levels of staff as well as carrying out the necessary organisation for internal courses.

Course delivery
She prepared all the training materials and carried out the actual course delivery (shared on occasions with internal staff or consultants).

The internal course evaluation forms indicated that the courses were well received and the thorough and professional approach was appreciated. Some were held in the regions and some at the small training centre at the head office.

Career development

In 1989, immediately prior to her joining the company, Dave had obtained agreement for a graduate development scheme to aid the expansion of the organisation. Each year, between four and ten graduates were recruited, the majority of which would progress into the mainstream computer operations following an induction programme and two to three projects to assist their company orientation. A minority would move into other sides of the business such as finance, marketing or general administration. Interjit was given responsibility for the overall recruitment and early training in this programme. She organised the recruitment programme and the assessment centre for the short-listed candidates. This would conclude with a selection panel including a director and two managers. During the recession, there were two years of low or zero recruitment but, by 1994, 25 graduates were on or had passed through the programme. Seven had left the company but the remaining 18 had performed well and the programme had been seen as a success.

Interjit also had responsibility for overseeing the professional development of a further handful of staff in finance, purchasing and marketing who were aiming to obtain professional qualifications. In total, this took up 20 per cent of her time.

Personnel duties

The remaining 30 per cent of her workload was taken up with a set of general personnel activities, including:

- general recruitment of head office staff;
- recruitment of IT staff;
- developing personnel procedures, including areas such as exit interviews, grievance and disciplinary procedures, promotions and paid absence;
- monitoring statistics on absence and turnover;
- welfare matters;
- contributing to company magazine;
- advising on employment law matters;
- working on HR projects, such as ideas on flexible benefits; and
- office administration including dealing with her own correspondence and, on occasions, acting as relief secretary for Dave in the absence of the departmental secretary (who was sometimes 'requisitioned' by one of the directors).

The problem arises

As the first HR manager, Dave had slowly gained acceptance and influence in the organisation. By 1990, all major areas of HR passed through his hands and there was firm control over systems, procedures and advice. All, that is, except in one important area.

The operations division was divided into two parts. Sales consultants, who were a team, 50-strong, who liaised with new and existing clients and signed them up for IT development work. This could be adapting existing programmes for new business developments, re-vamping the entire IT set-up or providing staffing on a temporary or long-term basis.

The other part is the 150-strong team of programmers, system analysts, engineers and 'Solutionists' who were those staff who work out the entire IT solution for small businesses.

The staffing has always come principally from agencies with whom a close relationship has been formed. In 1990, the increasing difficulty of obtaining and recruiting staff with the right skills led to Dave gaining agreement for a more formal programme of regular recruitment both on the graduate development scheme and by the organising of a regular flow of ONC and HNC computer studies students from the local colleges to the regional centres.

Dave wanted to recruit another member of staff with IT experience for his department to run these programmes but, to his surprise, this responsibility was given to Harold Keys.

Harold Keys

Harold, an ex-sales advisor, had been carrying out the training for the sales advisors since the mid-1980s. He had not been a particularly successful advisor, lacking in the required drive and direction. After two years in this position, he had expressed his interest in the training activities and had been given the chance to prove himself. On appointment, he had put together, with the help of an external consultant, an improved training programme which had showed a modicum of success over the next few years. It was considered that Harold could add on these additional training responsibilities and he was keen to do so. He was supported in this move by Charles Brown, his immediate boss, who saw this activity as vital to the operational area and wanted to retain complete control here.

The job was described as:

1. Training (65 per cent of time):
   - course development, organisation and delivery. Designing and running initial training courses for sales advisors, together with consequent assessments and recommendations at course end. Developing remedial courses in specific areas;
   - designing and delivering initial training for new unit managers and operations staff;
   - career development. Designing and operating control processes for the career development of sales advisors and operations staff, including administering the regular appraisal system and implementing promotions and career changes; and

- external training. Identifying, arranging and evaluating external training course for unit managers, sales advisors and operations staff.

2. Recruitment, induction and other duties (35 per cent of time):
   - recruitment. Assisting in recruitment process for unit managers, advisors and operations staff including being a member of a panel on assessment centres for graduates;
   - induction. Planning and evaluating induction programmes for all new sales and operation staff; and
   - projects. Carrying out various projects on quality, communications and employee involvement in the sale/operations areas.

Dave was acutely disappointed by this decision but decided to bide his time, expecting that Harold would not be able to cope with the job. Within the next six months, he reached agreement with Charles on the process of recruitment and selection of IT staff, including using psychometric tests, in which he and Interjit played a substantial part in practice.

There remained, however, a tension between Harold and the HR department from that time onwards. Harold was intensely possessive of the IT training areas and dealt closely with Charles on details of new training and development arrangements. The new responsibilities gave him a new lift and he responded with increased dedication and enthusiasm, which was noted in the field. He attended a number of courses in training delivery and arranged the purchase of the latest training technology, in which he became quite proficient. His attendance at monthly sales and operation meetings became much more frequent and he managed for the first time, to produce an efficient looking IT training plan for the year ahead. It was suggested at one of his career development discussions that he might work towards the professional IPD qualification but he could see little relevance in this.

On appointment, he wanted to be called 'manager' but the company was going through a minor de-layering exercise and wanted to avoid any more manager titles. He would not accept the title of 'officer'. The compromise of 'IT training specialist' was supposed to be short-term but it remained in place as the years went by. He kept his former remuneration as sales advisor which had reached £25,000 by 1993. This included the bonus element of £1500 which had been consolidated on appointment. A sales advisor's salary range was £17,000 and rose to £26,000 after probation plus a bonus that could yield a maximum of £4000. He had the use of a Mondeo car and free petrol, the same car level as sales advisors.

At the end of 1992, after considerable and extended manoeuvring, he was successful in crossing the threshold onto the select group of managers who received an annual discretionary bonus. Dave had opposed this move but the chairman was persuaded at last by a detailed and well documented case put forward by Charles which dealt with his overall improvement and commitment. It coincided with an improved sales and profit performance. It was a fairly modest payment of £2000.

The claim

Interjit was indignant when she heard of this decision. She considered for some time that their two jobs were at a similar level. The salary difference between her and Harold, which had narrowed a little over the previous two years, suddenly widened again and the sense of unfairness became acute. She discussed her unhappiness with Dave on more than one occasion before realising that he could do little at this stage except to obtain rather vague promises about the future.

Although she enjoyed the job, she decided that it was time to move on. She was aware, in any case, that women were not well regarded in the organisation. The Directors were all male and she was the most senior female apart from a finance manager and a senior sales advisor who was a distant relative of one of the founders. She was also conscious that the mixed group of graduates tended to split up into males moving into the IT operations and females into other areas. The number of female sales advisors and operations staff was really quite small.

With the help of a couple of agencies, Interjit received a number of job offers by March 1994. She talked over her reasons for moving with the owner of the agency who had delivered the most attractive job. The subject of a possible equal pay claim came up at this point and the agency owner put her in touch with Julie, a friend who worked at a well respected legal firm.

Interjit had a long discussion with Julie as to the implications of such a claim. It was pointed out that they always took up a considerable amount of time and usually caused considerable stress for the claimant. Julie did feel, however, that Interjit had a good case and she would endeavour to gain the support of the Equal Opportunities Commission (EOC). They discussed whether a claim for racial discrimination should also be made but Interjit pointed out that racial minorities were well represented in the operations area and had started to make their mark in the management positions. In any case, she considered that her colour was not the issue – it was because she was a woman that the excess salary differential occurred. A few days before she handed in her notice, Interjit entered her IT1 form which caused considerable consternation in the organisation.

The procedure

The basis of the claim was that her job was very similar to Harold's ('like work') or, alternatively, her job should be rated at the same level ('work of equal value'). There was no formal job evaluation in the organisation, salaries being determined by the Board through advice from Dave and subjective decision-making.

LCS duly responded to the claim with the defence that the jobs were quite different, covering different areas, different levels of responsibility and different contributions to the organisation. To protect their position, they had been advised to also respond that, in the alternative, the difference in pay was due to a material factor other than sex, namely the market salaries for specialist IT trainers.

The preliminary hearing took place in September 1994. By this time, Interjit had left LCS and she had received confirmation that her case would be supported by the EOC. During her last two difficult months at LCS, the Chairman had tried to persuade her to drop the claim through a combination of charm, detailed argument and veiled threats over references. He was all too aware that the case would take up time and resources. There was an indication that some small form of compensation (around a month's pay) could be offered. Interjit discussed this with Julie and Samantha, the EOC barrister, but they all felt her case appeared strong and the compensation offered was derisory.

At the preliminary hearing, the case for both the 'like work' and 'work of equal value' claims were put by Samantha and countered by the barrister appearing for LCS. The tribunal decision was that the jobs were not similar enough to come under the category of 'like work' but there was a sufficient case made for the claim to go to an independent expert under the 'work of equal value' procedure. Arthur Jones was appointed to act as the expert and to complete the report by March 1995. As is customary in these situations, the EOC had their own independent report carried out by a trade union research group who had considerable experience in this field. The company also commissioned their own report.

Over the next four months, Interjit and Harold, plus their original line managers, were interviewed by the three experts. In each case, this took almost a full day as the experts examined each aspect of their complex jobs and attempted to obtain their respective views on levels of responsibility, frequency and contribution. There were also a number of follow-up calls when both sides had been seen to try to clear up areas where facts were substantially disputed. Interjit did not enjoy the process (nor did her new employer) but Harold found the whole affair extremely irritating. He felt that he had no alternative but to give his views fairly in supporting the company case.

The EOC received their report by late January and they were in the process of arranging with LCS to exchange their respective reports and to give a copy to the independent expert when the Tribunal office informed them that Arthur Jones had become ill and there would be a delay of two or three months. This subsequently became three or four months before the Chairman of the Tribunal informed the parties that Arthur could not complete the case due to continuing ill health. A new expert, James Williams, was appointed in June 1995 with a deadline to report in December 1995. This report was duly completed on time.

The reports

The Equal Pay Act encourages comparison between the applicant and comparator's work being made under factor headings commonly used in analytical job evaluation schemes and all three reports followed that methodology. The factor headings differed, however, and the three reports, not unexpectedly, came to different conclusions.

The EOC report

Five headings were chosen (see Table 6.1) and a straight comparison made between the two jobs on each of the headings with a judgment made as to whether the demand of one job was Greater than, Equal to, or Less than the demand of the other job. Each factor was taken as of equal importance so there was no weighting of factors. This approach (called GEL) was justified as appropriate where there were only a small number of jobs to be compared. It was argued that it was not appropriate to set up a complete factor-points system with a complex gradation just to compare two jobs. It was also pointed out that such a complex system would magnify the differences and minimise the similarities which was against the spirit of the Act.

The report's detailed analysis came up with the general assessment that a very large proportion of the two jobs was similar. These were the training skills, the resource responsibilities, the concentration and the physical effort/working conditions. The differences in favour of the comparator were the service responsibilities which could have a direct effect upon the sales performance and the reporting arrangements direct to a director. Those in favour of the applicant included the wider knowledge of the organisation, the contact responsibilities, and the wider field of problem-solving activities. In other words, the more focused training responsibilities with their immediate outcome of the comparator was balanced by the broader and more long-term outcomes for the applicant.

Table 6.1 *EOC report*

FACTOR 1 – KNOWLEDGE AND SKILLS REQUIRED FOR THE JOB	
• Training and other interpersonal skills	Equal
• Organisational knowledge	Applicant
• Other skills and knowledge	Equal
FACTOR 2 – RESPONSIBILITIES	
• Service responsibilities	Comparator
• Contact responsibilities	Applicant
• Resource responsibilities	Equal
FACTOR 3 – INITIATIVE/INDEPENDENCE	
• Reporting arrangements	Comparator
• Decision making	Equal
• Problem solving	Applicant
FACTOR 4 – MENTAL EFFORT	
• Concentration	Equal
FACTOR 5 – PHYSICAL EFFORT/WORKING CONDITIONS	
• Work locations	Equal
• Physical effort	Equal
• Hours of work	Equal

The LCS report

The basis of this report was an informal Hay-type approach looking at three key elements (see Table 6.2). This approach was chosen as both jobs were at a junior management level and therefore ideal for such a well-proven evaluation method. A simplified points system was put in place.

The result here came down in favour of the comparator due to the greater degree of impact of the job together with greater perceived technical and procedural knowledge where it really mattered. The applicant's apparent advantage of the freedom to act was not seen as sufficient to offset these points and the results were sufficiently different to justify a grade and salary distinction.

Table 6.2 *LCS report*

FACTOR 1 – KNOWHOW	Max points	Applicant	Comparator
Technical/procedural/professional knowledge/skill	150	110	120
Planning/organising and managerial skills	150	110	110
Human relations skills	100	70	70
FACTOR 2 – PROBLEM-SOLVING			
Thinking environment	100	70	70
Thinking challenge	100	60	70
FACTOR 3 – ACCOUNTABILITY			
Freedom to act	100	70	60
Magnitude – scale of events/job impact	150	110	120
Impact – the directness of impact	150	90	120
Total	1000	690	740

The independent expert's report

James Williams had access to both the previous reports before completing his own. His own experience, through running his own consultancy for some years, had been quite wide and, in recent years, he had tended to adapt the approach operated by KPMG with their EQUATE system where the methodology was designed with the equal-value legislation in mind. Simply put, the system for each organisation is unique but the key areas include five common factors (see Table 6.3).

Table 6.3 *Independent expert's report*

	Max points	Applicant	Comparator
Knowledge, skills and experience	200	150	150
Job impact	200	125	150
Thinking demands	200	125	125
Communication demands	200	150	125
Accountability	200	125	150
Total	1000	675	700

For each of the five factors, James Williams had devised a scale of eight degrees, each of 25 points and placed both parties at what he regarded as the appropriate level, taking into account a number of points made in the respective reports.

His conclusion was that a difference did exist between the jobs but that it was not significant enough to justify a difference in grade in a normal company job evaluation system.

The tribunal

The Tribunal took place in March 1996, two years after the claim was entered. It lasted for four days and ten witnesses were called, including the two founders, five other staff of LCS and three consultants brought by LCS, one on job evaluation and two on external salary comparisons on computer-based staff. Interjit herself spent six hours in the witness box, including four hours in cross-examination.

The main points that LCS emphasised were:

1. The independent expert's report was too simplistic and general. It was not related to the special nature of the company in question and there was no evidence that such a scheme had been applied in the computer sector whereas they produced evidence of the application of a Hay-type scheme.
2. The points awarded under communication demands was perverse. Both parties carried out course delivery and no professional trainer could survive without a high level of effective communication skills in the course delivery situation. Although the applicant may have a somewhat broader range of activities, the necessary communication skills here, principally telephone and writing, could not be compared in importance with the course delivery skills.
3. The lack of weighting in the EOC report substantially reduced its credibility.
4. Insufficient importance was attached in both reports to the 'bottom line' considerations. The heart of the business was the sales and operations performance and the comparator was a key person in improving and maintaining that performance. Should the quality of training slip, the implications in turnover and profit would be substantial.
5. Evidence was produced of the market salaries for computer trainers which showed that, on average, their pay was 20 per cent higher than trainers in other areas for the same level of experience and qualifications.
6. The applicant's job involved quite junior work, such as secretarial assistance and minute taking. Her training activities also involved lower level skills, such as desk-top publishing.
7. Comparative figures were produced of a number of other IT companies' sex ratios which showed that the company did not operate any form of sex discrimination.

In response, the EOC barrister put forward the following points:

1. The majority of the training carried out by the comparator was in sales and administrative training, not actual computer training. Reports comparing sales trainers with general trainers showed a difference, on average, of no more that two to three per cent.
2. The secretarial work took up a small and declining percentage of the applicant's work and should be discounted.
3. The level of impact of the comparator's work alleged was exaggerated. The overall control of the sales and operational work lay with the unit managers whose day-to-day informal training and control played the conclusive part in the company's final results.
4. There were disputed ratings in the LCS job evaluation scheme including the equal rating for HR where the applicant's breadth of responsibilities should have given a higher rating. There was also a lack of justification for a higher rating for the comparator on the 'thinking challenge' factor. The consultancy skills required for the applicant's position had been undervalued.
5. The qualification achieved by the applicant was higher (IPD graduate) and had not been recognised in the scheme.
6. The company appeared to operate an informal system of discrimination judged by the number of female staff in the sales and operations departments, particularly in positions of authority.

The result

The Tribunal reserved judgment and gave their findings five weeks later. In a 15-page majority report they rejected the applicant's claim on the following grounds:

1. The main findings of the report by the independent expert was accepted in that the jobs were essentially of equal value. The report was sufficiently detailed, was not perverse in the ratings and was appropriate for the company.
2. Although the number of females in positions of authority was disappointing, the applicant had not given any objective proof of sex discrimination in the company.
3. However, the company had established a 'material factor' difference which entitled the employer to pay a higher salary to the comparator. The tribunal, by a majority, accepted the necessity for the comparator to have an IT sales advisor background to establish credibility in the field. Given that the maximum rate for a sales advisor was £30,000, a figure of £26,000, including bonus, for the comparator was not an excessive figure and this was reflected in the higher overall market rate for sales trainers in the IT field. The actual salary difference of £6000 was higher than the average market rate but was within the bands of reasonableness, taking age and experience into account.

At the time of writing, the applicants have set an appeal in motion.

Student activities

1. On what basis is an appeal to the Employment Appeal Tribunal allowable and how would this apply in this particular case?
2. Identify the emotional, social and psychological effects on Interjit of taking this extended case and comment on any long-term career implications.
3. Compare the three 'expert' reports and identify weaknesses which could be exploited by the applicant and the respondent.
4. In what way would the balance between male and female executives in LCS be relevant to the case?
5. Would all the equal pay problems have been avoided if LCS had carried out a job evaluation exercise?

Standard reading

	Armstrong and Murlis	*Armstrong*	*Milkovich and Newman*
Pages	122 and 546-9	142-158	503-548

Further reading

ACAS (1996) *Annual Report*, London

Bargaining Report, (1996) *Equal Pay – More Successful Settlements*, No. 163, pp 8-13, July

Clarke, L (1995) *Discrimination*, IPD, London

Fagen, C and Rubery, J (1994) 'Equal pay policy and wage regulation systems in Europe', *Industrial Relations Journal*, Vol. 25, No. 4, pp 281-292

Gilbert, K and Secker, J (1995) 'Generating equal pay decentralisation in the electricity supply industry', *British Journal of Industrial Relations*, Vol. 33, No. 2, pp 191-207

Greenhalgh, R (1995) *Industrial Tribunals*, IPD, London

Hastings, S (1991) *Developing a Less Discriminatory Job Evaluation Scheme*, Trade Union Research Unit Technical Note, No. 109, Oxford

IDS (1994) *Equal Pay*, Employment Law Handbook Series 2, No. 3

Lewis, P (1997) *The Law of Employment*, Kogan Page, London

Rubery, J (1995) 'Performance-related pay and the prospects for gender pay equity', *Journal of Management Studies*, Vol. 32, No. 5, pp 637-654

Rubery, J (1992) *The Economics of Equal Value*, Equal Opportunities Commission, London

Case Study 28

Too Far Too Fast? The Telecorp Dilemma

by Chris Mills, Consultant

Located in the tropics, Malaysia straddles across the South China Sea. It is at the tip of mainland South-east Asia while the states of Sabah and Sarawak are on the island of Borneo. The population of the country is 19 million, comprising Malays, Chinese, Indians, Ibans, Kadazans and other races. Bahasa Malaysia is the national language and English is widely spoken. Islam is the State religion but there is complete freedom of worship.

The Malaysian economy has expanded tremendously with all sectors recording a strong output. Since 1987 the manufacturing sector has emerged as the leading economic sector followed by the agricultural and mining sectors. Leading export-oriented manufactured products are electrical and electronic products, textiles and wearing apparel as well as rubber-based products. Malaysia is the world's largest exporter of palm oil, natural rubber, tropical timber and the leading world exporter of cocoa beans and pepper.

In the manufacturing sector, investments to develop resource-based industries and selective heavy industries are encouraged. Incentives are also provided to support large-scale commercial agricultural ventures. The main thrust of economic development, though, is to stimulate greater and wider private sector growth. When it comes to such growth Malaysian entrepreneurs say that telecommunications doesn't just support growth, it makes it happen.

Transforming telecommunications

'Telecommunications no longer just supports development, it is actually a catalyst for development', says Mr Tajudin Ramli, Chairman and Chief Executive Officer of Technology Resources Industries, a diversified group of companies which has focused its resources on domestic and international telecommunications.

Malaysia has plugged into telecommunications as an industry to facilitate national growth, and as a valuable export earner. Cambodia's Department of Post and Telecommunications and Iran's Qeshm Free Area Authority are developing and operating telecommunications services with Malaysia's Technology Resources Industries Berhad. The US Navy chose Sapura

Telecommunications Berhad ahead of other international competitors to install and manage the telephone network at its base in San Diego.

Telecorp Ltd*

An introduction

Telecorp Ltd is one of the premier telecommunication solution providers in Malaysia. It has grown at a tremendous pace in the last few years. It has realised that staying ahead of its competitors can only be achieved by being superior in technology, marketing, customer service and innovation.

Telecorp's strategy has been to go after markets which seem to their American and European competitors to be too small or too far away for them to efficiently service. While they may be small opportunities for others, they hold significant potential for Telecorp. They can see nations in the Middle East, Africa and in the Asian neighbourhood which are ripe for telecommunications development right now.

Telecorp installed Malaysia's first privately owned cellular mobile telephone network, TEL 888, and operates it under the name of Telecorp. The network was set up in a record five months, thanks to what their chairman calls 'technological leap-frogging'.

It is this kind of development that has helped Malaysia achieve an average growth rate of eight per cent a year for the last eight years with the same increase projected for the next five years. The development of skills to install and operate the new technology is crucial. Malaysia is facing a manpower shortage so it must be flexible and creative in its approach to developing human resources.

Telecorp realises the importance of managing and developing its 2700 people. That is why their '26 Basic Winning Strategies' underline the importance of people.

The internal climate

In 1994-5 Telecorp conducted an internal climate survey. Sixty-one percent of staff selected responded to the survey. The study showed that everyone was proud of the company and had an idea of the direction and responsibilities of their department.

Corporate mission and identity:

- 95 per cent felt that Telecorp had a clear mission statement.

Organisation and job clarity:

- 90 per cent had a clear understanding of their job responsibilities and the functions of their divisions; and
- interestingly, 95 per cent of non-executives agreed whereas only 87 per cent of executives agreed.

---

*Telecorp Ltd is the fictitious name of a leading Malaysian telecommunication company.

However the climate survey identified some areas in need of development. For example:

Management/superiors:

- staff would like their superiors to be more accountable and supportive, someone who will guide, coach and develop them. 85 per cent of executives agreed, 92 per cent of non-executives agreed;
- 64 per cent of executives agreed that superiors listened to their ideas. Only 54 per cent of non-executives agreed; and
- 76 per cent of executives agreed that they were criticised more quickly for poor performance than praised for good performance. 79 per cent of non-executives agreed to this statement.

Favouritism/promotions:

- staff felt that favouritism existed and needed to be addressed for a better working environment;
- performance appraisal and promotion processes were not clearly established;
- only 54 per cent of staff agreed they were treated fairly and that there was no favouritism; and
- only 48 per cent thought there was a procedure for making sure all relevant staff were considered for promotion.

Service quality:

- employees felt that the company did not live up to its promise of outstanding and excellent service to its customers; and
- only 45 per cent felt it provided customers with outstanding and excellent service.

About working in Telecorp:

- executives said that the worst part about working in Telecorp was favouritism.

If I were allowed to make changes:

- eliminate overlapping job functions;
- have a clear job description and inform staff of their responsibilities; and
- enhance formal communication.

The response from top management

The Managing Director believed the company learnt a great deal from the employees' responses to help chart Telecorp's future:

> It is very pleasant to hear all the 'best things' about working in Telecorp, and a bit painful to hear the 'worst things'. But we have to be open-minded and use the feedback positively as you have given us a wealth of information to work on in our action plans.

The managing director added:

> ... Now that this survey has been completed, you must be wondering 'what next?' Well, the real work begins. The results of the survey show where we are today. The next step is to direct initiatives to build on our strengths and address our concerns. In the coming months, management will require your co-operation in setting and implementing action plans to address the issues. Even as I speak, several action plans are already underway. We will keep you informed of the actions to be taken.

As a result of the internal climate survey, action plans to address the issues raised were prepared, one of which was to probe into concerns relating to the quality of performance appraisal, promotion processes and staff feelings regarding favouritism.

An international consulting company well versed in performance management design was engaged to review current performance appraisal practices and make a proposal for change.

The consulting company recommended that employees complete a performance management questionnaire. This would cover all phases and aspects of the manager-subordinate relationship in the performance management cycle. The outcome would be an analysis of the present system and recommendations for development. The consulting company would compile the results for presentation to the management, use the data to gain participants' support at the start of any training and store it for comparison when reviewing the effectiveness of the training. It was seen as likely to have the added advantage of gauging Telecorp's return on investment.

The survey

So a performance management questionnaire to identify Telecorp employees' more specific concerns and needs was prepared in both English and Bahasa Malaysia. The survey used the same five-point semantic differential Lickert scale as in recent Malaysian, Singaporean and US national surveys conducted by the same consulting company. The questionnaire sought to explore levels of satisfaction and expertise in performance management/appraisal practices.

The areas that were reviewed were:

- performance planning;
- feedback and coaching;
- performance review;
- outcomes; and
- overall satisfaction.

Demographic data reviewed were:

- number of respondents;
- position in the organisation;
- role in performance management;

- number of years with Telecorp; and
- employee location.

In the report, charts were presented firstly in percentages and then compared in mean ratings with data from other companies in Malaysia (ie the Malaysian survey highlighted above). The survey collected 704 respondents or 26 per cent of the company workforce and revealed a degree of reliability above 0.7. It reinforced concerns which the internal climate survey had surfaced, especially the lack of coaching and being criticised more quickly for poor performance than praised for good effort. It also highlighted similar matters regarding lack of management accountability for employee development. A summary of respondents' views on the system included frustrations such as:

- 'the system is not objective';
- 'favouritism is apparent';
- 'performance appraisal is not tied to bonuses';
- 'different appraisers have different standards' and
- 'there is no action on recommendations'.

Resulting action

Consequently, it was announced by the management that:

> Telecorp are in an increasingly competitive business where premium growth, customer retention, excellent customer service and overall operational efficiency are critical to the company's success. Telecorp, therefore, now sees the need for an on-going business system that supports its strategic direction linking individual and team performance to business goals and objectives.

It was therefore agreed that an empowering performance management system was what was needed. This would be the business tool that would help the company communicate its goals to every individual within the organisation. Having clear measurable goals would thus enable Telecorp to identify, reward and retain high performers. Such a system would be self-regulating where each individual was empowered to track and monitor their own performance. At the same time interdependence should be built-in so those who needed coaching would get it to help meet expectations set for the year.

In addition, it was seen that an effective performance management system must support key organisational beliefs and inculcate core values like customer service, teamwork, etc. Telecorp's mission and values would be operationalized through the performance management system so that all employees understood what was expected and be made accountable for both results and behaviours.

A proposal was prepared outlining Telecorp's need to upgrade its existing appraisal system to a performance management system to help the firm achieve greater productivity, set clear accountabilities and clearly link rewards to performance.

Needs identified

Telecorp currently then used a trait-based performance appraisal system. The system had been in use for approximately five years. The major concerns with the current system related to it being seen as a 'compensation system' with salary increases expected irrespective of performance level. This was exacerbated by the climate survey, complaints of favouritism and no clear links to promotion.

One of the key factors critical for the success of the new performance management system was support by senior management. An organisational support meeting was held to describe the action taken since the internal climate survey. Results of the performance appraisal survey were highlighted and the phases of the new system's implementation outlined. It was stressed that the system should be communicated clearly to the people who used it. This would ensure that each person was then made accountable for its success. A discussion then took place to identify how managers could show their support during and after the system was in place. This included identifying possible road-blocks to be overcome.

The new performance management system's approach and methodology were described in four phases.

Analysis phase

This phase centred around a project planning meeting. The consulting company met with a steering committee of human resource and department representatives from Telecorp. This was primarily to agree on critical behaviours and activities for success in the skill areas to be addressed by the performance management system.

In particular the following areas were discussed, 'what are the expected results from implementing the system?', eg 'a system which will emphasise accountability and teamwork and develop self-empowerment skills'. In addition the agenda covered a review of the vision, values, business strategies and organisational issues. Naturally there was a discussion on the company's current performance appraisal practices and how they linked to other human resource systems. System design, system administration communication/internal PR strategy and programme roll-out were also planned. In addition project responsibilities, service contracts, deliverables and time frames were finalised.

Design phase

Materials were then designed that had been determined as integral to the system. This included the following:

- the design of an organisational-specific performance planning and review form;
- the design of an organisational-specific sample performance planning and review worksheet;

- the design of a performance management handbook to include policies, procedures and performance management process;
- the design of a performance management training manual plus a competency dictionary and application guide. Also instructor guides linked to organisational practices and covering administrative processes; and
- the design of Telecorp specific skill practices. These covered the business cycle from performance planning, tracking/feedback and coaching to performance review.

Training phase

Telecorp wanted to transfer the performance management technology from the consulting company to key staff responsible for the system's success. It was therefore decided to train 12 instructors. Such instructors were trained in performance management philosophy, skills and training techniques.

To kick the training off senior management went through a two-day session. The purpose of the workshop was designed to help Telecorp senior management understand and commit to all aspects of their role in an effective performance management implementation. This was done by linking the system to a strategic focus:

- establish or communicate organisational vision, values and critical success factors so that others know where to focus their efforts;
- translate organisational vision, values and critical success factors into their own performance plan; and
- coach others through the process.

Senior management then were introduced to developing their own Key Result Areas (KRAs). KRAs are the three to seven main areas of accountability such as profitability, customer satisfaction, business development, staff development and professional development. They went on to identify objectives and dimensions. They learnt how to write measurable objectives for their position. They then determined which competencies (dimensions) are important to support the achievement of the objectives.

All employees (managers and non-managers, appraisers and 'appraisees') were trained in performance management philosophy and skills. The workshops combined mini-lectures with group discussion, video models, written exercises and skill practices.

Specifically, the goal was for managers to have enhanced management and coaching skills and be capable of effectively implementing the cyclic performance management process with their subordinates. Appraiser training therefore consisted firstly of pre-work activities to develop understanding of the philosophy and rationale for the new approach. Workshop participation was encouraged through training sessions emphasising skill building using a behaviour modelling learning design. The behaviour modelling format consisted of:

- learning behavioural objectives;
- watching a positive model;
- practising the skill; and
- getting individual feedback.

Aside from skill development, these techniques heightened participant enthusiasm and demonstrated the high relevancy to on-the-job application.

Appraisee training consisted of understanding their role in the process, identifying key result areas, objectives, supporting dimensions and behaviours and a tracking process.

Review phase

The review process was seen as comprising two parts. There would be quarterly performance management review meetings of the steering committee to discuss key issues. Secondly, at the end of the first year of implementation, there would be a survey of the participants in the system. They would answer a questionnaire complementary to the instrument filled in prior to the workshop. The data would be processed and an analysis of the findings would highlight any change and recommend appropriate fine-tuning.

Concerns

At the first performance management review meeting it was reported that attendance in performance management training was 96.5 per cent. However the number who had completed and submitted performance management forms was only 51 per cent. None from senior management had completed theirs.

Staff focus group sessions revealed the following information:

- it was felt that there was no clear direction from top management. Some divisions' technical and clerical staff already had their KRAs but middle level managers in other divisions were still waiting for top management to cascade down business plans;
- due to restructuring some staff were unclear of their job description and function;
- some employees were still not clear how to complete the performance management form, eg compulsory KRAs were often not included even though both the training course and handbook covered this area, competencies were mixed into KRAs, objectives were not time bound or measurable, compulsory competencies were not included, tracking methods were not shown for both objectives and competencies and endorsement by appraisers should have been recorded but frequently was not evident;
- staff did not know how to track their performance and keep a record of their use of competencies; and
- staff did not relate the importance of performance management to their self-development and career. Some felt this was because of lack of

encouragement from their superior. Such managers were very busy and not always around.

It was clear that there was still some way to go! Each member of the steering team was asked to go away and consider the current difficulties and to come back with some specific solutions.

Student activities

1. As the HR representative on the steering team, what specific recommendations would you put forward to overcome each of these issues?
2. What method would you use to facilitate these recommendations?
3. How would you measure your success at achieving each recommendation?
4. Does the case study indicate any distinguishing features of Malaysian business culture with respect to performance management?
5. Indicate the next stage of development of the performance management system as it leads into the reward stage.

Standard reading

	Armstrong and Murlis	*Armstrong*	*Milkovich and Newman*
Pages	205-246	260-270	361-415

Further reading

Fisher, M (1995) *Performance Appraisals*, The Sunday Times business skills series, Kogan Page, London

Fletcher, C and Williams, R (1992) 'The Route to Performance Management', *Personnel Management*, November

Hartle, F (1995) *How to Re-Engineer your Performance Management Process*, Kogan Page, London

James, T (1995) 'Performance management in a changing context: Monsanto pioneers a competency-based developmental approach', *Human Resource Management*, Vol. 34, No. 3, pp 425-442

Walters, M (ed) (1995) *The Performance Management Handbook*, IPD, London

Case Study 29

Ambitious Rewards at an International Investment Bank

by Sarah Kelly, Senior Lecturer, Bristol Business School

Introduction

Grossman Bros International (GBI) is the securities trading arm of Grossman Bros Investment Bank. GBI employs approximately 120 people and is based in luxurious premises in the heart of the City of London. It operates relatively autonomously from its US investment bank parent, Grossman Bros, which has its headquarters in New York. GBI's profit targets and achievement levels are watched 'hawkishly' by the parent company in the US.

The head of the dealing room operation, Guy Salmon, is English, but there are a number of traders from the Bank's US dealing operation on secondment to London, applying their knowledge of the US bond market to Europe. The dealing operation has a team of 30 dealers in currency and bonds, the equivalent number of sales people, together with a 'back room' team of settlements and IT staff.

The City-based dealing room has been up and running since the early 1980s and the operation has a reputation for being both aggressive and highly successful in the market place. Grossman's best dealers are reputed to have earned bonuses of £1 million a piece in some of the most successful years of the mid 1980s. Graduate traineeships are highly sought after and prized. Careers at GBI may be short and brutish but highly lucrative. Successful traders in particular can command the highest total packages in the City. However, mediocrity is not well tolerated and GBI prides itself on recruiting and retaining the sharpest, best and most aggressive dealers. From time to time, other banks have been known to lure top performing teams and the organisation is keen to avoid this type of defection where possible.

The ECU bond dealing team

This team of three traders buys and sells ECU denominated bonds on behalf of the Bank for its own profit. In addition, the team buys and sells bonds on behalf of the Bank's clients, who are taken care of by GBI's sales team. The most senior member of the team, Roy Garner, is in his early thirties and, unusually, has been with the Bank since he joined as a graduate trainee. Roy is an Oxford graduate and has done exceptionally well as a trader over the

Table 6.4 *Salary progress for Roy Garner*

Year	Base	Bonus	Total
1991	£65,000	£80,000	£145,000
1992	£65,000	£65,000	£130,000
1993	£70,000	£40,000	£110,000
1994	£75,000	£50,000	£125,000
1995	£85,000	£85,000	£170,000

years, often earning bonuses of hundreds of thousands of pounds. He spent two years in GBI's French operation in Paris, where he met Francois Le Strang, the second member of the team. His salary progression is shown in Table 6.4, above.

Francois has been working with Roy since the Bank first set up an ECU bond dealing team in 1991 and finds the London market more dynamic and exciting than the French equivalent. Francois is married to an English woman and is planning to stay in the UK, unless GBI decide to offer him further overseas opportunities. The team's third member is Gary Smith, the junior trader. Gary started his career in the 'back room' operation as a settlement clerk. He has been with the Bank for three years, and persuaded Roy and Guy Salmon (the senior dealing room manager) to give him a trial as a trainee 12 months ago.

Gary operates under the watchful eyes of Roy and Francis, but runs his own position, which has a limit of £1 million and which he has to square off at the end of each week. This means that he must make sure that his position is not making a loss on a weekly basis, although any weekly profits are added to the team profit figures. Gary is 'a natural' and has so far impressed Roy and Francois with his nerve and skill, not to mention his ability to boost team profits.

The team has worked together now for a year and have been making record profits for the Bank. They record their performance on a daily basis according to how much profit and loss they have made of their own 'accounts'. Roy and Francois together calculate the profit that their team have made on a daily, weekly and monthly basis. This information is confirmed by the settlements team who make sure that every transaction is properly documented and accounted for and that the Bank actually receives the right funds from counterparts in the trades.

Roy and Francois calculate the profits they are making from day-to-day and have running totals of the profits they are making on each of their transactions. They know, from past experience, that the Bank usually calculates the bonus payments it makes on overall profitability of the trading operation. Traders can usually expect to get a proportion of what they have made in profit and the team would typically expect between 10 to 25 per cent of what they have earned in profit for the Bank. This year, so far, things are going well for both the Bank and the team. Profits are usually calculated in September and bonus payments paid out in December. Several of the most successful traders and salespeople will wait until bonuses are paid out in Christmas before considering approaches from, and entertaining more serious discussion with, other financial institutions or head hunters.

Reward package

Given their status and reputations as successful dealers, both Roy and Francois have high basic salaries which are considered to be extremely competitive in the market place. It is the Bank's stated aim to pay its dealing room staff in the upper quartile of salaries paid in this sector. Consequently, the compensation and benefits manager, Jeff Banks, participates in a club survey with other key City institutions to obtain the most up-to-date and reliable information on the prevailing salary levels in this sector. GBI compares itself to other US investment banks and the best of the UK merchant banks in the City. In addition, Jeff must monitor total package arrangements in the sector which means collecting and analysing information on incentive bonuses and benefits in order to make sure GBI can attract and retain the best people.

There is a great deal of competitiveness between institutions for the best traders and sales people and it is not infrequent that rival institutions try to out-bid each other in salary and overall package terms for a star trader or sales person. In addition to this, dealers will regularly talk to head hunters and to colleagues to establish what the best 'going rate' is for the job that they do. Performance bonuses enhance the compensation packages and can, in many cases, double potential earnings for a trader if successful and profitable. All dealing positions attract a package of benefits including a company car, private health insurance and pension contributions. Roy and Francois enjoy the Bank's lease car scheme. The traders talk endlessly about the latest, raciest and most expensive cars they can afford!

Despite the fact that cars are one of the most obvious and important benefits in the package, many traders are finding the larger more expensive models increasingly less cost effective, given that they do very few business miles and attract almost punitive tax rates as a consequence. Gary does not yet have a company car but, given his own success, is expecting to be 'promoted' to full dealer status fairly shortly. He realises that taking a car is not of great financial benefit to him, but is likely to want to lease a company car so that he can join in the dealing room debates about which model and make is the most prestigious. However, Gary, like other dealers, would also be prepared to take a cash equivalent and make his own arrangements. He is certain that he could negotiate an extremely good deal through the private leasing schemes which are becoming widely available.

Most dealers have set up private pension plans, which have the advantage of being portable when they move from one institution to another. Additional cash payments are offered to contribute to these personal pension plans. The Bank also provides life and health insurance for its employees which can be costly benefits to the Bank given that life assurance is calculated on the employee's total package. For this reason, potential employees undergo an extremely thorough pre-employment medical at a private clinic before their employment packages are confirmed. The nature of the working environment and the lifestyle involved with this work means that organisations take a great deal of care in assessing employee health and well-being.

Lifestyle and health issues are becoming more and more important in the relatively short careers of high flying dealers who could expect to stay at the top for 20 years at the most. GBI provides employees with corporate membership of a 'top notch' gym and fitness centre in the City. The traders' work and lifestyle involves significant amounts of stress and the organisation is keen that this stress is relieved in the gym as often, if not more frequently, than in the wine bar.

The role of HR

Jeff Banks, the compensation and benefits manager, has worked in the financial institutions in the City for most of his career. It is his responsibility to gather as much relevant and accurate market data as possible to inform the salary and bonus planning process. The Bank participates in a club survey along with other investment operations to establish the prevailing market rates and conditions. Jeff also likes to keep up with the latest trends and developments both at a 'local' UK level and through his colleagues in the US. He is also much involved with setting policy and calculating expatriate packages for the frequent secondees arriving in London from GBI's US and overseas operations.

In order for the Bank to remain profitable, the best traders and sales people must be adequately rewarded. Jeff knows that such people have relatively little loyalty to a given institution and that rewards must match perceived effort and success. He is always concerned to calculate a competitive bonus payment for each individual whilst at the same time ensuring the Bank's on-going profitability and success. Salary and bonus discussions with the head of the dealing room are handled by the unit's HR Manager, Debbie Elliott.

Debbie works closely with Jeff Banks and regularly asks Jeff for up-to-date information and advice. It is important that she keeps an eye on the market rates but sometimes gets frustrated that her advice on salaries is ignored as traders prefer to listen to the head hunter's views or, worse still, 'make markets' for their own salaries.

Debbie receives constant requests for exceptions on Bank policy from dealers who want to trade one benefit or another for cash. She also has her hands full in persuading senior dealing room managers to exercise restraint when trying to lure employees away from other financial institutions. There are a number of rumours flying around the dealing room at the moment that the ECU team lead by Roy Garner are about to quit and accept an offer from a major competitor. The senior dealing room manager, Guy Salmon, has called Debbie into his office to see what can be done to persuade the team to stay at GBI.

In preparation for the meeting with Guy, Debbie has been distilling information she has collected from her discussions with traders and sales people about their views on how they are rewarded. She has also consulted Jeff Banks about what measures the organisation might need to take to keep it as competitive as possible.

Information gathering

As far as salaries are concerned, Jeff's view is that the Bank's salary policy is effective once individuals have joined the company. However, from information he has gleaned from the market place, it seems that so called 'golden handcuffs' are becoming more and more prevalent. This means that individuals or teams receive a signing-on bonus, but, rather than give a one-off payment on joining, payments are made over a predetermined time-scale, usually locking the employees into the contract for as long as possible. This proves to be a very effective 'loyalty' bonus.

Jeff has also been reviewing the benefits package offered by GBI compared to the other institutions in the aforementioned club survey. Payment of mortgage subsidies to employees is common throughout the financial services sector. This usually means that employees receive either an in-house mortgage at special low rates or, alternatively, a cash amount which is calculated as the difference between the prevailing interest rate and a nominal, low rate as established by the bank's remuneration policy. Given present interest rates, the cash subsidy offered by GBI may be worth relatively little.

Jeff is inclined to retain this feature of the package as it costs the bank relatively little at present, although he will be watching political and economic changes quite carefully over the next few years in case the cost of this benefit should rise.

Debbie has been attracted to the idea of offering a 'cafeteria' of benefits to dealing room personnel. Given the amount of hassle Debbie constantly experiences from that quarter, she believes there is a strong case for letting employees calculate what is most important to them and what benefits they will value most. Jeff is less convinced that this will make life easier, as it is often difficult to calculate the value of a variety of benefits for tax purposes. He believes that offering such a choice will increase the amount of administration involved in providing benefits to staff.

Both Jeff and Debbie feel that the organisation's bonus arrangements may be falling behind the times and could be usefully reviewed. The present system allows for a lump sum cash payment to be made at Christmas time each year. Various City institutions attempt to stagger the timing of their payouts to their employees, some paying annually in August, October, December or April. Other institutions deliberately calculate profit figures and pay out bonuses at different times during the year to avoid paying out at the same traditional time.

Jeff has learned, through other compensation managers in the City, that a number of institutions have changed both the timing and frequency of the dealing room bonus payments. At one investment bank, traders are paid performance-related bonuses on a quarterly basis. Other institutions are said to be considering paying on a monthly basis. At the investment bank mentioned, sales people are paid semi-annually and support staff continue to receive bonuses on an annual basis at Christmas time.

Finally, Jeff believes that GBI should consider reviewing its bonus payment schemes and extending its stock option scheme (currently offered to a handful of senior executives only) to all of the sales and trading employees. He would like to develop a tiered structure where employees could elect to take part payments of expected bonuses in say, December and June, and to take instalments either partly or completely in company stocks. Debbie believes this would be beneficial to the Bank in terms of retention and could be motivational for employees by giving them a good reason to increase profits for both themselves and the organisation.

Student activities

1. Evaluate the organisation's reward strategy. How far does the external environment shape this strategy?
2. What motivates the dealing team? How can the organisation respond to these needs?
3. Assess the extent to which team-based pay is appropriate in this case.
4. Analyse and discuss the role of HR in this context. Comment on the function of the compensation and benefits manager.
5. Discuss Debbie's views on bonus payments and make recommendations on timings.

Standard reading

	Armstrong and Murlis	*Armstrong*	*Milkovich and Newman*
Pages	298-308	–	–

Further reading

Bok, D (1993) *The Cost of Talent*, The Free Press, New York
Churchill, C (1990) *Serious Money*, Methuen Press, London
Coggan, P (1995) *The Money Machine – How the City Works*, Penguin, London
Crystal, G (1992) *In Search of Excess*, Norton Press, New York
Gapper, J and Denton, N (1996) *All that Glitters*, Penguin, London
Smith, I (1991) *Incentive Schemes: People and Profits*, Croner Publications, London

Subject Index

Abbey National PLC 243
absenteeism 173, 176
ACAS 97, 104, 106
accelerator 183
accountability
  in performance management systems 147
Acquired Rights Directive 57
Alan Jones Associates 95
allowances 55, 56
'Anonymous Customer' 81
'Annual Incentive Plan' (AIP) bonus 92
appraisal 88
  360 degrees 94, 160, 232
  peer group 27
Arthur Andersen consultants 217
attitude surveys *see* employee attitude surveys

base pay
  pay range 80
  reducing 64–5, 81
  spot rates 97
benchmarking
  in job evaluation 90, 105
benefits 229–30
  advantages 233
  care responsibilities 238
  child care vouchers 239
  cost 229, 232, 242
  evaluation 242–3
  flexible *see* flexible benefits
  family friendly 238–43
  maternity and paternity pay 241
  mortgage subsidy 302
  rationalising 81
  reasons for introduction 239
  summer play schemes 241
  working hours flexibility 241
board room pay 17, 257, 258, 261–5
  FTSE plan 264
  justification 258
  Mining Plan 263
  need for change 262
  pay ratios 257
  types of payment 261
bonus schemes
  ceilings 53
  City traders 298–303
  discretionary fund 65
  difficulties with 53
  executives, for 261–5
  managers, for 57
  maximum payment 65
  operations staff, for 53
  overtime, for 53, 55
  sales staff, for *see* sales force pay
  self-regulation 57
  terminal 16
BP Oil 199, 211–12
breast screening 241
British Airways 49, 243
British Gas 17
broad-banding 9, 28, 85, 90, 93, 129, 168
  advantages 117
  difficulties 85, 117
Brown, Cedric 17
BS 5750 129
BSkyB 257
budgets, pay 28

Business Process Re-engineering 27

Cadbury Committee 258
Caesar 16
career breaks 242
case studies, use of 18
champions 64
change
  behavioural 16
  compensation and 61
  managing 61–6
  requirements in Vauxhall 267
Childcare Charter 243
childcare information on-line 243
childcare vouchers 239–40
  flexible benefits, in 235
Citizen's Charter 150
communication
  competence, as a 129
  Flexpack for employees 234
  job evaluation and 102
  links with profit-sharing 225
  new pay system and 82
company cars 17, 77, 236, 300
compensation *see* pay
competencies 28
  core 29
  framework 102
  multi-dimensional 33
  profiling 33
  specialist 33
  uni-dimensional 29–30
competency-related pay 9, 25, 101
competition 25, 45–9, 81
  co-operation and 48
  direct selling 190
  factory cleanliness 47
  framework 73, 164
  material saving 47
  objectives 191
  on-time factor 47
  prizes *see* prizes
  problems and solutions 193–4
Compulsory Competitive Tendering (CCT) 51, 145
  financial penalties and 52
  innovation and 59
  pensions and 58
computer pay package 78
contribution
  reward for 16, 23, 73, 79, 130, 206
Corfu 15
customer care 16, 49, 102, 129

Daily Mail 257
Dartford Borough Council 198, 201–8
David Webster Group 51–60
de-layering 85, 197
dental insurance 235
Direct Line Insurance 171
Disney Corporation 257
Dr Sophie Redmond Stichting v. *Bartol* (1992) 58

Eisner, M 257
employee attitude surveys 129, 141–2, 180, 236, 243, 290–1
empowerment 127, 293
  replacing command structure 159
  and salary determination 28
  and work-teams 28, 274
Equal Opportunities Commission (EOC) 282–5
EOC v. *Secretary of State for Employment* (1994) 219
equal pay 78, 98, 259, 277–88
  arguments put 286–7
  claim 282
  EQUATE scheme 285
  GEL approach 284
  independent expert 283
  like work 282
  outcome 287
  reports 284–6
  work of equal value 282
European Court of Justice 57
evaluation *see* flexible benefits, paying for performance, pay strategy
Everest Double Glazing 25, 42–50
excitement

as motivational element 49

fairness 49
family friendly benefits *see* benefits
families of employees 49
flexible benefits 9, 25, 229, 231–6
feasibility study 233
Flexpack 234
menu 234
origins 231
pilot 233
reasons for recent growth 231
scheme evaluation 236
take-up 236
taxation 230
flexibility
factor in job evaluation, as a 108
work practices and pay 43, 55, 58, 85
flexitime 229–30
Fordism 267
funding of pay plan 64

gainsharing 57, 199, 210–15
conversion to pay 212, 213
employee involvement teams 214
feedback 212
IMPRO-SHARE 211
outcome 212
Rucker Plan 211
Scanlon Plan 210
targets 212, 213
GEC PLC 257
Glaxo-Wellcome 25, 27–41
goal-setting 62, 64, 130, 133–4, 140, 147, 268
'golden handcuffs' 302
Greenbury Committee 258

Hay job evaluation scheme 88, 99, 180, 285
international alignment and 88
switching jobs and 88
healthcare 235
health insurance
pre-employment medical 301
Heysham Power Station 243
holidays 235

IBM 98
ICL 84
IMPRO-SHARE 211
incentives
comparison and evaluation summary 105–6
customers and 49
debtors, and 45
objectives 49
options 174–6
quality and 44
sliding scale 44
traditional 44–5
Ingersoll-Rand 199, 213–14
Institute of Personnel and Development 16–17
ISO 1902 56
internal equity 79
intrinsic rewards 123
involvement 49, 59, 214, 225, 274

job enlargement 55
job evaluation 73, 84, 88, 99
see also pay structures
anomalies 106
appeals 106, 129
competence-based 101
converting to salary structure 110
equal pay implications 164
groups of employees to include 100
integrating previous systems 129
is it necessary? 99
points system 101, 108
proprietorial scheme 100
publication 106
resolving disputes 104, 105–6
steering committee 103
tailor-made scheme 101
time-scale 109
training participants 104
upgrading difficulties 165
job families 28, 164, 185

job share 242
John Lewis Partnership 198, 222–7
Jones Associates *see* Alan Jones Associates
Jones grades 89

KPMG consultants 285

labour market pressures 51
league tables 45
Lean Manufacturing 267
levers for change 127
life assurance 235
local authorities' pay and bonus systems 53
Local Government Act 1988 51

market rates 78, 86
  exchange groups 90
  free exchange of information 86, 90
  Hay survey 91
  Jones surveys 90
  local survey 91
  pay club 300
maternity and paternity pay 241
Matthew Clark 257
MCB Ltd 191
McDonald's 84
Mercury Communication 217
mini-contractors in pay system 56
motivation 48, 86, 182, 217
MSD 88–95

national pay negotiations 145–6, 201
Newsday Corporation 61–7
newsletters 47
non-union companies 51
Northcliffe, Lord 257
NVQs 17

objectives *see* goals
on-time production 47
on-target bonus 80

Parents at Work 243
pay
  alignment with business objectives 42, 74
  change and 47
  communication and 47
  decentralised 76, 81
  earnings plateau and 44
  matrix 131, 141, 148, 169, 205
  powerful message 66
  relationships, base and incentive 64
  reinforcer, as a 129
  re-structuring and 70–3, 129
  scales 29
pay structures
  broadbanded *see* broadbanding
  changing 146, 180–4
  costs of implementation
    new 114
  movement within grades 116
  non-overlapping grades 110–11
  overlapping grades 114
  problems
    overpay, of 111
    underpay, of 113
paying for performance (including performance-related pay) 16, 39–40, 59, 79–80, 123–6, 127–51
  adding pay on to performance
    management system 159
  advice to practitioners 144
  association with other initiatives 124, 129
  behavioural issues 158
  construction of goals 148
  converting performance measures into pay 131, 148, 169
  cultural problems 157
  culture of organisation
  difficulties
    funding 150
    general 176
  employees' views 142
  evaluation 131, 149
  external influences 186

improve managerial attitude in police service, to 152
individual payments 175
versus team payments 149, 157, 160
introducing 131
judgment on effectiveness 125
Kohn's arguments against 123
local authorities, in 146
Murlis's list of difficulties 124
pay matrix and 131, 148, 169, 205
team payments *see* team pay
rating system 131, 147
relationships effect 156
safety scoring 158
union opposition 150
variation of judgments 149
wider focus 123
'working the system' 148
pensions 55, 81, 230, 245–50
comparison of schemes 247
CCT and 58
defined benefits scheme 248
employee views 248
flexible benefits, in 234
funding rate 247
merger and 245
money purchase (defined contribution) scheme 249
Pensions Act 1995 247, 250
private pension plans 300
performance management 27, 28, 38–9, 65, 74, 92, 124, 129, 172-4, 201, 289–97
basis for stock options, as a 92
employee attitudes to 293
difficulties faced 295
feedback 131
hard targets 130
issues 130
logistical problems 156
medium for communication, as a 155, 169, 294
measures under scheme 172–4
model 132
objectives 129, 153–4
options for schemes 130, 147
ownership 160
research in police service 153
soft targets 130
stages in system 154
success factors 160
training implications 155, 295
performance-related pay *see* paying for performance
Personnel Standards Lead Body 17
piece-work 56, 124
Planning and Land Act 1980 51
Portsmouth Hospitals NHS Trust 199
Price Waterhouse consultants 206, 243
prizes 46
cash and non-cash 252
hampers 47
sales contest, in 191–3
variety and size 176
problem solving 48
profit-related pay 216–21, 230
Burton Group, in 216–21
communication of scheme 220
cost to taxpayer 216, 230
part-timers, effect on 219–20
pay review, effect on 218
scheme operation 217
take-up 216
tax situation 216
profit-sharing 78, 222–7
factors influencing payment 225
links with participation culture 225
partnership profit 222
payments under scheme 224

quality and incentives 46

return on capital employed (ROCE) 57, 80
reward policy and strategy
assets earning their keep 211
company values and 74, 76, 293
customer focus and 84, 293

dysfunctional behaviours and 16
employee contribution and 23
external competitiveness and 23
external consistency and 85
evaluation of 206
by local authorities 145
internal consistency and 23, 79, 84–5
links
business strategy, to 9, 25, 77, 154, 217, 223
flexibility, to 232
individual and team performance 79
profit, to 217
shareholder worth, to 262
product innovation and 84
reinforcing change process and 259
underpinning philosophies 88, 274
what to pay for 165
renovating pay structures 25
risk sharing 25, 65, 254, 258
Royal Liverpool Philharmonic Society 243
RTZ PLC 199, 261–5
Rucker Plan 211

salary administration 16
sales force pay 40, 62–6, 178–87, 189–96
accelerator 183
competitions *see* competitions
direct selling 189
'fifth bonus' 183
incentives 45
links with business need 62
motivation 189
pay structure 190
performance pay and 125
SAYE schemes 230, 251–5
approved schemes 251
communication to employees 253–4
faults in scheme 254
risk sharing and 254
scheme
operation 252
performance 253
Scanlon Plan 210
sick pay 55
Simpson, George 257
skills-based pay 25
spot rates *see* basic pay
stakeholders 64
stock options 93, 262, 303
suggestion schemes 266–7

team pay and rewards 9, 25, 65, 175, 197–9
cascade of targets 202
conversion to pay 203
performance levels 204
research findings 199
scheme evaluation 206
size of teams 202
spectrum of approaches 198
strengths of team rewards 206
success criteria 199
targets, definition and numbers 203
weaknesses 207
teamworking 173, 274
Thomson Newspapers 172
Transfer of Undertakings Regulations (TUPE) 55, 97
Treasury 85
trust 47, 102

unionisation 44

Vauxhall Motors Ltd 199, 266–75
Employee Recognition scheme 267–72
award calculation 271
benefits 273–4
campaigns 272–3
eligibility 271
examples of ideas 271–2
improvement idea form 269
pilot 208
pointers to success 276

role of rewards 274
structure of responsibilities 268–70
need for change and innovation 267
video to communicate pay system 82
vouchers 46, 81

Watson Rask and Christiansen v *ISS Kantineservice A/S* (1993) 58
windfalls and bonus 64
Woolwich Building Society 76–82
Woolworths Ltd 84
'work beyond contract' 23
Working Parents Support Group 243
Wyatt consultants 78–81

Author Index

Abowd, J 126
Advisory, Conciliation and Arbitration Service (ACAS) 288
Adams, C 228
Adam-Smith, D 22
Aitkin, O 60
Anderson, G 161
Anfuso, D 228
Arkin, A 151, 275
Armstrong, M 22, 41, 50, 60, 75, 82, 94, 107, 120, 142, 151, 170, 177, 188, 196, 200, 208, 209, 215, 221, 227, 236, 243, 249, 255, 265, 288, 297, 303
Arthur Andersen 265
Ashton, C 26
Audit Commission 151

Barber, A 237
Bargaining Report 288
Barlow, G 161
Barrett, G 107
Barringer, M 94
Baron, A 107
Beam, B 230
Bevan, S 243
Boam, R 41
Bok, D 303
Brewster, C 259
Brignall, S 151
Brown, D 200
Butler, A 162

Callaghan, T 126
Cannell, M 187
Caulfield, S 230
Cave, A 259
CBI 230
Chaudhry-Lawton, P 66
Churchill, C 303
Clark, L 288
Coggan, P 303
Connock, S 41
Conoley, M 265
Conyon, M 260
Cook, F 87
Cook, S 177
Cooke, W 200
Cooper, C 200
Coopers and Lybrand 237
Coulson-Thomas, C 41
Crabb, S 260
Crofts, P 243
Crystal, G 303

Dale, A 161
Dawson, P 66
Denton, N 303
Doverspike, D 107
Dreher, G 230
Dugdill, G 41
Duncan, J 82
Dyck, B 215

Easton, G 22
Edmunds, J 125
Ekvall, G 275
Employers for Childcare 243
Ernst and Young 221
Evans, J 243

Fagen, C 288
Finch, S 243
Fisher, J 196
Fisher, M 297

Fletcher, C 162, 297
Fletcher, S 41
Folger, R 87
Foulkes, F 22
Fowler, A 60, 161, 228
Frohlich, N 215

Gapper, J 303
Geary, J 143
Gerhart, B 126
Gilbert, K 288
Golding, R 161
Goodman, P 215
Greenberg, J 196
Greenhaigh, R 288
Gregg, P 260
Gross, S 177, 200
Grundy, T 82

Hale, R 60
Haines, S 41
Hallman, G 230
Hampson, S 228
Hartle, F 297
Hastings, S 260, 288
Hay Group 41, 200, 237
Hawk, E 75, 200
Heery, E 125
Henemen, R 151, 170
Heshizer, B 237
Hewitt Associates, 94, 237, 265
Hill, S 121
Hillage, J 107
Howarth, C 66
Hunt, P 250

Income Data Services (IDS) 75, 87, 221, 244, 255, 260, 275, 288
Industrial Relations Law Bulletin 250
Industrial Society 82, 126, 170
Inland Revenue 221
IFF 221
Institute of Directors 265
Institute of Personnel and Development (IPD) 250
Industrial Relations Service (IRS) 75, 209, 215, 221, 255, 265

Jackson, C 255
Jacques, E 87
James, T 297
Johnson, N 177
Johnson, R 237
Jolson, M 196

Kalleberg, A 259
Kelly, A 170
Kent, S 255
Kessler, S 143
Kessler, I 125
Kilbride, P 82
Klein, K 255
Kohn, A 50, 125
Kossen, S 41
Konovsky, M 87
Kruse, D 200

Labour Research Department 151
Lancaster, G 177
Langley, M 187
Lawler, E 82, 162
Le Blanc, P 121
Leggatt, C 260
Leigh, A 82
Lewis, P 126, 288
Lewis, W 259
Lincoln, J 259
Littlechild, D 151, 259
Lloyd, G 275
Lummis, R 275

McAdem, J 50
McAdams, J 200
McFadden, J 230
McLean, H 221
McCoy, K 41
McGoldrick, A 22
McHale, P 107
Mackenzie, T 161
McLaughlin, D 22
Maitland, I 60

Marsden, D 125, 143, 162
Marx, A 275
Mason, B 143
Mavin, S 161
Mejia, L 215
Merrick, N 188
Milkovich, G 22, 26, 41, 50, 60, 66, 75, 82, 87, 94, 107, 120, 126, 142, 151, 161, 170, 177, 188, 196, 208, 215, 221, 227, 236, 243, 249, 265, 288, 297, 303
Mitrani, A 41
Monks, K 170
Morden, A 188
Murlis, H 22, 41, 50, 60, 66, 75, 82, 94, 107, 120, 121, 126, 142, 151, 161, 170, 177, 188, 196, 208, 215, 221, 227, 236, 243, 249, 255, 265, 288, 297, 303

National Police Training 161
Neathey, F 107
Nelson, W 161
Newman, J 22, 26, 41, 50, 60, 66, 75, 82, 94, 107, 120,142, 151, 161, 170, 177, 188, 196, 208, 215, 221, 227, 236, 243, 249, 265, 288, 297, 303
Nicholl, V 255
Nortier, F 66

Obolensky, N 83
O'Byrne, S 259
Oldfield, M 250

Peacock, A 22
Peel, M 177
Pfain, B 177
Pickard, J 275
Piland, W 187
Plant, R 66
Prescott, B 41
Pritchard, D 170
Purcell, I 143
Reardon, A 250
Reiner, R 162
Richardson, R 125, 143, 162
Ridgeway, C 60
Rosen, C 255
Rubery, J 260, 288
Rubin, P 126
Ruh, R 215
Ryden, O 94
Rynes, S 87

Sable, R 94
Sadler, P 83
Saunier, A 75
Schuster, J 26, 215
Seaman, R 50
Secker, J 288
Self, R 250
Sheehy, P 161, 162
Siminitiras, A 177
Simmons, S 177
Smilansky, J 75
Smith, A 209
Smith, I 303
Smyth, R 187
Sparrow, P 41
Spence, P 60, 151
Stewart, G 50
Stewart, J 60
Summers, L 41
Suter, E 221

Terry, M 143
Thatcher, M 41
Thompson, M 125, 143, 161
Towers Perrin, 230
Townley, B 162
Tyson, S 259

Vroom, 187

Wagner, J 126
Wakely, J 215
Wallace, B 60
Walters, M 297
Watling, R 237
Weightman, J 121

Weinrauch, J 187
Welbourne, T 215
Whitlam, P 60
Wilkinson, B 260
Williams, A 260, 265
Williams, M 194
Williams, R 162, 297
Winstanley, D 22
Wood, L 259
Wood, S 50, 187
Woodhall, J 22
Woodley, C 230
Wright, V 265

Young, K 255
Young, M 161

Zingheim, P 26, 215